SEAN

SEAN

EILEEN O'CASEY

EDITED WITH AN INTRODUCTION BY

J. C. TREWIN

COWARD, McCANN & GEOGHEGAN, INC.
New York

TO NIALL

Contents

Illustrations follow pages 128 and 224

Acknowledgements

I WOULD like to thank all who, during the writing of this book, answered my questions so patiently, and all who have permitted me to quote from letters.

In the first group: Brooks Atkinson, Ronald Ayling, Lord Bernstein, Ernest Blythe, Tom (Thomas Quinn) Curtiss, Dr and Mrs Doran, Barrows Dunham, Mrs Earle, Leonard Elmhirst, Lillian Gish, Miss Chris Hatch, the Rt Hon. Harold Macmillan, Gjon Mili, Barbara Nivan, Breon O'Casey, Shivaun O'Casey (Mrs Laurence Kenig), John O'Riordan, Mrs Harvey Ross, Commander H. P. Sears, R.N. (retd), Wolfgang Suschitzky, Richard (Dickie) Watts, Jnr, Ella Winter (Mrs Ogden Stewart). To which I must add the late Geoffrey Dobbie and Tyrone Guthrie.

In the second group: Miss Dorothy Dickson for the letter from C. B. Cochran; the Rt Hon. Malcolm John MacDonald, for the extracts from the letters of Ramsay MacDonald; Admiral of the Fleet Sir Caspar John, G.C.B., for the extracts from the letters of Augustus John; Mr C. M. Grieve, for the letters of Hugh MacDiarmid; Major Richard Gregory, for the extracts from the letters of Lady Gregory; the Society of Authors, for the Bernard Shaw Estate; Lawrence, Graham & Co., acting on behalf of the Trustees of the Will of Mrs Bernard Shaw, for the letters of Charlotte Shaw; the Estate of Eugene O'Neill for the extract from his letter.

Also I want warmly to thank Alan Maclean and Teresa Sacco, of Macmillans, for their great encouragement. My last and warmest thanks to John Trewin.

E. O'C.

Introduction

SEAN O'CASEY and his much younger wife, Eileen, were married for thirty-seven years. A month before his death, in Torquay at the age of eighty-four, he wrote to Eileen the enchanted letter printed towards the end of this book: a letter in which he thanks her for the ideal companionship ('You are, and have been, indeed, . . . the pulse of my heart') that had survived the decades of insecurity, 'constant closeness to poverty'. It was a union that Eileen O'Casey remembers today with unwavering affection. In her Hampstead flat there hangs Augustus John's portrait of Sean as she knew him first, the candid, watchful, and combative Dubliner in London: Sean himself spoke of the face 'set determinedly in contemplation of things seen and heard'. His books are all round her: his Elizabethan and Jacobean plays, valued by a man who was himself an Elizabethan reborn; the small, ill-printed volume of George Crabbe's poems that he prized so much; and his own plays and autobiographies and essays, the massive work of more than forty years' single-minded devotion to his craft. He was a compulsive writer, a man ready to make 'gold embroidery out of dancin' words': the language he could heighten as once they heightened it on Bankside where an audience looked for sound and imagery, the phrase that could kindle like a spark in tinder.

His compassion would be as enduring as his humour. To an eloquence Dublin-bred and prodigal in the unexpected epithet ('It always gives meself a kind of thresspassin' joy to feel meself movin' along in a mournin' coach'), he added the imagination that could take him, like Claribel of Tunis, ten leagues beyond man's life. After his first Dublin plays he was ahead of his time. We prize

Juno and *The Plough and the Stars*, the great twin brethren; we must
think also of *Cock-a-doodle Dandy*. Sean loved Shakespeare and –
sometimes obtrusively – he loved, too, what he called the 'colour
and stir' of the Boucicault melodramas. Who can blame a genius,
pledged to the theatre theatrical, for the scene that is tumul-
tuously larger than life? Where he failed, he failed at least like a
master.

In politics he would not compromise. To the last he was thrusting at religious bigotry. But he was never either a routine Communist or a routine rationalist. 'His was a truly Christian nature,'
said Harold Macmillan in *Winds of Change*; 'one of the kindest and
most genuine men that I have known. He and Ronald Knox – in
their very different ways – were saintly men.' The phrase might
have startled Sean O'Casey; but he would, I think, have been
grateful.

II

When he and Eileen Carey were married in 1927 he had written
only three of his major plays, and she had acted in London productions of two of them, as Nora Clitheroe in *The Plough and the
Stars* and as Minnie Powell in *The Shadow of a Gunman*. She would
watch the rest of his work flourish like a vast garden that, for all its
seeming wildness, yet had a proportion, a shape, and a style; it
glowed and glittered into colour, and its terraces looked towards a
far horizon. Though in the end Sean's sight had practically failed,
he could still command his world and write of it with the 'radiant
energy' that Masefield said, in another context, was a poet's gift.

Eileen Carey came upon his name first in New York. As a young
and beautiful actress of the lighter stage, wondering about her
future and straight from a trifling Cohan farce, she happened to
read the script of *Juno and the Paycock*, then running in London.
Overwhelmed, all she wished to do was to return home at once and
to meet the author, this Sean O'Casey of whom she had never
heard.

He was then forty-six years of age. Son of Michael Casey, a

commercial clerk from Limerick, and Susan (née Archer) from Wicklow, Sean, christened John, was born in working-class Dublin on 30 March 1880, the youngest of thirteen children: eight had died in infancy, 'for at that time', as he would write later, 'the death-rate in Dublin was as high as in the plague-spots of Asia'. John was six when his studious father died after an accident, a fall from a ladder in reaching up to a book on a top shelf; soon the family, under its indomitable mother, was to face the rigours of the north Dublin tenements, and John contracted a chronic and painful eye-complaint that hampered him to the last, and in childhood made it hard for him to read the books he adored. With a minimum of formal education he became a life-long student: 'I am a student still,' he said when over eighty.

His earlier working years had to be a sustained fight in the Dublin that, after his self-exile, continued to haunt his mind: 'A gold-speckled candle, white as snow, was Dublin once; yellowish now, leanin' sideways, an' guttherin' down to a last shaky glimmer in the wind of life.' Beginning in the stock-room of a hardware store, and moving to minor clerical work, he went on to a variety of tough manual jobs. His longest spell was as a labourer on the railway. At twenty or so, by then a fluent Gaelic speaker and a member of the Irish Ireland movement and of the Gaelic League which took the place of the secondary education he had missed, he had changed his name to Sean O'Cathasaigh: from the Abbey Theatre's staging of *The Shadow of a Gunman* in 1923, he became Sean O'Casey. In boyhood he developed a passion for the drama, reading Shakespeare, watching Boucicault; his brother Archie was an amateur actor, and later Sean himself made tentative appearances; one part, surprisingly, was Henry VI. If the Royal Shakespeare Company, many years on, had needed an epigraph for its production of *The Wars of the Roses*, it could have done no better than to borrow from Sean's words in 'Shakespeare Taps at the Window' from *Pictures in the Hallway*:

Battles, castles, and marching armies; kings, queens, knights, and esquires in robes today and in armour tomorrow, shouting their soldiers on to the attack, or saying a last lone word before poor life gave out; of mighty men of valour joining this king and reneging that one; of a king gaining a crown and of a king losing it; of kings and knights rushing on their foes and of kings and captains flying frantic from them.

Politically, Sean grew into an ardent left-winger, much influenced by the almost legendary Jim Larkin (we find him in Eileen's story), founder of the Irish Transport and General Workers' Union, and Labour's leader during the protracted Dublin lock-out of 1913: *The Star Turns Red* is dedicated to the men and women who fought through this. For a while Sean was secretary of the Irish Citizen Army which would fight in the streets of Dublin, and of which one day he wrote the history. His mother, whom he dearly loved, died in November 1918, on the day after the First World War ended; he revered her all his life and remembered her in the dedication of *The Plough and the Stars* 'to the gay laugh of my mother at the gate of the grave'; in the finest pages of his autobiography; and in the strongly personal play of *Red Roses for Me*.

At the age of forty-three, still a manual labourer and still trying to write a play for the Abbey, with the encouragement of Lady Gregory, much more sympathetic to him than Yeats, he reached success with a few performances of his 'tragedy in two acts', *On the Run*. It was retitled *The Shadow of a Gunman*: in spite of sudden Dublin excitement, he made from it just four pounds. Sean had little time for Joseph Holloway, the local theatre-diarist, but Holloway's journal can remind us of the occasion: 'The author is a thin-faced, sharp-profiled man, with streaky hair, and wore a trench coat and a soft felt hat. He followed his play closely and laughed often, and I was told he was quiet-mannered almost to shyness, and very interesting in his views.'* The following year brought *Juno and the Paycock*, one of the major plays of the twentieth century, a tragi-comedy set during the Troubles of 1922. Sean was never simply a recorder at large, a wandering notebook; rather he used his city as the Elizabethans and the Jacobeans used Athens, Venice, Amalfi, as a hearth for the glowing imagination.

* *Joseph Holloway's Abbey Theatre*, ed. Robert Hogan and Michael J. O'Neill (Southern Illinois University Press, 1967).

In an interview during 1925 he said: 'They tell me that *The Shadow of a Gunman* breaks all the rules. If the characters live, and the play holds the audience, it's enough.' He continued, triumphantly, to break the rules.

III

Juno and the Paycock was the script Eileen Carey discovered in New York on a cold and miserable March day in 1926: *Juno*, with its pattern of all loyal wives; her husband, that peacock-strutting taproom waster, the so-called 'Captain' Boyle; and his jackal, Joxer Daly. Eileen found the already famous scenes between the Paycock and Joxer:

> JOXER: God be with the young days when you were steppin' the deck of a manly ship, with the win' blowin' a hurricane through the masts, an' the only sound you'd hear was, 'Port your helm!' an' the only answer, 'Port it is, sir!'
>
> BOYLE: Them was days, Joxer, them was days. Nothin' was too hot or too heavy for me then. Sailin' from the Gulf o' Mexico to the Antanartic Ocean. I seen things, I seen things, Joxer, that no mortal man should speak about that knows his Catechism. Ofen, an' ofen, when I was fixed to the wheel with a marlinspike, an' the wins blowin' fierce an' the waves lashin' an' lashin', till you'd think every minute was goin' to be your last, an' it blowed, an' blowed – blew is the right word, Joxer, but blowed is what the sailors use. . . .
>
> JOXER: Aw, it's a darlin' word, a daarlin' word.
>
> BOYLE: An' as it blowed an' blowed, I ofen looked up at the sky an' assed meself the question – what is the stars, what is the stars? . . .
>
> JOXER: Ah, that's the question, that's the question – what is the stars?
>
> BOYLE: An' then, I'd have another look, an' I'd ass meself – what is the moon?
>
> JOXER: Ah, that's the question – what is the moon, what is the moon? (Act I)

Eileen found also the final lament of Juno that echoed the cry
of the bereaved mother during the third Act:

> Maybe I didn't feel sorry enough for Mrs Tancred when her
> poor son was found as Johnny's been found now – because he
> was a Die-hard! Ah, why didn't I remember that then he wasn't
> a Die-hard or a Stater, but only a poor dead son! It's well I
> remember all that she said – an' it's my turn to say it now:
> What was the pain I suffered, Johnny, bringin' you into the
> world to carry you to your cradle, to the pains I'll suffer carryin'
> you out o' the world to bring you to your grave! Mother o'
> God, Mother o' God, have pity on us all! Blessed Virgin, where
> were you when me darlin' son was riddled with bullets, when
> me darlin' son was riddled with bullets? Sacred Heart of Jesus,
> take away our hearts o' stone, and give us hearts o' flesh! Take
> away this murdherin' hate, and give us Thine own eternal love!

It was an astonishing play, and Eileen knew it. She had not met
then the even finer *The Plough and the Stars*, with the figures of
Fluther Good and Mrs Gogan, Bessie Burgess and the Covey, and
the last bitter moment when the English soldiers' chorus of 'Keep
the Home Fires Burning' rises above the fire and grief of Easter
Week. This was the piece that during the same spring had been
so furiously and inexplicably received at the Abbey Theatre that
W. B. Yeats, on the fifth night, took the stage to quell the rioters
with his scorn: 'Is this going to be a recurring celebration of Irish
genius? Synge first, and then O'Casey. Dublin has once more
rocked the cradle of a reputation.'

Understanding what he could do, Sean resolved to leave Dublin for London and, he hoped, for the life of a full-time writer.
The Irish Players in *Juno*, presented by James Bernard Fagan, were
still exciting the town. He had been in London only a few weeks
when Fagan told him that there would be a meeting at the Fortune
Theatre that afternoon with a young actress, Eileen Carey. How
this came about Eileen now describes in her book; actually there
were two meetings, the second to arrange for her appearance in
The Plough and the Stars. Sean would telescope these in a chapter of
Rose and Crown, the fifth volume of his autobiography:

Sean's Irish eye was as keen in the choice of a pretty lass as the
American eye of George Jean Nathan, so he stood staring at her
for a long time. He had rarely seen a lovelier face or figure anywhere in this world, and didn't expect to find anything better
in the delectable world to come. She was nervous. Sean saw that
she was sensitive, for the talk about wages embarrassed her, so
he helped by demanding that she get the same as had been given
to the girl whose place she had taken – for Fagan had offered
her five pounds a week less, reproaching Sean when she had gone
for adding to the expenses of the production. But Sean was well
pleased to be of service to such a delightful girl. . . .

Emerson has said that a pretty face is a great gift to a woman,
an attractive figure a greater one, and a charming manner the
greatest of all; and when one gets these in a *trio juncta in uno*,
then one has been promoted in life by the gods themselves,
especially when their grandeur is subdued by a gloriously
human sense of humour. There's nothing lovelier in life than a
lively laugh.

In September of the following year, 1927, they were married:
the Dubliner from the tenements, who in so short a time had
written himself into stage history, and the young actress of
English upbringing but Irish descent – 'as Irish as the heather on
Howth Hill,' said Sean – whose career had been fantastically unlike her husband's. Now, with candour and affection, she has told
the story of their remarkable life together.

IV

Here, first, is the controversy over *The Silver Tassie*, begun by
Yeats's letter ('Dear Casey') that, in retrospect, is as absurd as
Clement Scott's views on Ibsen. Here are the years of Sean's long
struggle as a writer, with Eileen at his side; his visit to America;
the friendship with G.B.S.; the move to a country town in
Devon; the tale of a family united, Sean and his room at the heart
of all; the coming of the autobiographies, unchronological and en-
grossing, which illuminate so much in the major plays; the deep
tragedy of the younger son Niall's death; the sustained endeavour

under the coloured cap – unceasing to an hour when the mere act of typing had become 'a per ardua ad astra task to me'.

Sean was content to write and write. Apart from the Hawthornden Prize for *Juno*, he accepted no honours. During his last decade he refused, with gentle dignity, offers of the C.B.E. and of various academic awards. He was content to be Sean O'Casey, quintessential Irishman and one whose lips were royally touched:

> Then every rib o' grass grows into a burnished fighter that throws a spear, or waves a sword, an' flings a shield before him. Then Ireland crinkles into a camp, an' kings an' sages, queens an' heroes, saints an' harpers stare me in the face, an' bow, an' pass, an' cry out blessing an' vict'ry too, for Heber's children, with the branch of greatness waving in their hands! (*Purple Dust*, Act II)

This is spoken by a Second Workman: Sean freely conferred the gift of speech.

His friends remember his courtesy, his fastidiousness, his fun, and the Dublin voice that curled into every crevice of every phrase. Moreover, in his presence, you thought instinctively of the Bridge of Vision – the sunset transfiguration of Dublin and its people in *Red Roses for Me*. (It appears, as an autobiographical narrative, in *Pictures in the Hallway*.) A few words from *Red Roses* hold the spirit of Sean: 'Praise God for th'urge of jubilation in the heart of th' young.' His hatreds, as Brooks Atkinson has said wisely, 'were confined to people and institutions that, in his opinion, impeded or impaired the normal joyousness of human existence'.

However fierce he might be on paper, his kindness was sovereign. Before we met, and when I was editing the *West Country Magazine* on a tiny budget, I asked him for a message. Promptly, out of sheer goodness and sent almost diffidently, there arrived the bounty of a thousand words on the town of Totnes. In this he wrote: 'The market-place is still a weekly blossom of the town, but its petals are no longer of a rich texture, and the colours are gone. Now it seems to be but a collection of a few green leaves and a handful of berries. God be with the time when the place was *giddy with profusion*.' That, too, speaks for Sean O'Casey.

V

Often, when an important writer dies, his reputation seems, transiently, to crumble. After the last of the elegiac tributes, the death-watch beetles move in; and for fifteen or twenty years (if we have nothing better to do) we can watch the trickling dust, the deliberate hollowing-away of a man's fame. If he is a genuine master, no harm ensues. He is 'rediscovered'; the riddled timbers become as sound again as those of the magically wrecked vessel of *The Tempest*, and the death-watch shifts elsewhere.

Sean O'Casey, his genius acknowledged, has been spared the post-mortem ritual. Today, the world over, he is acted more than he has ever been; his fame is safe with the generation ahead. What he said of Shaw, one Irishman of another, can be turned rightly to himself (and Eileen O'Casey's loving memoir confirms it): 'He made the most of life. The earth was his home and he loved it. He was at home among the mortals. His epiphany was the showing forth of man to man.'

J. C. TREWIN

SEAN

CHAPTER ONE

Eileen

BOTH my father and mother were Irish. What I write of them now is really hearsay, as it was told to me by my mother at odd moments. She was Kathleen Carey, born in the west of Ireland at the little town of Ballina in the north-eastern corner of County Mayo. Her parents, good middle-class people and strict Catholics, had a family of twelve children; I think about eight of them survived, but the only one I knew well was my Aunt Alice who lived with us in London when I was a small child. My mother had a firm Catholic education at a convent where her aunt – very strict, she used to tell me – was the Reverend Mother. Bored with life in the remoteness of Mayo, she wanted badly, after leaving school, to train as a nurse, a course which took about three years and for which in those days, I believe, one had to pay; her parents agreed to this, and she went to live in Dublin, working at one of the hospitals and staying in a small boarding-house.

My father, Edward Reynolds, came from a farm in Athlone, County Westmeath, not large but well stocked. He was the eldest son and would naturally have been expected to carry on the place. But, hating the life as much as my mother had hated the boredom of Ballina, he asked whether he could not give up his share and take a sum of money instead so that he might study in Dublin. His father told him to clear off; and presently he found himself at the same boarding-house as my mother, who was then a beautiful girl with dark brown hair and classical features. Soon they fell in love, to the displeasure of my mother's people who considered that, socially, Edward Reynolds was beneath them. For all that, he was a clever and diligent young man who read every book he could find, studied languages and, being excellent at mathematics, helped to support himself by doing various people's accounts: once he did those of the old Dublin Gaiety Theatre.

When he had been in Dublin for about a year he got a job as accountant to a South African stockbroking firm in the diamond business. He told my mother that, as soon as he had made enough money, he would send for her to join him in Johannesburg, and in fact, within two years, he did send her both the fare and money to buy her trousseau. Once they were married, my mother, with a bungalow to live in and coloured boys to wait on her, was very comfortable for a time. Certain things, even so, were deeply disturbing. One of the two sons born in South Africa died shortly after birth. (The other she adored.) Moreover, as soon as they were married, my father gave up his religion, and this must have distressed my mother, a devout Catholic who would have nagged at him to go to Mass. She used to tell me, when I was older, that he was an atheist and read dreadful books. They discovered, I imagine, that they were not suited to each other.

South Africa just then was desperately unsettled. When the Boer War loomed my parents decided to return to Dublin with their small son. Mother must have been a kind person because, so she told me, one of their coloured boys was so upset at losing them that he tried to swim out after the boat that was taking them away.

I was born in Dublin where my father had bought a house and intended to settle. In the event, we did not stay. Father, wild and reckless at times, was a gambler: one day he gambled his house, with all he had in it, the lot, and lost. After this we travelled to London and lived in lodgings. There my mother developed rheumatic fever and her son bronchitis; she could not cope with this, and a nurse looked after them both in one room. Over and over again, Mother used to tell me how she could not be moved and how she longed to go to her boy who was coughing. I believe that if she had been well herself he could have lived, but during her illness he died, and she never got over it; the thought of the agony she must have gone through helped me to try to love her. True, she did love me in her own fashion, yet I had, inevitably, to be second-best; when I was a child she would say to me so often, 'If only my son had lived!' I was then her only child, and she had nothing like the comfort she always wanted. Father had resolved to go back to South Africa, realising that at least he could earn enough to send a monthly cheque.

We were in lodgings now in West London, at Brook Green, Hammersmith; a pleasant sitting-room, bedroom and kitchen. I must have been happy. Certainly I recall that Aunt Alice, Mother's sister and, unlike her, really cheerful, came to live with us for a while. Try as I may, I can never picture my mother as young; I cannot see her playing or larking round with me as I would later with my own children. Instead I associate her with tidiness and with tears over hair-brushing. She was neat, clean, and a good cook; we had fires and warm clothes; food was never scarce, and I cannot remember wanting for anything. Father's money must have served.

Then – and this is the first part of my life I do remember sharply – Father came back from South Africa; he had a nervous breakdown, and before long he had to enter hospital. It was a sad homecoming, for Mother, who was a strangely difficult character, could make the running of a home a burden to everybody; there was such a dreary hustle-and-bustle that I wanted to run off until it was over, and I am sure Father felt like this. Two memories of him are still plain. One I shall come to; the other was when he took me on a bus ride to the West End to buy two sailor-suits of white holland with pleated skirts that I could twirl round, and, of course, with wide sailor-collars. I was happy that day; he called me a lovely little girl, perhaps because I looked like him, as Mother used to remind me sorrowfully. At last he went to hospital; Mother found a post as a nurse-companion; and relatives who were nuns helped to get me to school. We tried several: first the Sacred Heart, which was too expensive, and then the Daughters of the Cross, no use again because he could not pay the fees. It was lucky that I was naturally gay; the changes, as well they might, were making me feel insecure.

Finally I reached a London orphanage that was run by the Sisters of Charity. There were a hundred or more children, all living in dormitories; about six of us seemed to be on the 'better list', favoured in various ways, so I suppose our parents had paid. I cannot say that I was worried, for I had no kind of punishment, and one of the nuns, Sister Frances, genuinely loved me. Some of the food I disliked as much as anything, boiled fish especially, and the Friday meal I dreaded. Toys were scarce. One of my favourite games was to tear out paper dolls with great care and to play at schools with them, arranging them in a semi-circle and carrying on an imaginary conversation. When they had been collected into a tiny box, or folded patiently into a piece of paper, I managed somehow to carry them round with me until the next playtime.

Life was much harder, of course, for many other children in the orphanage. A few unpleasant things stick in my mind; thus if a child wetted her bed, she was made to stand with the sheet on her head and the wet patch across her face. Any sort of corporal punishment took place on a Saturday evening. I discovered this by accident on going to a room in the basement where we changed our everyday shoes for our Sunday ones. The small girls went down first; and one Saturday, having lost a shoe and stayed to search for it in the corridor, I realised suddenly that some of the older children were being whipped. Girls who had done wrong, or what was called wrong, must have been told to line up after the others had gone upstairs. I was so frightened about it that I held my hands over my ears and hid until it was possible to creep out unnoticed and weeping. I do not know whether the whippings were severe; probably not, but I hated the idea, and it disappointed me terribly to find that my beloved Sister Frances was giving the punishment.

While at the orphanage I became ill. They sent me for a while to a branch at Dover, and it is from Dover that I have the second strong memory of my tall, handsome father. He had travelled from the hospital where he had been sent after his breakdown to take me out for the afternoon. I sat with him on a bench by the sea, clutching his hand; it may be romantic imagination but I must always think of his sadness and his nearness to me then; I was so alone, and I remember my screaming and fright when he left me again. Though in these days his ailment would have been treated and cured, they regarded him as a mental patient and he grew more and more depressed; his must have been loneliness indeed. I saw him only once after our parting in Dover. That was in hospital just before he died; we held hands quietly, saying little. I had developed a romantic love for him; throughout life I would look for a father-figure rather than a husband.

II

After my father's death, Mother, who was troubled about my education and the orphanage life, wrote to her wealthier relatives about the possibility of paying for me to go to a better school. One of her cousins was Lord Macdonald; his wife decided to take me from the orphanage and to send me to the Ursuline Convent at Brentwood in Essex. I had still only the orphanage uniform, a plain dress and a pinafore, and the clothes which I had worn at my father's funeral and had been put away. These were now unearthed from somewhere. The only thing I recall was the hat, a large black beaver, probably my mother's pride; I can never forget it, I felt so self-conscious and silly.

It was hard to leave Sister Frances who had mothered me affectionately; both of us cried at our goodbye. I heard afterwards that she had been planning to have me well educated at a neighbouring school. I must have seemed an odd sight on arrival at the Convent, wearing clothes too small for me and a hat, the beaver, too big; I was a plump girl, quite nice-looking I gather, with good hair, eyes and eyelashes. The Convent had given to Lady Macdonald a detailed list of the clothes I should have; all of these clothes, in their twos and threes, were put into a new trunk and I did not see them until, to my pleasure and excitement, they were unpacked. It turned out that I would stay at Brentwood for some years. Cheerful by disposition, I put up a front. After all, I sang well, danced well for my age, and had no complexes, even if it did worry me to say who I was and where I came from. Most of the children were from fairly comfortable families, and, having a vivid imagination, I would tell fancy stories about my own home. I had no home.

Several things I appreciated, We slept in dormitory cubicles:

mine, at the end of the room, had a large window that looked out on to the lawns and the trees beyond. There was a coloured eiderdown with a matching mat beside the bed; I had a small wardrobe and a built-in cupboard, a jug and basin on the top of a smaller cupboard, and a mirror on the wall. After curtains had been pulled across the cubicles at night, each of us was safe in her own little space.

Our Reverend Mother was fond of the theatre. Our large Assembly Hall had at one end a platform that made an ample stage; it was fitted, too, with footlights, and it was easy to arrange entrances and exits through doors on each side which led into a passage used as a dressing-room. When we acted, as we did on most Sunday evenings during the term, one group or another would do a play; I was supposed to be very good at comedy. I also sang in the choir, thoroughly rehearsed by the Reverend Mother, who understood and loved music. Dancing and painting were extras, but somehow I managed to slide into the dancing class and enjoyed it.

One problem sorely bothered me. I hated to receive parcels from Lady Macdonald because generally they contained velvet or silk dresses of hers or her daughter which had to be cut down and remade. Fortunately they did not come often, but when they did I hid them at the back of the cupboard in my cubicle, hoping nobody would see them. I never learned to ride a bicycle because I did not have one. I did not learn to play tennis because I had no racquet. I never even learned to roller-skate properly because I had no skates, though occasionally I could borrow a pair from a friend to use on the Convent rink. Having nothing but essential things, I could not help feeling inferior. Holidays, with nowhere to go, were a trial. Even if I could visit another girl's home sometimes, mostly I went into digs with my mother who would give up for that period whatever job she had. Apart from my uniform, I had only a made-over dress or so; and, except on one occasion, I do not remember much about clothes during all my school years. There was an older girl named Carrie Rose who saw that my hair was brushed, and who fussed over me in various ways; she awed me because her mother was a French actress. After leaving the Convent,

Carrie went on the stage, into C. B. Cochran's production of Bruce Bairnsfather's war-time musical play, *The Better 'Ole*. Excited when she asked me to come to see her, I remember sitting enraptured in her dressing-room at the New Oxford Theatre; she gave me some underwear and a coat she had altered to fit me, the first clothes anybody had given to me with understanding. Having longed for such things as these, I felt proud at being able to return to school with them.

III

Around the age of sixteen I had a bad nervous breakdown, accompanied by blinding headaches and bouts of sleepwalking. My mother took me to a doctor who was horrified at my condition and told me I must not go back to school. All that happened was that my 'periods' had stopped; we never spoke to anyone about these matters, in fact lived a curiously deceitful life as though they could not possibly have existed. In secret, I had been pleased; but the consequences left me really ill. I was ordered to recuperate at a sanatorium in Brighton where I was not unhappy and struck up a friendship with two girls of my own age from Roedean. Later, when my doctor said I should work in the open air, I went up to a large house in the Sussex village of Billingshurst, ostensibly to learn gardening; in fact I weeded the flower-beds and detested it all, feeling that the wasted days would never end. This was a curious place, owned by a strange couple with whom I had meals, and who kept as pets two monkeys that scared me. On Sunday I went to Mass at a neighbouring convent in Burgess Hill which was a home for rich mental patients; an immense place in its surrounding acreage of gardens. The Reverend Mother, who was particularly kind to me, suggested that I should work there, and I did; it meant that I picked the flowers for the entire convent and helped to arrange them. With nobody but the nuns to talk to, I felt lost and lonely, though I did get on with some of the younger nuns and now and again went out driving with the milder patients. My room and bathroom were pleasant; but, being alarmed when

on my own and hating the dark, I could never turn out the light
on going to bed. It would burn until morning.

The interlude did not last. My mother, who was working as a
nurse-companion, brought her patient, a Miss Kay, down to
Sussex and left her there for a time with me. I was supposed to
have a country life but I had not bargained for Miss Kay who,
though not certifiable, was in a state of utter depression. An odd,
silent woman of unpleasant appearance, she terrified me. We had
a charming cottage at Wivelsfield Green, with a housekeeper to
cook for us. But, except for those few hours when I could chat or
lark with a few youths and girls on the village green, I hardly
talked at all; Miss Kay herself would give an intermittent grin or
grunt. Though I scurried through books by the dozen, romantic
novels usually, I was not allowed to read in the sitting-room
before meals. At length her brother, coming to see her, was dismayed that so young a girl was in charge; hastily he made arrangements for Miss Kay to be taken back to London and to a hotel
where my mother would go daily to look after her. So once more I
was with Mother in rooms. She decided at this stage that she was
not fit enough to keep on working. I suppose she had a little
money from my father's insurance, and possibly a small pension
from the firm in South Africa; anyhow, there was enough for her
to live on, and because I seemed to have recovered I went to a job
as a tracer in the Lincoln's Inn office of an architect, Morley
Horder, where I worked all day.

My great ambition now was to be a singer; I had a good con-
tralto voice and wanted to have lessons. Here Lady Macdonald
must have enlisted her friends to help because a wealthy Mrs
Jones, who was kind and not difficult to talk to, fixed up weekly
lessons for me with an admired singing teacher, de Lara. Later a
Lady Parsons introduced me to a pianist and a soprano, much older
and more professional than I was; we practised at a celebrated
Hanover Square studio and booked several after-dinner engagements at private houses. There the soprano and myself would get
a guinea each, and the pianist two guineas, and we would have
dinner in a small ante-room. Afterwards, though invited to join
the guests, we preferred as a rule to catch our buses home.

The same Mrs Jones took me to a dressmaker who made me several dresses for wearing on these engagements; at the time I had high ideas of being an opera singer. Somehow I earned enough to keep my mother and myself. Noticing one morning an advertisement for a concert-party singer on the outskirts of London, in the evenings and on Saturdays, I applied for the job and got it, joining a troupe of eight dressed as pierrots and pierrettes; we came in turn to the front of the stage to sing our numbers, otherwise we worked a kind of dance routine, fun to do though I hardly think we can have been good. After three weeks it was over. The man who ran it had a brother much older than me, about thirty-five I would say, a baritone employed at an Italian bank in Haymarket. We fell in love, and though he never intended to take engagements he would come along to my practices in Hanover Square. My mother objected, firstly because she did not think he was a gentleman, and secondly because she thought he was immoral. Drawbacks, probably; yet with his charm she could hardly help liking him. One of his uncles was the celebrated music-hall comedian, Gus Elen, the singer of coster songs; his other uncle, a butcher, made sure that we had our week-end joint, something at least that Mother was ready to accept. The romance ended as all my early romances did. He was not a Catholic, and in those days I was steadily of the faith.

IV

I ought to say how I regarded my mother. She never neglected me; she loved me in her own manner, and it was by no means as easy then as it is now for any woman left alone with a child. Not from the working class, she had never experienced real want. She had kept her looks. But I had to agree that, besides being difficult, her notions of sex were puritanical and Victorian; it was plain to see why she did not remarry. Until she died, only two years before Sean, I was responsible for her; at her death I simply felt grieved that she had never had the type of middle-class home she wanted. Her loneliness seemed to be her own fault. Obviously, she was intelligent. Sean, who did not like her, said often: 'If only this woman had used her brains in the right way!' The qualities I recognised were wasted; I did my best but we were miles apart, and in meeting we never failed to set each other on edge.

In those early days I resolved that it would be better to leave her and to live on my own. How to do it was the trouble; I explained that for a while I had to go out of London to work. Actually I was in London still, engaged upon tracing for Doultons, the pottery firm; this could have been why I gave Stoke-on-Trent – an inexplicable choice otherwise – as the place where I was assumed to be. Having supplied Mother with a post-office address that I had carefully looked up, I found myself a room in Goldhurst Terrace at Swiss Cottage in north-west London; a bright, tiny attic with gas ring and kettle, crockery for one, and a curtain behind which you hung your clothes. I never cooked, preferring to live on milk and cornflakes and an odd cup of tea; friends asked me out to various meals. It was fine while it lasted, which was not long; within a week or two, my mother, who had tracked me down without much searching, was there waiting for me. She made a scene.

It was useless; I would not go back to her. My landlady, an understanding woman, had not complained, but I knew that I must discover a permanent home. A Catholic canon, who was a friend of the Macdonalds, introduced me to a hostel called Nutford House in Seymour Place, Marble Arch, where one needed first-class references. These I got and my life at the hostel settled into reasonable shape. At first I had a single small room until I met a Canadian girl, Stella Greer, a commercial artist, who was in the same circumstances and who appeared to be unhappy. We decided to share a large room which was both better and cheaper for us. Stella, I learned, was an artist's daughter and a relative of the actor, Raymond Massey. Because her parents disapproved of a love affair, she had been sent to London on an allowance that she added to by designing for catalogues. Soon we made friends with two Scottish girls, Isabel and Alison Duncan, who had lost their parents and who were left with a fair amount of money; Alison I got on with especially, and still do. At that time we were all

quite stupid about the problems of life; I think practically anything could have happened to us.

I was sent with an introduction to Sir Woodman Burbidge, of
Harrods. Had he a job for me? The poor man must have been at
his wits' end to fit me in; still, he tried, and for two or three
weeks I was measuring counters and taking the results back to the
Drawing Office for drawings and tracings to be made of them. I
must have been as good as a sick headache at this. Next, another
man interviewed me and found another job. I was instructed to
go round the departments and to buy various things, all of which
– except perishable food and flowers and an occasional length of
material – would be returned later to store. I was to report how
the assistants served me, whether or not they were helpful,
whether they were curt or polite, slow or quick. I did not like
this at all; it was a bore, and in effect I had to spy upon girls who
were at work as I was. My only consolation was having food sent
to Nutford House; I chose tins because of our limited cooking
facilities, a few gas-rings on each floor, used for stray cups of tea.
Our meals we took in the main communal dining-hall.

Throughout, Mrs Jones had continued to pay for singing lessons.
Now my latest teacher heard of an audition for the D'Oyly Carte
Opera Company which performed only the operettas of Gilbert
and Sullivan; one had to be at the Savoy Theatre at two o'clock in
the afternoon. Instead of going to Harrods, I rehearsed my song all
the morning. Alison and Isabel spent a lot on clothes, so I borrowed a dress from one and a simply cut fur-coat from the other.
Stella was waiting at the Savoy with a bunch of violets for luck.
She dressed in a most dramatic, arty style with a cape and
feathered hat; sometimes she had embarrassed me, but that afternoon I felt grand to be there in my borrowed finery and to be
receiving her flowers. It was even better after the audition had
been successful; they accepted me for the chorus under my name
of Eileen Reynolds, summoned me to the stalls, and said that
rehearsals would start in a month's time; Lady Dorothy D'Oyly
Carte asked me to tea in her Mayfair flat. I never returned to
Harrods to collect my old tracing pens and box of compasses,
though I did write a note to say I would not be coming back.

Because nobody on the stage was allowed to live in Nutford House, Stella planned to go when I did. Ultimately we got a room in Sydney Street, Chelsea, with an old piano in it that would be right for my practising. Having a bad throat, I was sent before rehearsals began to Geoffrey Carte, the specialist, who decided to remove my tonsils – grave news, for the very thought of an anaesthetic terrified me; immature and daft, I had horseshoes and every kind of lucky charm on a string round my neck, muddled up with holy medals. Nothing went wrong, and when I was due to leave hospital, where they had treated me as an important person, Geoffrey Carte offered me a lift home to Sydney Street. I had fallen in love with him. Excited, I asked Stella to bring me one of my nicest suits; but being in an arty, up-in-the-air mood, she brought nothing but an old skirt and jumper. I was so upset and determined not to be seen that I slipped out through the bathroom and by the hospital back-stairs, and went home alone.

v

My singing teacher, combining a holiday with intensive lessons, arranged to take her pupils for a fortnight to a village in Brittany near St Malo. I discovered there was time for this. Who paid for me I cannot remember – I had just enough for the journey and the fees – but in Brittany I met a young girl, Helen Seldon, who was lonely and rich; her parents had died, and she was a Ward in Chancery, living in Cavendish Square with a guardian until she was twenty-one; she had an elder sister. Helen did not have much of a voice. Our teacher hoped that the lessons and the need to mix with other girls might help her confidence. It was my first close acquaintance with someone so rich. For years I had been frustrated, the poor girl whom her wealthy friends pitied; for years I had been in and out of big houses without getting to know the people. Yet here I was, much gayer and more carefree than this girl with all her wealth. We had a splendid holiday; Helen, able to draw on what money she wished, spent it generously.

Presently it was time to join the D'Oyly Carte tour. The

Repertory Opera company, which undertook it, was led by such
famous players as Henry Lytton and Bertha Lewis, Leo Sheffield,
Sydney Granville, Darrell Fancourt, and Winifred Lawson. I did
not want to share with anybody else in the chorus, so my first
room was awful, an over-heated conservatory where I was surrounded by plants. In consequence, with a wretched cold, I had no
voice for rehearsals. Wisely, after this week I went in with two
other girls, and we kept together in much better and cheaper
accommodation until the tour ended. Though in no sense
depressed, for it was a likeable company, I knew that I could not
stay with the D'Oyly Carte; I had other stage ambitions than
these fairies and *contadine*, schoolgirls of Titipu and General
Stanley's daughters. That aside, I enjoyed some of the towns; we
remained normally for two weeks, longer sometimes, which gave
me a chance to explore. At the end, when I asked to be released,
Rupert D'Oyly Carte himself said: 'Is this wise?' I could have a
secure job for years and already showed promise as an understudy.
But, in spite of his persuasiveness, I was determined.

Back in London, I enrolled for dancing classes with a noted
teacher, Carlotta Mosetti, in Soho. After various auditions I was
engaged, as Eileen Carey, for the chorus of a musical comedy, *The
First Kiss* (1924), a piece with some vague Spanish origin, that
starred Désirée Ellinger and ran for only six weeks at the New
Oxford Theatre (where I had once seen Carrie Rose). More auditions; and another musical with a wild title, *Love's Prisoner*, that
had an even shorter run, three weeks at the Adelphi in the spring
of 1925: this piece, set in Cornwall during the Napoleonic Wars,
had Harry Welchman in the lead. Among its chorus-girls was
Mona Warren, the beginning of our prolonged friendship; she
married B. C. Hilliam, the writer and pianist, 'Flotsam' of the
'Flotsam and Jetsam' act. With *Love's Prisoner* fading so swiftly,
we hunted together for other work and heard that everybody was
discussing auditions for a big new American play, *Rose Marie*, in
preparation for the Theatre Royal, Drury Lane, not yet a regular
musical-comedy house. Both Mona and myself applied at once. I
took great care to dress in a plain polo-necked sweater and a short
pleated skirt so that I would be ready for my audition dance when

the time came, with no bother about changing. When I got to Drury Lane I must have been half-dead with practising; the place was crowded, and we were summoned, ten together, to wait in the wings for our call. Usually at that time you both sang and did a routine dance to the chorus of your song.

I had never been more nervous; it was a miracle that I did not lose my voice or fall flat on my face. Somehow I did get through; but even then, as soon as my turn had ended, I was walking off in a daze. Suddenly an American voice spoke from the darkness of the stalls: 'Hey! Don't you want the job?' I went back and said feebly, 'Thank-you.' I was in, and deliriously happy.

CHAPTER TWO

Eileen and Sean

I LOVED those strenuous rehearsals for *Rose Marie*, believing that here I had started stage life in earnest. Our American directors were expert and thorough: they made us rehearse morning to evening, and I was learning to work well. A good deal of this 'romance of the Canadian Rockies' depended upon its dancing. A spectacular number, one that invariably roused an audience, was the Totem Dance at a lodge in the Kootenay Pass, to the music of 'Totem Tom Tom': *Rose Marie* is still famed for it. Sean would write, in *Rose and Crown*, that of all the plays he saw during his early weeks in London, he remembered one thing only, the Drury Lane chorus, 'the extraordinary, beautiful slide and slip, shimmering with colour'. After we had opened, Edith Day, our leading lady, who was warmly approachable, asked me to several parties. The Prince of Wales was at one or two of these, and more than once he would be at the Café de Paris, that smart night-club of the twenties, when I went to a supper and dance after the show: to me he was a quiet, ordinary young man, unobtrusive among his party of three or four.

Billy Merson, our *Rose Marie* comedian, who got through a lot of burlesque dancing, was a small, gay Cockney, frequently around joking with the girls; I liked him. He had relatives in to help him as chauffeur and dresser; and it seemed to be a jolly family. Derek Oldham, our leading man, was reserved by comparison.

I had several young men who took me out, one in particular who was in the Navy. Another, Ben, who was extremely rich, would take me to cricket at Lords and to race meetings where we lunched in the special enclosure. I spent several week-ends with his people. They were not forthcoming; after all, I was simply a chorus-girl. Moreover, besides being on the stage, I was modelling hats and furs for two major photographers, Dorothy Wilding and Janet Jevons, which meant that my name was printed under advertisements in the *Tatler*. There would be a picture of me, looking solemn and dopey in a fur or hat, with the caption, 'Posed by Eileen Carey'. My country week-ends would be perfectly all right during the day when we could go about and visit the people Ben knew; but the evenings were just dull. The talk was of nothing but horses, or hunting, shooting and fishing, and as it was all foreign to me I could merely sit and listen – at least sit.

Visits to the Navy boy's parents were far better. Delightful people, they lived in an old Gloucestershire rectory; the father was a Protestant canon. We responded to each other, and these were always cheerful meetings. I was enjoying life, with a job made to last – *Rose Marie* had moved into a safe run – and extra money to be earned in modelling. I had lessons in dancing and voice production. Most evenings after the show I was at a supper-dance. My only problem was my mother; I could not bring myself to live with her, so I used every week to give her money and she would live in a series of rooms where I visited her with Stella; Helen went also. It was now that Helen's trustees in the City asked me to call. She wanted, they said, to get me a flat of my own; she had plenty of money, and apparently they considered that if this was what she wished to do she should do it. Eventually we got a flat behind Baker Street – it was in Dorset Street, St Andrew's Mansions – and chose the furniture for it. Though Stella lived there to begin with, she left quite soon because she needed a studio. It was not a big flat, a sitting-room, two small bedrooms, kitchen, and bathroom: very dark, and quiet as well because the flats looked out upon a courtyard where a porter was on duty at the gate.

After Stella left, I did try for a bit to have my mother with me. It proved to be hopeless. I would come home late, tired after my work at Drury Lane, and sometimes supper and dancing; and at nine o'clock in the morning she would pounce into my bedroom, pull the curtains, throw the window open, and say: 'No girl of your age should be in bed at this hour. This awful life you are leading. . . . This unnatural life.' I saw it could never last. Finally a hat caused the break. I loved hats, especially an affair of soft velour which came down over my eyes and had a bobble on top; I fancied myself in it greatly. One morning after a singing lesson, when I rushed in to get ready to lunch with a boy, having left my hat and dress on the bed, I found that Mother had cut off the bobble, and some of the velour from the brim; there was nothing to do but scream. 'You must go,' I cried; 'I know you will drive me mad if you stay.' And she went. She had never been happy in the flat; after all, I was away from it most of the time. Temporarily she found rooms with somebody she knew in Brighton where she had other acquaintances.

II

Rose Marie had been on at the Lane for six months when Helen, who was going to New York, asked me to accompany her. There were people she wanted to see; and she was thinking of getting married. Naturally, I would have liked to go; but how to leave my work? I could not abandon my contract. After talking it over carefully, Lee Ephraim, the *Rose Marie* manager whom I was very fond of, said he could arrange for me to move straight into the chorus of *Rose Marie* at the Imperial in New York: I was a good worker, and the method in each production was the same. At that period it was customary, and I am sure still is, for an author or producer to ask some of the girls out to lunch or dinner. I went frequently at first with Oscar Hammerstein, Junior, part-author of the *Rose Marie* book; then this stopped and I was more and more in the company of Lee Ephraim, going out at night to dance with him at the Café de Paris, the Kit Kat Club or the Gargoyle. A man of perhaps forty, kind and attentive, he was married. Not markedly well read or interested in art, he was less cultured than C. B. Cochran but certainly a cut above Jimmy White, the Lancashire impresario, who was a power in the theatre. I recall mostly the huskiness of Lee's voice; he dressed conventionally and quietly, and entered a room without fuss. In appearance he could have been taken for a prosperous Jewish businessman. As a rule we talked of the many musical shows he was doing; it never bored me because I had ambitions to be a leading lady in a musical play. You might think he would have given me a small part somewhere, but I was wholly a beginner and, except for the little I had done at the Convent, and for dancing lessons from Carlotta Mosetti, I had no kind of dramatic or stage training. Further, I had not practised in any detail high kicking or soft-shoe techniques, simply ballroom steps and, at the Convent, country dancing: these did give me a sense of rhythm, and I loved to dance for its own sake. Lee was anxious to make sure that I should continue to work when I got to America; later, he said, when I had more experience, he would help me.

Eagerly, I prepared for the American trip, let my flat in St Andrew's Mansions, and arranged for agents to bank the rent and for the bank to send a weekly sum to my mother. Once I had conquered my sea-sickness, which lasted only a day and a night, the voyage was fine: Helen had booked first-class in the *Mauretania*, and we were at the Captain's table. Joseph Duveen, the art connoisseur, was a passenger; so was the explorer Amundsen; they were in the parties that Captain Rostron used to invite to coffee in his cabin after dinner. Because Helen had a weak heart, the voyage upset her and she had to go to bed early; but I seized any fun that was around, from fancy-dress balls to singing at the ship's concert.

When we had reached New York and booked in at a large hotel, the noise was the first thing I noticed: after London it was terrible, more especially as our hotel was close to the 'El' railway where the trains every five or ten minutes would make a shattering row. I resolved after a few days not to ask at once for a job in *Rose Marie* or to show the management Lee's letter, but to hunt for something else, possibly a small walk-on or a part. It meant a round of the agents. At the first of them, while running up the stairs, I nearly knocked a man down; apologising, I said that I must hurry on as there was an audition to catch. 'Are you English?' he asked. 'No,' I said; 'I'm Irish.'

'Well, if you don't get into the show you are auditioning for, come and do an audition for me.'

He gave me the number of his room and a card. The audition I wanted was over, so I glanced at the card to see where this one might be and was startled to find the name of the famous George M. Cohan, actor, author, director and composer. Recovering, I found the room where Cohan himself greeted me with a grin. Why was such a pretty girl roaming about New York on her own? What did I want, and who was I? I explained that I had been only in the chorus, and that I would probably join the Broadway *Rose Marie*. At once he gave me a script with the few lines of a maid's part; I repeated them again and again, and after reading them with me he promised to let me have a contract – to play this part and to understudy a principal in the comedy he was taking on the road. I would hear where to sign the contract and also when rehearsals would begin.

The comedy, *American Born*, had had its short New York run. Set in England at somewhere called Malbridge Hall, with Cohan playing the Master of Malbridge, it contained besides such figures as a 'real estate broker' and 'Lady Bertram, of the District', a remarkably large domestic staff: housekeeper, butler, second butler, under butler, groom and 'Annie, a maid' (myself). There was time to spare before rehearsal. I intended to earn my own money, not simply to stay with Helen; so I tried advertising agencies and was engaged to model clothes and some négligés. Dozens of us were at it; we worked at speed, and the money was appropriate, but there was an astonishing difference from the orderly method in London. A big room held several screened-off sets for the various advertisements. I remember reclining in a négligé on a soft, furry couch. Under highly professional direction you took up several postures as if it were a film; and if you were wrong they simply shouted at you. I did several days in this studio; maybe I would have gone on with it, but rehearsals were called for Cohan's play, and I signed off at the agency.

By this time I had moved with Helen to a small hotel on 74th

Street, the Berkeley. Rehearsals before the tour opened were not exacting; I had only a couple of sentences, 'feed' lines for Cohan which in effect would alter at every performance. Lee had come over from England, and I saw him whenever I could; he was worried about my circumstances and wished that I could be in a New York musical, with more company and more practice. After the first weeks I saw that he was right; there would have been better fun in New York and the chorus than in *American Born* which had no young people in its cast. It was dreary sitting around waiting to utter a sentence or two.

While our company was at Atlantic City, I would catch the midnight train to New York where Lee met me; we were deeply in love then. I had not lived with him before; now he chose the best hotel on Park Avenue, quiet and elegant; strangely, in those days we had separate rooms. In order to keep me contented Lee had to be discreet because I was full of fears bred of a Catholic conscience, fears I must say that I overcame well; my upbringing had been hypocritical, my main rule never to be found out. Lee's wife had poor health; he did not want to hurt her, and care was necessary. There was no problem in New York, but he had at length to return to London, and I was left to carry on with the tour of an unexciting play and my occasional odd lines as a maid dressed in a smart, short black taffeta dress, with a small white apron.

Cohan, a Bohemian character and a notable figure of his time, clearly liked me a lot; even so, he was not nasty when he understood that I loved another man. In fact he grew fatherly, taking me to the cinema on non-matinée afternoons, and often in the evenings giving supper in his hotel room to five or six others and myself. When again the play got close to the outskirts of New York, I returned to my room at the Berkeley and travelled nightly to the show in terrible weather, icy and snowing. Only a few weeks remained. Cohan was doing another production in which I could have a minor part; or, had I wanted, I could have attended other auditions. By now I was despondent for I had no close friends in New York, only people who came over from England. When Ben arrived to see relatives, we often went out together. He had a most attractive uncle, so I would ask another girl to make up a foursome. Indeed I got on better with the uncle than the nephew; I liked older men and he was an excellent talker. I had leisure also to find some of the art galleries whose names Joseph Duveen had given to me on the voyage. I had always enjoyed these visits; in the dressing-room they used to tease me about my fondness for pictures. Moreover, I could go on Sundays to the theatre. It was now, at the Neighbourhood Playhouse, that I saw Mary Ellis – a musical comedy lead until something harmed her singing voice – as the girl Leah, possessed by the devil in *The Dybbuk*.

Time passed; but what, I kept asking myself, should I be doing with my life? At the moment it was aimless. Though, if I married, it would presumably be my naval boy, I seemed to be in a muddle. At this point my mother wrote to say that she was seriously ill, and would I return; and I thought that on the whole it would be wiser to get home again while I had the fare.

One miserable day, glum and cold, the girl I had understudied in *American Born* handed me a play to read. 'Can you speak with a brogue?' she asked. No, I told her, explaining that though Irish by birth I had been brought up in England. Nevertheless, she left the play with me and I found that I was reading *Juno and the Paycock*, a tragedy by the Irish dramatist, Sean O'Casey. Forgetting everything else, I read it straight to the end, profoundly moved. Suddenly I became as happy as I had been miserable; overcome with excitement, I wished above all else to meet the dramatist himself. Here I was, imagining myself as an O'Casey actress, a girl with no experience except the chorus and the tiny part I had just done.

How were we to meet? I had booked my passage to Southampton for a week later. Lee would be waiting for me, and he must take me to see *Juno* in the West End; after that he might arrange for me to see the author. A few days previously I had been to a fortune-teller supposed to be as reliable as she was expensive. She insisted that I would go to England almost at once to meet there a man with piercing eyes and heavy boots, a man who would be world famous and whom I would marry. Furious and thinking that my money had been wasted, I could hardly sit still while she babbled on; I had no intention of going back. Most likely, I would accept the job in the next Cohan show. Anyway, the description of the man I was supposed to marry sounded entirely unromantic.

My last week-end in New York was full. A girl named Babs Dodge, whom Helen had come across to meet, was to sail home with me. On the evening before we left I was asked to a party at Mayor Walker's, crowded, gay, and full of theatre people; I got to the hotel in time to finish my packing, then out to the boat in the early hours: again the *Mauretania*, with the same captain. It ought to be a pleasant trip, and, in spite of a tiresome bout of sciatica, so it was.

Lee was at the docks in Southampton. After dinner we drove to London. Glad though I was to be with him and to be back in the flat, one thought obsessed me: how to get to *Juno and the Paycock*? Lee fixed it at once. On the next night I was sitting with him in the stalls of the old Royalty Theatre in Soho, with no imaginable idea that I would soon have to choose between the man sitting beside me and the author of *Juno* who was a complete stranger. It underrates my feelings to say that I was excited. These Irish players, Sara Allgood as Juno, Maire O'Neill as Maisie Madigan, Arthur Sinclair as Boyle, Sydney Morgan as Joxer, were astonishing individually and as a cast. At Sara's last speech, 'Sacred Heart o' Jesus, take away our hearts o' stone, and give us hearts o' flesh! Take away this murdherin' hate, an' give us Thine own eternal love', the theatre was held in absolute silence. Applauding, with tears of emotion, I could not think of the man who had brought me to the play but only of its author and where and how we could meet.

Within a few days my telephone rang. It was Lee's voice: 'Eileen, I have done what you asked. I have arranged for you to see J. B. Fagan, and Sean O'Casey will be there.' He gave me the time and place, fixing our own rendezvous afterwards. At the hour, extremely nervous, I reached the little Fortune Theatre where the manager of *Juno*, James Bernard Fagan, had his office. He was sitting at his desk, but to this day I have no really clear picture of how he looked or how he behaved. I centred my whole self on the man who sat beside the desk: the dramatist, Sean O'Casey.

III

Sean, then aged forty-six, was a lean man with hazel eyes that were weak but strangely penetrating: he looked directly at you when he spoke. Now he stepped forward, took both my hands in his, and said in his rich and lovely Irish voice, 'There is no need to be nervous.' It was obvious that I was, but only for a minute: he put me at ease with the immediate unspoken suggestion that he genuinely admired me. The office was not warm. I noticed that Sean kept on a trench-coat and had an orange-coloured muffler loosely round his neck. He wore heavy boots; but it was not for many years that I remembered my New York fortune-teller. How the interview went, I cannot say, though I struggled on, trying to say that I had read *Juno* and had been overcome by it, that I had seen it and thought it wonderful, and that though I had done so little I wanted to act in it if it went on tour, and would like to play Mary Boyle. Throughout I concentrated on Sean because somehow he was talking to me all the time. When the interview was over, and James Fagan had probably said, in the polite formula, that he would let me know – certainly he asked me to leave my address – I was reluctant to go. Realising that Sean was equally reluctant, I knew that this man, so unlike any other I had ever met or gone about with, was attracted to me. Though it might not have been love at first sight, he fascinated me and I could not stop thinking about him. We did not marry for more than sixteen months. Yet from that first afternoon until his death thirty-eight years later, I don't suppose I ever lost him.

We had met. What would follow? I went dining and dancing, started to think of work, considered the possibilities. If I were stuck I could always return to *Rose Marie* which was running on to full houses, many of my friends still in it. Then of a sudden I had a telephone call. It was Sean, asking me to come again to the Fortune Theatre to see Fagan and himself. This was the meeting that really settled my fate and my life with Sean O'Casey: Kathleen O'Regan, it seemed, had been taken ill, and he invited me to play Nora Clitheroe in *The Plough and the Stars* which was due to open within ten days at the Fortune – just across the road from Drury Lane and *Rose Marie*. Sean himself compared the theatres, big and small, to Falstaff and the little page.

Astounded by the offer, I argued that I had no experience for so difficult a part. Whether Sean loved me already and was resolved to help me, blinded by his admiration, or whether the management was in a spot and could get nobody else, I cannot say. On reading the script I was even more alarmed. Nora is a young married woman in a Dublin tenement, with a desire, that the neighbours deride, to improve herself and her home. When her husband is summoned to the Irish Citizen Army as a commandant at the time of the Easter Rebellion in 1916, he leaves Nora, who is having a child, to live alone. Fighting across the city is fierce; after she has tried to find her husband and has had an emotional meeting with him, he is killed. In the last Act Bessie Burgess, formerly so opposed to Nora, is nursing her, for the girl is mad with grief at the loss of her child. ('Her eyes are glimmering with the light of incipient insanity; her hands are nervously fiddling with her nightgown.') It is a most testing scene; my terror and reluctance can be understood. Sean was patient; he used every persuasion, we read through the part together, and at length I agreed, something only a foolish and ambitious girl would have done. I was doubly handicapped because the sciatica which had hit me on the voyage from America had recurred.

Now I ceased to go out with anybody; even to learn the part inside two weeks was a strain. Sean was infinitely helpful during rehearsals that were far from cheering. I did get some aid from Kate Rorke, the former actress, who was giving voice lessons and who steered me through the part. But though, when I did go to her, she was my prop and encouragement, I could not manage it often. In the cast of *The Plough* were the major Irish players. Sally (Sara) Allgood, whose work I venerated, was unsympathetic to young girls, and the fact that Sean was making such a fuss of me hardly told in my favour. Her sister, Maire O'Neill, was invariably kind; so were Sinclair and the men, but most of my scenes were with Sally. Oddly, the mad scene, the hardest, was the one I got through best, and there both Sally and Arthur Sinclair praised me.

The Plough and the Stars opened at the Fortune on the sixth day of the General Strike of 1926: no newspapers appeared except the official *British Gazette*, and in a way this was lucky for me; at first few critics came to the theatre. *The Plough* was a success with the public: an even better play, I thought, than *Juno*, and it pleased Sean to hear me say it. He did not send me large bouquets or baskets of flowers, as other friends did for the première. Instead he came back to my dressing-room and talked, trying to make me confident about myself – as Eileen Carey, dear Sean – though he could not have guessed that it was a task practically impossible: I was paralysed with nerves. Lee called for me when the play was over: we went on to the Savoy for a quiet supper, with only a few friends, and Lee, who was truthful and recognised my worries and want of assurance, urged me not to fret; I had brought it off well, considering my lack of experience and only brief rehearsals, a beginner thrown among the top professionals of the time. 'I think you'll find', he said, 'that as you go on with this, every night will be like an extra rehearsal; you'll improve enormously as the run develops.'

My first gift from Sean was a box of six macaroons. Glancing into my dressing-room before a matinée, he had asked if he could get me anything – anything at all. As a joke I said vaguely, 'Some macaroons for my tea.' There, at the interval, they were: he told me that an intelligent taxi-man had driven him to the right shop. Afterwards, for tea in his flat, he would always try to buy macaroons. When he took me home in a taxi, he would ask, 'Have you enough money? Are you sure?'; many times, if I had wanted them, he would have given me bundles of notes. Receiving his royalties, he had no idea what money meant; through life he never cared for it. He was not reckless, not a drinker. Naturally generous, he longed, without attempting the usual kinds of gift, to show how much he loved you, to be with you and to talk. We passed much of our time in restaurants or in the park; it was a joy to be with him and to listen.

The first letter I had from Sean was an invitation to tea in the rooms where Mrs Sparrow was his landlady, at Trafalgar Square, Chelsea: rather a misleading address, for when he forgot to say Chelsea people were in the habit of taking a cab towards the National Gallery. This was my first visit to him, in a large, dismal sitting-room. He was as shy as I was. Mrs Sparrow had laid the tea, and after she had carried in the teapot we were able to relax a little. But every time Sean made any approach to me there was Mrs Sparrow: 'Do you want any more milk?' or 'Do you want any sugar?' She came in at least four times. After tea we sat on the sofa and Sean was about to kiss me when Mrs Sparrow reappeared: 'Have you finished with the tea-things? Can I clear away?' Once more we sat strained; I had a struggle not to laugh. Then she went; Sean, beginning to tell me what a lovely girl I was, again prepared to kiss me, and again Mrs Sparrow entered: 'Do you mind if I leave the door open so that I can hear you if you want anything?' We gave it up and left for a walk in the park. That room in Trafalgar Square was the only one I recall without a trace of Sean's personality. His coat and cap hung on the back of the door; a few books and papers were scattered round; so were his ash-tray and cigarettes. Otherwise it might have been any dreary hotel lounge: not at all like Sean.

From Trafalgar Square he wrote his second letter to me:

My dear Eileen Carey,
Be brave and be confident of the power and possibilities that are in you. Fight firmly against the disadvantages that are wrestling with you, and the effort will give you a strength that will bring you a strength that is greater still.

You have done well, and you will do better.

If you should want any help in any way, any advice about a particular phase or incident, ask me and all the fullness of sympathetic help that is in me will be freely given to you.

With best wishes,
SEAN O'CASEY

I saw more of him once *The Plough* had begun, and when the Strike was still on: no buses, no Tubes, no trains, a general hold-up. Having fought so much for workers in Ireland, he was keenly excited, expecting to find a riot outside his windows or, at the very least, some form of shouting protest. But when he rose early to see what had happened it was all quite orderly; private cars were stopping to offer lifts, and if anything the streets seemed to be quieter than before. Sean, bitterly disappointed, felt let down; he could not fathom why I took no interest in politics. True, I hoped that the strikers would win what they asked for, more money and better conditions, but I was by no means as roused as Sean had wished me to be.

After I had been playing Nora for about three weeks, Kathleen O'Regan, who had recovered, turned up at a Saturday matinée. Improving daily and knowing that the audiences were responsive, I was less nervous; that evening I had asked people to come in to see me. But after the matinée Kathleen decided to appear at night herself. Being easily intimidated, I left without either seeing or speaking to her, and with no question of returning as an understudy; I just wanted to go.

Lee helped presently by offering me the soubrette in a tour of *The Street Singer*, a frothy musical comedy with a book by Frederick Lonsdale. I was a young milliner, opposite the comedian who played a butler, and we had a duet and dance routine. Sean wrote to me before the tour began: 'Remember the advice of Saint Teresa – "Pray as if everything depended upon God; work as if everything depended upon yourself".' Throughout the engagement I was ill. Fate, I reflected morosely, could never have meant me to act; in some way I must be handicapped and doomed. Our production kept to a twice-nightly tour of theatres and music-halls in the London suburbs and on the fringe, a twelve weeks' circuit of such places as Croydon, Lewisham, Penge and Stoke Newington. Several times Sean, who found it a very poor business and who was worried about my health, journeyed out to see me and to bring me home. He had lately moved from Trafalgar Square to a flat in Clareville Street in the Gloucester Road area of South Kensington; his desk and books were forwarded from Dublin, and with the advice of his friend Billy McElroy, he had bought the essential furniture.

Stella, as well as Sean, chanced to be in front on a Saturday evening. By then the sciatica was so painful that the other girls were ironing my leg with a hot iron and brown paper. Before each entrance I swallowed aspirins, and at the end, when I had lost my voice entirely and could only open and shut my mouth, the comedian carried me along. It was like a mime; the audience, with no hint that I was ill, found it extremely funny. I came off and passed out. Stella got me to my flat where later the doctor arrived to save me – luckily, because all day I had been taking aspirin upon aspirin. Sean rang up, asking what had gone wrong; Stella, without telling him everything, said simply that I had been ill. Happily I could rest on Sunday and most of Monday, and by the next performance I was again all right.

IV

In this touring period Sean by no means dominated me. I went out a lot with Bill, who was in the Navy and stationed at Greenwich. Also I saw a good deal of Lee and other friends, one of them a banker's son. Often I got home late; Sean would ring me up, warning me that I needed more sleep and rest and that the other person I had been with was not worth it. Sometimes I would meet him for supper, loving the affection, tenderness and praise in which no one could compare with him. But generally we would have tea in the Clareville Street flat; although it was good to be with him, I did prefer a supper and dance in the evenings.

There came a week when I had not met Sean for quite a time and was torn emotionally between him and Lee – each so utterly different. While walking in Bond Street, miserable after a visit to a doctor about my sciatica, I suddenly noticed Sean passing me; we were overwhelmed. 'My dear child,' he said, 'you look ill. Come and talk.' We found a teashop and I released all my troubles, glad to relax in his ready sympathy. Afterwards he accompanied me home, begging me to give up the tour which, he said, was not worth a damn anyway. No doubt he was right, but it was impossible to break my contract, and the tour would be ending soon.

Early in December it did. That Christmas I went to the Riviera with Helen and her husband, Yule Elliott, at whose wedding in St Margaret's, Westminster, earlier that year, I had been a bridesmaid. Though it was a glorious holiday, it brought my real severance from Lee. One evening, with Helen and her husband, I had gone into Monte Carlo to dine with Lee and his wife, an attractive woman to whom he was most attentive; she appeared to have trouble in walking, and moved slowly. Somehow I saw that my position was false. While out with Lee on the next afternoon I told him that we should end our relationship. We were both exceedingly upset – at the moment, in fact, I felt broken-hearted – and agreed to do nothing more until we had got back.

In London, after a variety of auditions and photographic modelling jobs, I reached the Royal Court Theatre in Sloane Square, controlled by Sir Barry Jackson. The Devon comedy of *The Farmer's Wife* had run through more than 1300 performances. Now a new play, by the same author, Eden Phillpotts, was wildly diverse: a serious piece, *The Blue Comet*, about a Hampstead family facing the destruction of the world. A critic said logically that if the world did not end the last Act was bound to be an anti-climax; and it was. I had a small bit in this Act, besides playing a newspaper boy (shouts of 'Evening paper!' under the stage and off) and understudying the leading lady, Cecily Byrne. Towards the close of *The Blue Comet*, which struggled on for barely a month, *Rose Marie* reached its last night after nearly two years at Drury Lane, and Lee was eager for me to be there at the curtain. I had to stay for my bit at the Court; but a frantic rush by taxi got me to the Lane just in time to join a packed house in the farewell to *Rose Marie* and to reflect on what had happened to me during its run.

Again I was not working. Some evenings I spent with old friends, Ben among them, though we were never truly in love. Bill had gone to sea; certainly I would have wanted to marry him if Lee and Sean had not entered my life. Lee himself was in the midst of auditions for his new musical, *The Desert Song*, which was opening at Drury Lane, with Rudolf Friml's score, early in April. Having continued my singing lessons, I auditioned for the understudy to the leading lady – she was Edith Day once more –

and got through a stiff test. But Sean did not approve and I knew that I had to make an alarming choice.

If I chose the musical, I must stay with Lee, who was sad about my recent behaviour. Yet Sean now was dominating. Conscious though I was that it would mean a life utterly remote from anything in my experience, I did not stop to ask whether I would be happy or not. His power of words, in his letters and in our talks, had won me, and at last I turned down the offer from Drury Lane. Soon after this Sean and Lee arrived simultaneously one evening on the doorstep of St Andrew's Mansions, Sean frail but almost ready to knock Lee down, Lee stockily built and resolute. Glaring at each other, they said that they were going to walk round the block to talk things out. They vanished; then, after a while, Sean reappeared to tell me that he wanted us to marry and that he had made it clear to Lee. Much later that night Lee telephoned, profoundly upset but saying that if this was what I desired I had played with his affections long enough. So, though my distress about him remained, it was settled. I was pledged to Sean.

Now we went everywhere together, to picture galleries and theatres, to Kew and Richmond, and into the country. None of my friends were pleased. My mother came to Sean to tell him that it was wicked and wrong of him to marry a good Catholic girl; he was ruining my life and spoiling my chances with more suitable men. Sean, who never liked her but who kept his patience, could not feel that her concern was real. Throughout his life we had to provide for her, and as she was exactly opposite to all he believed in, this could cause a lot of unhappiness.

V

A new play, in which I was not acting, had an even shorter run at the Court than *The Blue Comet*. Finally, Barry Jackson resolved to present the Irish Players in Sean's early tragedy, *The Shadow of a Gunman*, which had not yet been staged in London. It was short, in two Acts only, so at first Synge's *Riders to the Sea* was put on as a curtain-raiser. To my mixed delight and fear, Sir Barry asked me

to play Minnie Powell in the *Gunman*; again I was in the great
Irish company and again in a flap of nerves. During rehearsals I
met Sean daily; on most evenings I would dine with him at a
table always reserved for us in the corner of a restaurant, the
Queen's near Sloane Square, that was popular with writers and
artists. Here I saw first the tall, leonine figure of Augustus John
with whom Sean, who called him 'strong and kingly', got on very
well; both were intolerant of anybody they did not like. They met
frequently at the Queen's with Billy McElroy, backer of Sean's
plays in London; and during the run of the *Gunman* I would join
them after the performance.

Minnie, my second O'Casey part, was a young, pretty and
aspiring girl living in a Dublin tenement house during the summer
of 1920. Seeking to help a fellow-lodger, a poet, whom she
believed wrongly to be a gunman in hiding, she was shot by
English soldiers after a tragedy of errors. By this time I was able to
act more confidently with Sinclair and Sydney Morgan, Sara
Allgood and Maire O'Neill, and Harry Hutchinson who was the
poet Davoren. In *Riders to the Sea* (Sean called it 'a lovely melody of
pain'), where Sara Allgood had a famous part as the bereaved
island-mother, I played a 'keener' at the wake besides understudying the daughter. Like certain other great actresses, Sara
Allgood could be unkind to her younger colleagues. Though in
Riders I was not considering my appearance at all, she would hold
my arm tightly, almost pinching it, and whisper, 'Keep your head
from the audience. They're not looking at *you!*' After which,
leaving me like a jelly, she would turn to the house her own face,
full of warmth, and speak her lines. True, she did not always
behave like this; when I had begun to improve, she would act with
me, on equal terms, which made me feel proud. I watched her
from the wings, observing how beautifully she used her hands to
express rage or grief or affection, and knowing that the throb in
her voice never failed to excite me. After my marriage to Sean we
became friends.

It must have been in these days that Sean went to James
Fagan's production of his own play, *And So to Bed*, a comedy of the
Restoration, with Edmund Gwenn as Pepys, Yvonne Arnaud, and

Fagan's wife, Mary Grey. Sean, who did not like the piece (he wrote later that it was 'moribund') tried not to tell Fagan so, but when pressed he said what he thought. He was always courageous in this way; I admired it, but he hated to give an opinion to a personal friend unless he was urged. His candour with Fagan meant a slight cooling-off.

Sean had come to know all my problems and background, the bills I owed for my dresses, my helplessness with money. Nobody but he must pay my debts, though they must have sounded outrageous to him. He did not comment; he only wanted for me to be free from worry. This, I remember, was a period when, because I was scared of dogs, I had been given a wire-haired terrier in the hope that I might forget my fear. Bobbie was engaging and affectionate, but I continued to be uneasy, though somehow we managed to get on. He never obeyed me when I called; off the lead in Hyde Park or Kew Gardens, he just scampered wildly. With footballers he could be amusing, even if they failed to see the fun when he tore into the middle of a pitch and ran after the ball, keeping everyone in chase until we could trap him. Sean appreciated him because he was so game. We were not allowed to have dogs in the Court Theatre, and Bobbie had to be tied up in the stage doorkeeper's cubby-hole; somehow he always got free to find his way up the stairs, and at the dressing-table I would feel a wet lick on my leg; in the end the doorkeeper took no notice. Bobbie was around throughout our engagement. He appears in Sean's letters; in this, for example, from Clareville Street on 4 August 1927:

My dear Eileen,
Oh – my – God! Yes, I believe, I'm sure of it – before you sat down to write the letter you sent to me, you were charged full with gallons of Golden Guinea. It bubbled and sparkled, glittered and gleamed and shone. You'll have to learn to write as you talk, for as the Psalmist says somewhere, 'Thy tongue is the pen: of a ready writer.'

I'm so glad to hear that you are feeling fit again. Grapple that feeling to thy soul with hooks of steel.

Myself, I've done no work. I have spent the passing hours

sitting, walking, rambling, idling voluptuously in Kensington
Gardens: Sean and carelessness have met together: idleness and
he have kissed each other. Hallelujah!

Sorry, but not surprised, to hear that Bobbie has had a
'terrible fight'. It is said that the Millennium will be heralded in
by the lying down of the lion with the lamb. It's a damned
egregious error – it will be when Bobbie lies down with a cat.

I am going to try to do a little work today; to put a stone or
two on the tottering wall, and repair the broken hedge.

And so farewell, my dear little Eileen, till Friday:

SEAN

And again (undated):

I am very glad to hear that Bobbie's much better. I had visions
from what your mother said of Bobbie flying round the flat like
a roaring lion seeking whom he might devour, and crowds of
citizens, firemen, soldiers and police watching him through the
window, while they waited for the heavy artillery to come up.

VI

At Billy McElroy's suggestion Sean bought me a ring. They went
off together to Regent Street to choose it: a simple platinum ring
with a sapphire surrounded by small diamonds. In years ahead it
would have a history of its own, it was so often pawned. Those
days I was in Clareville Street far more often than in St Andrew's
Mansions. Now and again Tallulah Bankhead, a beauty (as
Augustus John painted her) and a natural wit, would join Sean at
tea. Olga Lindo was another guest: an actress Sean also respected
as a talker. Neither of them was in search of a part; they came for
Sean's warmly courteous welcome. Even if we kept it from each
other, both Sean and myself were nervous about our decision.
His side is shown in a letter he wrote to me on 10 September, a
fortnight before our marriage. I had gone to Bognor to visit Mona
Hilliam for a long week-end and to try to convince myself of our
wisdom.

Sean said:

I suppose you and Bobbie got down to Bognor safely, Eileen – I
fear neither you nor he nor Mona will do a lot of dancing in the
sun. . . . I have missed you, and am missing you now. I wish,
I wish, I wish you were here with me. I have my play – I did
quite a lot of work today – my thoughts teeming in my head,
and all the books, and yet I miss you, miss you, miss you very
much indeed, darling.

I have just got your letter which tells me you wish to be with
me and that you love me.

This frightens me a little – oh, not because of reasons that
may flicker through your mind – but because of the possibility
of pain and disappointment to you. Day by day a dread of
giving pain to others flickers in me to a fuller strength, and how
much to me are you above all the others!

And yet, when I read your dear words, my darling, a glow of
joy unstemmed went through me, for I love you, Eileen, and I
cannot help it. Your loveliness and your charm have broken
down defences built by reason.

Be at ease, unquiet spirit – I dined this evening at the
Queen's. Your pen-picture of myself and all of my movements
is very good, and as I think, very true indeed.

Yes, indeed, you are a strange girl, Eileen, and very lovely too,
and charming, sweet, and very dear indeed to

SEAN

The question now was where and when we should be married.
Sean was not a Catholic; and, even if I was about the most
bewildered Catholic ever, I did want to be married in a church.
We had to call upon a priest to plan everything; by coincidence,
Father Howell in Sean's parish, which was Chelsea, had known
me at school. Genial and obliging, he ordered matters as simply as
possible; Sean respected him; and it was decided that we should
be married on 23 September 1927 at the Church of the Most Holy
Redeemer in Chelsea. I had also to notify a priest in my own
parish, at the church in Spanish Place. While we were waiting,
just before the priest came in, Sean leaned back in his chair and it
broke; we had hardly a minute to stick it together, prop it against
the wall, and stop laughing. The interview was quick and formal;

Sean had accepted my wish for a Catholic marriage service, a wonderful thing to me, realising his opinions as I did, and all the routine a mixed marriage would involve. Soon reporters were ringing up, and photographers taking pictures of me, while Sean avoided as much of the publicity as he could. Telephone calls never stopped, invariably someone to ask where the wedding would be. Sean would say gravely anything that occurred to him. 'The Chelsea Baths at midnight' he told one reporter, and the man, who must have been a serious type, asked him if he were certain. 'Absolutely!' Sean replied with conviction.

On the night before the wedding I stayed at Helen's, near Berkeley Square. Next day Mrs Earle, formerly my dresser and like a mother at the time, helped to get me up expensively in blue chiffon and a blue coat in woollen material with a grey fur collar: both the dress and coat gifts from Helen. Captain Corby, the only man I knew apart from Lee and my boy friends, was to give me away; since I had worked for him in the Doultons tracing-office he had kept in touch with me and had entertained Stella and myself to meals. Having gone to see Sean when he knew I was to be married, he was probably the one person really pleased.

Sean, after a bout of bronchitis a few days earlier, was not too well on the wedding morning. He wore a dark suit that he liked to call plum-coloured. The daily girl who cleaned his flat had ironed his trousers, and I saw the mark of a burn on the seat; luckily the jacket covered it. My mother arrived at the church in black from hat to shoes, and in tears; somehow she was prevented when she tried to speak to Father Howell. She was distracted that she had not stopped the wedding, and maybe her worry over me was genuine. Only twelve or so of my nearest friends attended. Billy McElroy, Sean's best man, lost the ring, according to custom, and fumbled around for it. A camera, shooting the service for a news film which would be shown at the cinemas that evening, made a buzzing noise in the background.

Such a mixed marriage as this, between Catholic and non-Catholic, begins with the ordinary wedding ceremony and proceeds to the State marriage which is a formal business, merely a few words and the signing of the register. During our walk down the aisle after it was over, I felt composed, almost at peace. Fleetingly then, as I caught sight of Lee in a back pew, a surge of emotion returned; Sean held my hand firmly, as if in persuasion; and by the time we were outside the church I thought only of him. It was little more than sixteen months since that reading of *Juno and the Paycock* in New York when I vowed to meet the man who wrote it, and now we were married; nearly all of this within the life of a single musical play, *Rose Marie.*

CHAPTER THREE

Dublin Honeymoon

WE drove from the church to a wedding breakfast at Helen Elliott's in Charles Street, Berkeley Square: the kind of grand, precise occasion that Sean must have loathed, though he stuck it out until four-thirty, talking to Billy McElroy and Captain Corby, and several young people I had known in the theatre. We were leaving at once for our Irish honeymoon, so it meant a return to Clareville Street to change and to collect Sean's luggage. I dreaded the crossing and my invariable sea-sickness. Sean himself was an entirely untroubled sailor; when at Holyhead I disappeared at once to my cabin and lay down, fearing what might come, he began to walk round the deck, enjoying himself thoroughly. Billy McElroy's son, Willie, travelled over with us. Oliver St John Gogarty, the surgeon and writer, was to operate on his throat in Dublin; and when in the early morning we drew into Dun Laoghaire there Gogarty was, waiting to drive us to Howth.

At this fishing-village, nine miles north of Dublin, Sean had booked rooms in a hotel; he had told me of Howth many times and was longing to show it to me. Everything was fresh, for though born in Ireland I had never been back since leaving it as a child, whereas Sean had been away for less than two years. Heaven knows what I expected to see. The romantic stories I had heard from the Irish nuns at school, from my mother, and especially from Sean who had described the beauties of Ireland so eloquently, had led me to picture something unimaginably fine; but Dun Laoghaire pier on a grey September morning was disheartening. I felt sick, sad and practically in tears. Poor Sean!

Oliver Gogarty seemed to be in a frantic hurry, typical of his progress through life: Sean would write later of his 'whirlwind of restlessness'. We were off almost before we knew we had started, and he drove us to Howth at furious speed. There had been no opportunity to arrange ourselves, We had to tumble as best we could into the back seat of the car before Oliver got going, and one or the other of us must have sat on Sean's over-night bag, a small fibre suitcase containing his brush and comb and toothpaste and not much else. After a few miles we noticed that a long, white stream of toothpaste was oozing out on to the floor of the car. We had no possible hope of attracting Oliver's attention, for the moment we were off he had begun to talk, and he never paused. The paste had to go on oozing; when we reached the Howth hotel nothing was left in the tube though there was plenty on the floor and the car seat. Sean's case, battered out of recognition, we could only carry upstairs, and that was the end of it. Still talking, Oliver waved goodbye and roared off towards Dublin at the same headlong speed, with Willie McElroy by him in the front seat, wondering no doubt what the operation would be like with such a tumultuous personality as his surgeon.

Our room, we found, was as big as it was cheerless, and filled with solid Victorian furniture: I remember a huge wardrobe. The gas fire, on the other hand, was so small that it did nothing whatever to warm the vast spaces. Though we could admire the view – a wide, spreading panorama of Dublin Bay and the sun rising across the Irish Sea – more than anything at that moment we wanted warmth. Good though it was to sense something of the beauty of Ireland, I was happier when Sean asked for a coal fire to be lighted, and a pretty maid came in to lay it. The scene changed immediately; flames blazed in the grate; a breakfast table was placed in front of them. After hot tea, eggs and toast, we felt thawed and ready to get on with the day.

Actually, I got on with a bath: in this hotel a full-time operation. The geyser was old and tired, the trickle of water little more than tepid. When I complained, several charming people arrived promptly to investigate, and after a pause the geyser condescended to work – at least to supply enough water at nearer the right heat. The bathroom was cavernous and cold; the bath lacked much of its enamel. When you rose from it you were stamped with something like a map of Ireland. Yet I could not be annoyed; everybody was being as kind as possible, and they had to remain so while I was at Howth; I took a bath daily and sometimes twice. Sean thought I was bath crazy.

In late September, and out of season, the hotel had few guests; on our first night the dining-room was almost empty. Sean wanted me to have wine; what we ordered I cannot recall – I drank little then and it would have been something sweet. Nothing happened; we had all but finished dinner when our waiter hurried up solicitously with a plain bottle carefully wrapped in a napkin. Though they had not got what I had asked for, he had been (we assumed) over the entire village and had found this. Would it do? It was appalling. Still, with so much goodwill around, I felt I had to drink it. We did not order wine again; in fact, it was better for us to eat in our room by the fire, and anyway at night we were usually in Dublin.

Next morning we had another view of the amiably relaxed Irish hospitality. On our walk we called at a sweet-shop which was temptingly full of old-fashioned sweets, acid drops, bulls-eyes, lemon drops, in big glass jars. Behind the counter sat a dear old lady enveloped in a pinafore. The sweets I wanted were high on a shelf, and when I pointed to them she said mildly, 'Ah, I can't be bothered getting those down. If you want them, you must get them yourselves.' Obviously she served nothing unless it was in reach of her hand; the customers helped themselves and were glad to do it. Sean scrambled up obligingly and brought the jar; she put the sweets into a paper bag; we paid; and she said with unabated charm, 'And now would you mind putting the jar back again?' Sean obeyed; he and the old lady had performed the entire exercise with the gentlest courtesy. Clearly, I thought, this was Ireland.

II

Though we were enjoying Howth, it was convenient after the first week to move into Dublin. Every night we were at the theatre, and we had either to catch a last little train that ran between Dublin and Howth, or, expensively, to hire a car. So we moved into the Hotel Russell on St Stephen's Green; Lady Gregory had told Sean about it. Unpretentious in 1927, it later became smart. Now Sean could really show me the Dublin he loved, the places where he had lived, and the bookshops along the quay where, when he could, he had bought his first secondhand books: Dickens and Scott and Balzac and Ruskin, and the Globe edition of Shakespeare. A marvellous companion, Sean was humorous, watchful, and content to be with you, never wishing to stray; later I would be the restless one, needing at times to be on my own. In Dublin he was eager for me to meet his friends: Barry Fitzgerald (his real name was William Shields), the Abbey Theatre actor, who created the Paycock and Fluther Good; Gabriel (Gaby) Fallon, who, like Barry, acted at the Abbey part-time and was a Civil Servant; and Dr Joe Cummins, the eye specialist.

Because of poverty and malnutrition, Sean's sight had troubled him since birth. When he was older and began to write his plays, his eyes were seriously ulcerated and he had again to attend hospital; Dr Cummins, who treated him, recognised his personality and invited him back in the evenings to his house in Merrion Square. Only the doctor and his housekeeper lived in it, and he did little entertaining. Passionately devoted to modern medicine, he would travel to Vienna and other places on the Continent to study the latest methods in eye surgery. In Dublin he and Sean used to sit into the daybreak, talking about drama and music. Sean said of Merrion Square that it 'looked as if it had been knighted by king exclusion and queen quietness, separating it from the lumbering, trade-tired streets of Dublin', and elsewhere he praised Dr Cummins as 'delicate in word and phrase and manner, sensitive to a high degree, but a true bohemian, all the same'.

Living with Sean, I understood his problem. Every morning his eyes would be sore and hard to open until he had bathed them in hot, nearly boiling water; he was worried about my touching his special lint for fear it affected my own eyes, though I did not believe this could be possible. When I first went round with him in London, he would call periodically on Bishop Harman, a Harley Street specialist Dr Cummins had recommended. He told me that when Harman had given him a prescription for spectacles, and he replied that he didn't want to be bothered with the damned things, Harman had said, 'I don't give a damn myself whether you get the glasses or not. They are simply what I know you need. So if you do get them, come back and let me see if they are right.' Sean, who appreciated straight talking, went at once from Harley Street to a Wigmore Street optician. He wore glasses for a time before we were married; after that, always.

Dr Cummins was the first person to ask us to dinner on the evening when we came from Howth. After Jammets, the restaurant where distinguished visitors to Dublin – especially in the arts – would be taken in those days (it is no longer there), we went to his home for coffee. I realised that he was sympathetic to me and would be the man to help in my sudden dilemma. I was pregnant and had begun to feel very sick. Having wanted a child of Sean's so much, I had panicked and took all and sundry to get rid of it. Nothing had had any effect and Sean was so upset about my health that he asked Dr Cummins for a first-class gynaecologist. I cannot remember who this expert was, but he was wonderfully soothing and said how foolish it would be to harm a healthy child: to have Sean as its father would be perfect. At once I became as happy as I had been miserable; thenceforward I could think of nothing but to sit in the sun when possible, eat fresh fruit, and talk and plan endlessly with Sean, who was equally happy for me.

III

One day, following a gay lunch with Gaby Fallon and his gentle wife Rose, Sean suggested a jaunting-car ride into the country. The jarvey had a thin but intelligent horse that stopped dead at every pub, a cue for his owner to leap down, exclaiming: 'Won't be a minute; must just call in here. The horse won't move an inch, so don't any of you worry.' At the third stop he returned to

the car a little slower; by the time we had had tea and turned
back to Dublin, he was singing merrily. Not that there was anything to worry about, for the horse knew its way without guid-
ance; Sean, admiringly, gave the jarvey an extra tip for the oats
that were obviously needed. Another day we hired a dilapidated
motor-car, held together, I thought, by bits of string, though its
owner seemed to manage anything that went round on wheels. He
longed to go to London, and after driving us several times he
believed, I imagine, that we had the means to engage him as our
chauffeur. He drove us one morning over the Dublin mountains to
Glendalough in County Wicklow. At the hotel by the lake a
porter who greeted us, explaining what a lovely day it was and
how lovely it was for us to come to the hotel, turned to me and
said, 'We've a wonderful lot of hot water. We've just had a new
system installed, and it keeps on the boil all the time.' This
tickled Sean because since London we had had only one difference
– over my resolve to get a hot bath that was comfortable. Sadly,
I said no to the porter; but when about to wash my hands I saw
over the pipe, in large red letters: *Danger. This Water is Boiling.*
There must have been a similar notice elsewhere, for Sean met me
in pealing laughter, asking if I had seen the Danger sign. When
we had had lunch – the mountain lamb almost sweet in flavour –
we hired a boatman to row us out over the big lake enclosed by
high trees that made it eerie and dark, cold even on a warm day.
We scrambled perilously into the cave of St Kevin, the hermit, a
gloomy place where it was awkward to stand upright; I was glad
to get back into the boat. While we waited for the car to collect us,
we wandered into the fields. Terrified of cows, I was startled to
see not a cow but a bull in the distance; though Sean tried to
persuade me that before it came near I could easily make the stile
and get over into the road, I lay flat in a ditch – dry weather,
luckily – and refused to budge until the bull, which had sheered
off in another direction, was far away. Then I rose with some
dignity, covered in dry mud, and rushed to the stile where Sean
was laughing his head off. Back in Dublin I had, naturally, to
have a bath, and only the hot tap worked; it was boiling. Timidly
I asked Sean if he would get a man to mend the cold tap. 'God,

Eileen!' he cried. 'These baths again! However often do you have to take one?' However, he did ring, and the cold water did flow.

Proud of Dublin, Sean wanted to display everything the city had. Dr Owen Sheehy-Skeffington, of Trinity, showed us over the College. Conspicuous for his independent liberal ideas, and a man who had a lot in common with Sean, he became an Irish Senator; his father was the pacifist and patriot, Francis Sheehy-Skeffington, shot by British military forces after his arrest as a hostage during the 1916 rising. At Trinity, as a privilege, they turned for us many pages of the illuminated eighth-century manuscript, the Book of Kells; as a rule, only one page is shown to the public daily. Sheehy-Skeffington also took us to Leinster House in Kildare Street where the Dáil was discussing housing in a lively and argumentative debate. Hearing Sean was there, the Lord Mayor (Alfred Burns) asked to meet us; a Dublin character, short and odd, proud of his office and of the huge mayoral chain that fell to his stomach and that he wore nearly all the time.

Much else we visited: the Art Gallery at Charlemont House, with its John painting of his son Robin, its Epstein bust of Lady Gregory, and its attendants so excited to talk to Sean; the National Gallery of Ireland in Merrion Square, whose curator would write to me after forty years to ask if John's portrait of Sean could be added to the collection; and the National Museum where Joe Cummins urged me to see the eighth-century Tara Brooch. One of our high days we gave to the Botanical Gardens and the Phoenix Park Zoo. Whenever I walked in the Park, I noticed how free and easy a normal Irish mother would be, and how wild and natural her children. It was so, too, in hotel lounges; the children, running round quietly, laughing and playing without self-consciousness, and the grown-ups apparently unaware. I liked this, though I could not miss the other side: children of the slum areas sleeping in their prams in doorways late at night. Some of them, in the poverty-stricken parts Sean took me to, might have a woollen shawl criss-crossed round them, and literally nothing else. Beautiful children, they did not appear to me thin or under-fed, though I suppose they must have been. Perhaps, as G.B.S. wrote to me several times, love is as important to a child as food, and it was clear that they had a great deal of rough-and-tumble affection. It was a worrying sight, but somehow Sean helped me to accept it, as he helped me to understand much in the city he wrote of in a famous phrase: 'A gold-speckled candle, white as snow, was Dublin once: yellowish now, leanin' sideways, and guttherin' down to a last shaky glimmer in the wind of life.'

He kept on telling me that nothing in the world could be lovelier than the Silver Strands outside Dublin. The boy chauffeur motored us there late on an October afternoon. With the tide out and, at this time of year, hardly any people around, the immense stretch lay empty, with a streak of sea in the distance; I could take off my shoes and stockings and walk straight to the other side. That was enchanting. It was less so when in Dublin Sean got me to see the tombs in the limestone vaults beneath the church of St Michan's. This was something I did hate, the horrible damp smell and the nun and crusader said to be so well preserved. Sean, not minding it a bit, peered with enjoyment into the ancient and leathery faces.

IV

We had been a long time in Dublin, and he had now a strong desire to get on with his writing. The play of *The Silver Tassie*, which had been roughly shaped before our marriage, was clamouring for release. Often, while we were walking in London, he had said that in some way he must break from his present style of writing and try one that would employ music as well as words. He told me how he had had the original inspiration on an afternoon when he had visited his coal-merchant friend, Billy McElroy. There, in his London office, Billy, whom Sean called 'a great soul lost in the flood of its own hilarity', was singing a Scottish song:

> Gae bring to me a pint of wine
> And fill it in a silver tassie,
> That I may drink before I go
> A service to my bonnie lassie.

Fascinated, Sean got Billy to sing this over and over until he had learnt the air himself. From that song came the footballer, Harry Heegan, who won the cup and went to war, and the entire narrative of *The Silver Tassie*. I know most of the play must have been contemplated before we were married; Sean had spoken with great excitement and urgency of his treatment of the second Act 'in the war zone' on the Western Front.

Back then to London. For the last day of our honeymoon we returned to Howth and walked over the hills. Though the hotel where we had stayed was all but shut for the winter, they gave us lunch graciously – and it was not difficult, for somebody had told me that if I ate only fruit for a day before I went in the boat, all could be well. That night we sailed from Dun Laoghaire to Holyhead; in the morning we were beginning our London life together. To Sean's pleasure my love for Dublin had grown. We had gone there for a fortnight's honeymoon, and we had stayed six weeks.

CHAPTER FOUR

32, Clareville Street, S.W.7

BACK from Ireland, we made our home in Sean's small Clareville Street flat; my own in St Andrew's Mansions had again been let furnished. To begin with it would be a strange life for us both. He had gone to Clareville Street when *The Plough and the Stars* was running in London, and some of its furniture belonged to his Dublin room; the rest he and Billy McElroy bought in Victoria Street. Cosy, warm and carpeted, the flat had a front room that looked pleasantly upon a tree-lined road; a little kitchen, a larger back room, and a conservatory off it with a bath in the middle. To say the bathroom was cold would be the under-statement of all time: it was freezing.

Sean had the front room: his desk beneath the window, a divan against one wall, a folding table at which he ate. There were as many bookshelves as the room would hold, a big gas-fire, and a number of prints. One, bought in Dublin, was over the mantel-piece, the 'Sleeping Venus' of Giorgione that is mentioned in *The Plough*. Mrs Gogan is completely overcome: 'God bless us, it's a naked woman!'

FLUTHER (*coming over to look at it*): What's undher it? (*Reading*) 'Georgina: The Sleepin' Vennis.' Oh, that's a terrible picture; oh, that's a shockin' picture! Oh, th'one that got that taken, she must have been a prime lassie.' . . .

MRS GOGAN: God forgive us, it's not right to be lookin' at it.

FLUTHER: It's nearly a derogatory thing to be in th'room where it is.

MRS GOGAN (*giggling hysterically*). I couldn't stop any longer in th'same room with three men, afther lookin' at it!

(Act I)

To be in any way at home here, I had to find some space for my clothes. My notions were extravagant, so I made for Harrods. There, as a wardrobe or dressing-table would not fit into the back room, we bought an old-fashioned chest. I had several shelves made which lifted up, in order that I could lay out my clothes flat; and we bought a long mirror and a wall mirror as well, with a shelf beneath it for my make-up.

Bobbie had been left at Helen's while we were in Dublin. On our wedding-day Helen had had him done up at some 'dog parlour', and he looked a misery. I had to leave him behind because of quarantine regulations; he ate hardly at all, I believe, but simply lay huddled on my coat, and when we saw him he was thin and pining, though he jumped with excitement on recognising us. We took him back to Clareville Street; sadly, he had developed an incurable throat affection and Sean did not like my bandaging the throat with our baby coming. The vet. thought it was hopeless, so one day I had to take Bobbie out and he was put to sleep. Sean was deeply distressed. We never had another dog.

II

As soon as we had fully settled, Sean began to work. Most of his writing he did in the evenings. Mornings were leisurely; we got up about half-past nine, and during the day we would go walking, or I would shop, or we would visit a gallery together, roam round the bookshops in Charing Cross Road, or spend hours in Zwemmer's basement, turning over modern prints and thinking of those we might buy when we had more house-room. Every afternoon, even at that early time, Sean had to rest his eyes, bandaging them from the light for a few hours. Never strong, he would occasionally feel faint when we were out. In consequence he took up the habit of an afternoon's rest until about four o'clock after which he would get up and have tea, and his working day would begin. Curiously his personality would change. From being rather casual and relaxed in manner, he would grow brisk and alert and get down to his writing. I would know – instinctively, for he never had to say it –

that he would prefer to have the room to himself without a disturbing presence. Every night, about eight, he would pause for a
meal. If he were really in the middle of his writing and had no
inclination to talk, we would merely have a snack where we were;
I was still not much good at cooking, though Sean was better,
boiling eggs to perfection and making an uncommon cup of tea.
On evenings when he did need a change, we went to the Queen's
Restaurant so familiar to us before marriage. Infrequently we
might have a few friends for the evening, or else go to the theatre.
I remember that, at various times before and after we were married, we saw Robert Loraine in his two Strindberg productions
('his bewildered agony, rage, and blindness in *The Father*,' Sean
wrote; 'his terror, selfishness, and decay in *The Dance of Death*');
Edith Evans, coming straight from the Restoration as Millamant
in a revival of *The Way of the World*, and Mrs Sullen in *The Beaux'
Stratagem*; and the full range of Shaw's *Back to Methuselah* when it
was done at the Court (Edith Evans again, as the Serpent).

In Clareville Street Sean had a daily girl named Ethel, who had
worked both for him when he was living alone, and for Billy
McElroy. A fine, red-haired Cockney, she was a disastrous cook.
Her bacon always floated in fat: neither of us could eat it, and as
a rule we settled for an egg on toast which at home came to be
our staple diet. Ethel had the direct Cockney approach. While I
was sitting one morning on the edge of the divan, looking as grim
as I felt, she said to me, 'Oh, my dear, you *are* in for a packet!'
(She was right.) She was also concerned about Billy who, at the
time, had a rage for lemons that he thought essential and health-
giving. Daily he drank large glasses of lemon juice; and, as he had
a shock of white hair, Ethel declared that it was getting whiter and
whiter every day and that if he were not careful he would soon
be an albino. Billy owned a few racehorses which he kept at a
stable near Lambourn on the Berkshire Downs. One of these he
called the Silver Tassie as a compliment to Sean; we travelled
down on a Sunday to be introduced, and Sean, who said that like
most Dublin men he knew a good horse when he saw one,
believed poor Silver Tassie to be rather bow-legged. Proudly Billy
told us that he had given instructions for the horse to have a

certain amount of lemon juice every day to bring him up to racing
standards. Once, indeed, the Tassie did run second; otherwise, I
hardly think poor Billy made much from him.

III

During our engagement, Lady Londonderry, who, besides being a
political hostess, held many parties for musicians, writers and
artists, had told Sean to bring me to one of them. Now we were
married, and aware that I was used to going out a lot and enjoyed
it, he asked me if I would like to visit Londonderry House. The
place today is a lavish modern hotel in Park Lane. Generally,
when passing it, I think it was a shame not to have left it as an
example of a graceful English town-house and to have established
it, if necessary, as a hotel on those lines. It would have appealed
to many visitors as a contrast to the strictly modern type, the
Hilton, say, or the Dorchester. I stayed once as a guest at a New
York apartment-hotel, Hampshire House, expensive but serene
and gracious; Londonderry House could have been a counterpart.
Possibly, remembering the place as it was, I am being wistful
about it.

Though Sean and Lady Londonderry were so absolutely opposite in politics – she diehard Conservative, he firmly Communist
and Labour – their friendship was lasting. They argued continually, and Sean would be emphatic in his views; but both remained
faithful to their opinions. Sean, of course, was the last person to
yield in any fight for the working class; this was purely a theor-
etical difference between two people who got on well with each
other.

I met some fascinating people at Londonderry House which
Sean called 'richer England's tapestried tavern of the Rose and
Crown'. Thus there might be much talk with James Stephens, the
Irish poet; with the former Socialist Prime Minister, Ramsay
MacDonald; and with Rutland Boughton, the musician who
composed the opera of *The Immortal Hour*. At these parties, after
we had stood around politely and chatted, Sean and James

Stephens, Ramsay if he were there, and Lady Londonderry's daughter, Lady Margaret Stewart, would move off towards the same corner. James Stephens ('the jesting poet with a radiant star in 's coxcomb' as Sean said later in the dedication of *Cock-a-doodle Dandy*) would tell the most riveting stories in the manner of his books: he must have let half of his talent go in conversation, and it was a pity that nobody in those days had a hidden tape-recorder. One night Lady Londonderry came across to us, patted Sean on the shoulder, and asked him – knowing he drank little – if there was anything he would like. In his most beguiling fashion he said, 'I wonder if it would be a great deal of trouble if I had a little pot of tea?' 'Of course!' she said quickly; but, recalling the times when I was a protégée in rich houses, each with its vast, orderly kitchen usually like a vault, I wondered who exactly was going to make that tea. Still, it arrived, with a single cup and saucer. It was not long before several people murmured tentatively, 'Do you think there'll be enough for me to have a cup?' and soon there were more cups and another pot. It is surprising how many people do enjoy a pot of tea about midnight. I am not saying that, ever after, Lady Londonderry provided it for her innumerable guests, but I do say that she would always whisper to Sean, 'If you would like some tea, there will be a pot in the small room at the back.' And there Sean, with five or six others, would sit for hours and hours.

Conventional friends, whom I had known earlier in my life, would ask, 'Don't you think you should persuade Sean to wear evening dress?' It never occurred to me to try; it would have been foolish to propose it, and, discomfort apart, he would have never agreed. Quiet in his dark, plum-coloured suit, he felt at home; so did everyone he met. His own personality was all that mattered; even when he attended Covent Garden Opera House where dress regulations were rigid, nobody objected to a man wholly unforced and genuine. Before my day there had been one tricky occasion. Lady Londonderry had asked James Fagan to bring Sean along to an evening where he would be the guest of honour: an invitation often extended to Celtic writers and artists. Sean duly arrived in his dark suit. 'Sorry, sir,' said the doorkeeper, barring him, 'no-

body is allowed in without evening dress.' Calmly Sean made his
way back to Chelsea and settled to work again; but he had not
been there long before Lady Londonderry telephoned to apologise; the new doorkeeper, she said, had not realised that Sean was
the guest for whom the party was given. Would he please return?
And I think he did.

When I got to know Lady Londonderry better, she called up
one afternoon, inviting me to an evening party that I gathered
would be particularly grand. 'Eileen', she added, 'I wonder if it
would amuse you to watch the people as they come in?' While
Sean read a book in her private sitting-room, some of us sat up in
a gallery at the head of the stairs. It was a fine picture: the Lon-
donderrys receiving, and a procession of people in full evening
dress, the women glittering with jewels, slowly ascending the
broad staircase ('up which a column could march without touching the banisters', said Sean). The scene, staircase, guests, the lot,
reminded me of a musical-comedy last Act, with a butler
announcing 'Lord and Lady So-and-so', or 'Sir Something-or-
other', or even 'Mrs So-and-so'. The only difference was that
musical-comedy entrances would be made down the stairs,
whereas everybody in Londonderry House was walking up. The
hall, wide, stately and lit by chandeliers, was like an opera-
house foyer; it had the same pervading excitement. Sean, who did
not enjoy this kind of evening, appeared unobtrusively towards the
end of it. This was about the last of the big functions we went to;
they could be formal and solemn, and the dancing on the staid
side, and I did not find them all that entertaining myself; it
seemed ridiculous that Sean should be taking me to something I
did not thoroughly appreciate.

In *Rose and Crown*, fifth volume of his autobiography, Sean
describes his Londonderry House talks with Stanley Baldwin,
Lord Carson and other guests. He wrote also in a letter to David
Krause during 1963:

Lady Londonderry had to live through a decline and fall; a
shock, for she, and all of her class, refused to believe that social
evolution was bound to write Ichabod on the lintel of every
grandee house in the land. Lady L. had formed a society of her

personal friends; a society to which she gave the name of THE
ARK. Each member received, or chose, the name of some animal.
On being accepted by 'Circe', the animal received a badge, a
bronze square piece, having the image of Noah's Ark on it,
surmounted by a broad ribbon-bow of the Stewart tartan. I
think Eileen still has hers. Quite a number of persons of the
time wore these badges of an inner acceptance; I saw Stephen
Gwynn and I didn't join in, refusing to get entangled in anything like a coalition of antagonistic forces. Lady Londonderry
was a charming woman, and I was content with her friendship
without even seeming to agree with political affinities. She
escaped from the scheming rascality and hypocrisy of power
politics by sinking herself into a misty Gaelic dream – the
poetry of Fiona MacLeod, the Over the Sea to Skye condition
of romantic thought; dreaming that the Gaels were really the
children of the foreworld; that they led the way to knowledge
and civilisation. Maybe they did, too. I don't think she ever
heard even the name of [Sir David] Lindesay, author of the play
[*The Three Estates*] that frightened so many thousands when it was
unexpectedly put on the stage during an earlier Edinburgh
Festival.

IV

Sean had completed *The Silver Tassie*, his anti-war play written in
a new style for him, with a symbolic second Act. Always he sent
his own rough typescript of a play to a professional typist for a
fair copy: three were made as a rule, one for himself, one for his
publisher, a third for any would-be producer. The Abbey Theatre
people had asked him to be sure to let them have his next play;
Lennox Robinson, the director, had been insistent when he visited
us in London, and a copy was posted at once to the Abbey where
Sean fully expected it would be staged. Already, with the *Tassie*
over, he was considering his next work. Since he reached London,
Hyde Park, and Speakers' Corner especially, had stirred his
imagination, and he intended to write a play of four seasons that
would be set entirely in the Park.

For the moment, between plays, he was less strained. Billy suggested to him that we should look for a house; hence a variety of bus rides and walks round several districts, particularly St John's Wood in the north-west which we both liked, though the first houses we inspected were too expensive. Then in Woronzow Road, off Acacia Road and near Primrose Hill and Regent's Park, we discovered the small Georgian house that suited us, Number 19, which we took on a seven-to-ten-years' lease. My first real home; I loved it. Built on two storeys, with a semi-basement, it stood in a road adorned with flowering trees: a beautiful lilac was in our front garden, and apple trees, lilac and laburnum grew at the back. A large garden backing onto ours had a building in it that was formerly a detached classroom belonging to a school. This, nearly twenty years on, would be the earliest Mermaid Theatre, started privately by Bernard and Josephine Miles in Acacia Road.

Moving was a perplexity because my Dorset Street flat, with some of the furniture we had hoped to use, was still occupied, though the agents were unable to get any rent from the tenants. Even so, we got busy on our decorating in Woronzow Road and laid carpets in one bedroom and in Sean's study. We had nothing but his furniture to start with, but it did mean that his room would be equipped with chair, divan, desk and bookshelves: he could have either an electric or a coal fire. Once more the plan was precisely that of the Clareville Street room – in other words, as with all of Sean's rooms, just as it had been in Dublin. From his desk beneath the window he looked out on the garden and the trees beyond. Though in Dublin he had had a large table, neither of the rooms in Clareville Street or Woronzow Road was big enough, and he had to write at the desk. He was much happier, I would learn, with a table over which he could scatter his papers in what seemed to me, or to anybody else, utter untidiness. For Sean the pattern was clear enough; he could tell you at once where anything was. It was only when the table had been dusted that panic and chaos ruled for half an hour until he could put his papers again into the perfect order which to the rest of us was perfect disorder. One had to understand that his sight was extremely poor. Mentally he knew where his various books and documents were – some in files on the floor, and bundles of newspapers set apart in which he had noted passages for reference.

From our earliest meeting I recognised that he must have some room, wholly his own, in which to write and think. Wherever it was, it would be full of his personality, even to the fact that he hung his hat and coat behind the door, never in the hall. He would change his boots when he came in, so his slippers stood ready by the fire. Thrown across the chair was generally an odd sweater. Sean regarded the room as his home. In the rest of the house he walked about, but this was where he lived. He explains in his autobiography that after his mother died he broke away from his brother and made several journeys with his books to a room in Mountjoy Square, Dublin, that he occupied with a Gaelic-speaking Aran Islander, Michael Mullen. As he earned more money, he got his own room; and it is this we see in the frontispiece of *Inishfallen, Fare Thee Well*, the coal fire, a table pushed close to it when he wrote, a bed along one wall, chairs, books, cups and saucers, a few cooking-utensils. I am certain of one thing: he never failed to contrive some sort of fire. A coal fire is the soul of any tenement room; a joy wherever it burns. (Today we exclaim 'A coal fire!' as if it were a rarity, which usually it is.) Anybody might have begun with us by having tea or dinner downstairs; afterwards, if he found the visitor likeable, Sean would say in his winning manner, 'Why not come up to my room where we can feel really at ease?' It was as if he were conducting the guest into his own part of the house. An armchair would be waiting by the fire; and Sean, taking his own chair opposite, would get down to smoking, telling stories of Dublin life, or enlarging on any topic that might arise.

At length my flat in St Andrew's Mansions was empty. Its tenants had flitted to Australia without paying the rent, though my agent got a very small sum from them, just enough to settle his expenses. The place was left in a terrible condition, carpets and kitchen equipment unusable and some of the furniture badly marked. As Sean wrote, 'The tenants had plonked hot saucepans on divans, carpet, and chairs; the carpets were torn and stained and the kitchen-ware had never been cleaned from the day Eileen had handed over to them.' In the event, we did have two good bedroom suites, one of walnut, one of oak, a dining-room table and chairs, and enough to furnish the sitting-room; moreover, as I had studied singing, I owned a Bechstein piano. Until these things arrived, we had to do the best we could. It was ironical that in the half-empty house we had two superb Augustus John paintings, one the head of a Gitana and the other the portrait of Sean. John – whom I had met before our marriage – asked us to tea at his Chelsea studio in Mallord Street which I had never visited: Sean had been many times during the sittings for his portrait. At the door John greeted us; the studio, large and beautiful, had a grand piano in it and an alcove with a table where we had tea with him and Mrs John and the art critic, Tommy (T. W.) Earp. Though he could be silent sometimes, that day he was in one of his talkative moods, and he even showed me a number of his paintings – a privilege, so I heard later. About half-past six, after a drink, he became quiet. Then, exclaiming suddenly, 'Sean, I have a wedding present for you,' he led us across the studio to his portrait of Sean and gave it to us: a princely gift that I continue to treasure. It was the second portrait; an earlier one had been sold to America, but John considered the second to be the better. Sean described it himself: 'Blue-green coat, silver-grey sweater, with a gayer note given by an orange handkerchief flowing from the breast-pocket of the coat; the face set determinedly in contemplation of things seen and heard, the body shrinking back right to the back of the chair, as if to get farther away to see and hear more clearly; a sensitive and severe countenance with incisive lines of humour braiding the tightly-closed mouth.'

This was one of the pictures we had taken with us to Woronzow Road. The completion of our furnishing was far from simple. Carpeting and curtains proved to be far more expensive than we had imagined; I had no damned sense of money at all, my taste being far beyond my means; and when we went to Tottenham Court Road to choose curtains that satisfied my sense of colour, and a plain hair-cord carpet that, plain or not, cost a great deal, Sean, too, would be supremely unconscious of price: sitting patiently by me, he would say simply how such-and-such a thing appealed to him. I had not the slightest idea of the mounting bill. Though there was no hint of ostentation, it does take a lot to buy simplicity. Further, we had an orgy with prints at Zwemmers: some Van Goghs, a Cézanne, a Renoir, a Manet, two lovely Gauguins, and prints by a young man named Marc, who had done fine animal studies; he was killed in the First World War. I was so mad that I bought some for friends who did not like them and who would hang them away in obscurity, in dark passages and pantries where they would not be noticed. Personally, I had been happy to look at paintings since my first days in the theatre; however busy I was, there would be time for the galleries. Now, when we had brought our prints home to Woronzow Road, we spent hours roaming round the little house that was so full of colour, making up our minds just where each picture should hang. Sean's books, too, were all in order. The first that he gave to me were Thomas Hardy's novels, beginning with *A Pair of Blue Eyes* and ending with *Jude the Obscure*. We used to talk about them and I read them all during my pregnancy. I had begun to read plays as well: those of Eugene O'Neill whom Sean intensely admired, and to whose work the Irish labour leader, Jim Larkin, had introduced him. Maybe, if I had not been married to Sean, I might have been crazy enough to say, 'Somehow or other, I must meet Mr O'Neill. . . .'

V

Lady Ottoline Morrell, who maintained her own literary salon, invited us to dine in Bloomsbury one evening with Oliver Gogarty and Dr Julian Huxley and his wife. Oliver visited us whenever he was in London, but the Huxleys I had not met. Far on in pregnancy, I wore a dress of black lace which was pleated from the neck and hung round me; it went with an underslip in heavy silk. When we reached the house the maid showed us into a long drawing-room down which Lady Ottoline advanced to meet us: a tall, striking figure wearing a white satin dress to her feet, with a deep lace fichu. As she swept forward, I realised in

horror that I had forgotten my silk slip and that the transparent
lace revealed all my underclothes. It must have been ridiculous.
Sean burst out laughing; so did I; and Lady Ottoline, joining in,
sent the maid for my coat which I wore during the rest of the
evening. Luckily, we were the earliest arrivals. The dinner itself
was a trifle difficult. Sean, his sight being so poor, did not notice
that with the fish he had helped himself to lemon which he
loathed; tasting it, he gave a horrified squeak. For some reason, the
talk switched to music. Oliver Gogarty hummed a few tunes, all
on one note, and we inferred, simultaneously but politely, that he
was tone-deaf. Still, singing hardly counted, for he was an
irresistible talker; Mrs Huxley was pleasantly animated, and Sean
in his liveliest mood. In the end, though I sat fairly silently in my
coat, the dinner was a success; everyone relaxed in the drawing-
room, and the Huxleys, whom Sean liked greatly, planned to visit
us in Woronzow Road.

Daily now, Sean was concentrating more closely on the play,
Within the Gates, which had been christened 'The Green Gates' in
draft. Busy with first-baby shopping, I was fortunate to have
generous friends; Helen Elliott gave me the pram and cot, and
other people sent necessary furniture. During pregnancy I had
tried to see as little as possible of my mother who upset me as she
always did, not entirely through her own fault. She had a room in
the district – invariably she stayed near me – and we gave her a
weekly sum.

Because of the baby's size, the birth proved to be more complicated than I had thought. After a visit to Dr Harold Waller one
afternoon, he told me that he would come round in the evening
with a specialist. No, I said, it was not very convenient. I was
going to the theatre. Would another evening do? He was sorry but
advised me to cancel the theatre. My mother, who was having tea
with me that day, told me in her morbid style that I should prepare myself for the fact that the child might be mentally afflicted:
my father had been unbalanced, and the child's father was an
eccentric. At this I dissolved in hysteria and practically pushed
her down the stairs. Sean tore out from his room. My old dresser,
Mrs Earle, who was living with us and who had known my mother

a long time, rushed up in astonishment. Sean exclaimed, 'What the hell are you up to, woman?' and the gentle Mrs Earle led my mother away, saying soothingly, 'Now, now, you mustn't upset your daughter at this time.' Mother left the house, repeating that she was simply trying to warn me.

When the specialist came that evening, he said that a little risk would be involved, and that he must ask whether, if there were an emergency, the mother or the child should be saved. Sean unhesitatingly declared for me. The anaesthetist arrived; two doctors delivered Breon; and it was over.

Sean during my last weeks of pregnancy had had an ordeal. I was sleepless at night, and it fell to him to make tea endlessly, or play cards, or sit and talk until perhaps in the early hours of the morning I might doze. On the night of Breon's birth, Dr Waller – who was a leading gynaecologist, among the most advanced of his time – proposed that Sean should stay with a friend; they telephoned him later with the news that I was well and that he had a son. Returning in the morning to Woronzow Road, he saw a pile of letters on the hall table, one of them with a Dublin postmark; it was from the Abbey. After reading it, he went upstairs to my room and embraced me. He was excited about the baby; it was a glorious morning, and round us in St John's Wood the lilac and syringa and acacia trees were in bloom. I was glowingly happy. It was not for a week that Sean told me of the shock he had kept to himself; the letter was from W. B. Yeats, and the Abbey Theatre had rejected *The Silver Tassie*.

CHAPTER FIVE

The Silver Tassie

SEAN'S disappointment was tragic. I could not credit that Yeats had written as he did: a condescending letter to 'Dear Casey' in which he said, among other things, 'You have no subject. . . . You are not interested in the Great War. You never stood on its battlefields or walked its hospitals, and so write out of your opinions.' Sean answered at once, 'Your statement is to me an impudently ignorant one to make, for it happens that I was and am passionately and intensely interested in the Great War. Throughout its duration I felt and talked of nothing else; brooded, wondered, and was amazed.' Point by point, he refuted the criticisms and ended with the words, throwing back and transforming a line from one of Yeats's own plays: 'You say that after the first and second acts of *The Silver Tassie* there is . . . nothing. Really nothing? Nothing, nothing at all? Well, when there is nothing, when there is nothing – there is God.' Sean did not hide the facts. As he wrote to Lennox Robinson, 'There is going to be no damned secrecy with me surrounding the Abbey's rejection of my play.'

Soon, Barry Jackson, then at the height of his London management, telephoned for a copy. After he had read it, he rang again to ask if he could see Sean. Hope for a while; but, though when he came to tea Jackson told Sean it was one of the most wonderful plays he had met, it was so frightening that he felt he could not stage it. It was another acute disappointment, slightly mollified by a letter from Sir Barry on 22 June 1928:

Dear Sean O'Casey,
    . . . I am turning my mind back to your play: I am convinced that it is one of the greatest of post-war plays and is certain to

be widely read – and, although perhaps this is not the desired result of a work written for the public stage, it is at all events a very good stepping-stone.

Very sincerely yours, BARRY JACKSON

Sean, meanwhile, had taken Yeats's letter to Daniel Macmillan. If, he said, after reading it, Macmillans would rather not publish the *Tassie*, he would be willing to withdraw his contract. Daniel, who had read the play admiringly, examined the correspondence, did not agree with Yeats, and told Sean that Macmillans would be proud to publish. Just after this, Mrs Bernard Shaw had written from Passfield Corner in Hampshire where she and her husband were staying with Sidney and Beatrice Webb:

G.B.S. and I have read *The Silver Tassie* with *deep interest*. We are both greatly impressed by it – I am most enthusiastic! – and we want to have a chat with you about it and the whole business. Could you and Mrs O'Casey come and have luncheon with us at Whitehall Court on Thursday next, the 21st, at 1.30? Do if you possibly can. We would be alone so that we might talk freely about our friends! – *no* – about the play!

Two days later Shaw's own letter (19 June) reached Woronzow Road:

My dear Sean,
What a hell of a play! I wonder how it will hit the public.

Of course the Abbey should have produced it – as Starkie rightly says – whether it liked it or not. But the people who knew your uncle when you were a child (so to speak) always want to correct your exercises; and this was what disabled the usually competent W.B.Y. and Lady Gregory.

Still, it is surprising that they fired so very wide, considering their marksmanship. A good realistic first act, like Juno, an incongruously phantastic second act, trailing off into a vague and unreal sequel: could anything be wronger: What *I* see is a deliberately unrealistic phantasmo-poetic first act, intensifying in exactly the same mode into a climax of war imagery in the second act, and then two acts of almost unbearable realism bringing down all the Voodoo war poetry with an ironic crash to earth in ruins. There is certainly no falling-off or loss of grip: the hitting gets harder and harder right through to the end.

Now if Yeats had said 'It's too savage: I can't stand it,' he would have been in order. You really are a ruthless ironfisted blaster and blighter of your species; and in this play there is none righteous – no, not one. Your moral is always that the Irish ought not to exist; and you are suspected of opining, like Shakespear, that the human race ought not to exist – unless, indeed, you like them like that, which you can hardly expect Lady Gregory, with her kindness for Kiltartan, to do. Yeats himself, with all his extraordinary cleverness and subtlety, which comes out just when you give him up as a hopeless fool and (in this case) deserts him when you expect him to be equal to the occasion, is not a man of this world; and when you hurl an enormous smashing chunk of it at him, he dodges it, small blame to him.

However, we can talk about it when we meet, which I understand is to be on Thursday next week. This is only to prepare you for my attitude. Until then,

Cheerio, Titan,

G. BERNARD SHAW

I felt exceedingly nervous about the visit to G.B.S. But when we reached the main door of Whitehall Court he was waiting for us and hurried forward to take both my hands in his, the same gesture, the same warmth of feeling I remembered from my first meeting with Sean; by the time the lift had taken us to his flat I was at ease. He and his wife would prove to be staunch friends. At luncheon Charlotte did try to tell Sean that he should not be quite so angry in the Press, so firm in argument. Mildly I said that Sean could hardly alter his personality, and that being naturally resentful about the whole thing, he must express his feelings. G.B.S., on Sean's side but not wishing to contradict Charlotte, did his best to smooth the problem over. There was no lull in a conversation that lasted until well into the afternoon. Sean reminded G.B.S. that, some years earlier, after writing a work that had not been published, he had had the temerity to ask for a preface, and received the following reply from 10, Adelphi Terrace (3 December 1919):

Dear Sir,
I like the foreword and afterword much better than the shouts which are prodigiously overwritten.

Why do you not come out definitely on the side of Labor and the English language?

I am afraid the National question will insist on getting settled before the Labor question. That is why the National question is a nuisance and a bore; but it can't be helped.

Of course the publishers will publish it with a preface by me; but how will that advance *you* as an author? Besides, my prefaces mean months of work. I am asked for prefaces three times a week. It is quite out of the question. You must go through the mill like the rest and get published for your own sake, not for mine.

You ought to work out your position positively and definitely, this objecting to everything else is Irish, but useless.

In great haste – I am busy rehearsing.

G. BERNARD SHAW

Shaun O'Casey, Esq.,
18, Abercorn Road,
Dublin.

Sean told G.B.S. that he had carried round this letter in his wallet for many years until it was creased and frayed. Now, more than eight years later, he was equally moved by the salute to *The Silver Tassie*. After we had lunched at Whitehall Court, Sean wrote to G.B.S. on 29 June to ask if a part of the *Tassie* letter could be sent to Macmillans:

When I got the quires of criticism from the Abbey I galloped off to Macmillans and told them they could withdraw the book if they thought the criticisms more important, and though they held on to the book, I felt they got a shock, so when your letter came I sent it on to cheer them up, and they have asked me to seek your permission to print some passages.

Besides as far as I can see at the moment, the coming year must be financially filled up with whatever the sale of the book may bring in, and any help in this way is a gift from God.

I confirm my assurance that I have no vindictive feeling to the Abbey – I refused four offers to have the play produced in

Dublin – and that I should be glad to have *The Silver Tassie* performed there subject to all conditions mentioned which I think are fair and just in all circumstances.

Shaw replied (3 July) on the foot of the letter:

Yes: Macmillans may quote the passage as above.

I have just heard from Lady Gregory. I gather that she has been really on your side all through: so there will be no difficulty there.

Don't *disparage* L.R. [Lennox Robinson] or 'make conditions'. Say that he is the rottenest producer on God's earth, and would kill a play even if St Luke and St Gabriel collaborated to write it. He won't mind that, or at heart won't resent it; and the conditions will follow spontaneously.

Playwriting is a desperate trade. £300 a week for just long enough to get you living at that rate, and then nothing for two years. Your wife must support you (what is she for?), and when she is out of work you must go into debt, and borrow, and pawn, and so on – the usual routine.

Ever, G.B.S.

On 8 July I heard from Charlotte about their difficulty in coming to Woronzow Road for a while:

We are just starting off abroad for a holiday. I am the more sorry for this as I do feel Sean wants a lot of looking after just now. He is going to be very naughty and fierce and resentful – and he is a terribly hard hitter!

That idea of letting G.B.S. see his letters to his 'friends' is a grand one. Do keep him up to it. Any letters addressed to 4, Whitehall Court, will be forwarded *at once*, and I will send you our address the moment we are settled, and Sean must write about all he is doing, and G.B.S. will answer *quickly* and try to act as a lightning conductor! Directly we come back, we will go to lunch with you, and see Breon, if you will ask us again.

Mr Yeats didn't come to see us about the play, but about the Irish Literary Academy they are trying to get up. He never mentioned *The Silver Tassie*. It was *I* who insisted upon talking about it – and he was rattled, self-conscious and reluctant!

Sean was angry about the idea that Charlotte should look after any correspondence he received and was certain that G.B.S. would never want to advise him about the way he should fight for his own work. So no more was done about it. The script of the *Tassie* went to C. B. Cochran who was enthusiastic, but who had to set about finding backers before he could develop any plan. There, for a time, the matter rested.

II

During all this controversy, mother and child had been thriving under the care of Nurse Selby whom we had engaged by the month. No royalties were coming in from London, but money was owing on other plays and Samuel French had endeavoured to get it for us. We knew we could not pay the nurse at the end of the month; the simplest thing was to ask her to remain until we were in funds. It was an odd situation; week by week we waited for the money, and dear Nurse Selby had to stay at Woronzow Road until our French's cheque arrived and we could settle with her.

Soon we had been married for a year. On 23 September 1928, 'first anniversary of our union', Sean gave me a copy of the newly published edition of *The Silver Tassie*. He had written on the fly-leaf:

To lovely and darling Eily –
Remembering how pretty and alluring she was when she was first seen by me;
Remembering her torment in the part of 'Nora' in *The Plough and the Stars* when her charm was envied by the Players, the Producer, and the Producer's Wife;
Remembering her quick perception of Colour and Line and Form which helped me to a fuller feeling for the Glory of Art;
Remembering her courage and perseverance in the pain and danger of motherhood:
From Sean, with deep and intense love that has been wedded into a sweet and lovely companionship.

In the spring I always filled a large green vase with daffodils. Sean, who looked forward to this, dedicated the book of the *Tassie* to 'Eileen, with the yellow daffodils in the green vase'.

The rejection of the *Tassie*, the ensuing arguments, and the effort to get the play into London production, had not distracted Sean from other work. He wrote on steadily at the final version of *Within the Gates*, his symbolic play about Hyde Park from the opening of the gates in the morning until their closing at night; a day with its progress of nursemaids and children, guardsmen, whores, tramps, down-and-outs, chair attendants, speakers: a work 'written round life not from outside looking in but from inside looking out'. Originally he had imagined it as a film in which everything, from flower-beds to uniforms, would be stylised. Beginning at dawn and ending at midnight, to the soft chime of Big Ben in the distance, it would be 'geometrical and emotional, the emotions of the living characters to be shown against their own patterns and the patterns of the Park'. Having got so far, he wrote to Alfred Hitchcock, and when Hitchcock and his wife dined with us Sean explained his ideas to an apparently responsive hearer. Hitchcock and he talked excitedly. They parted on the same terms, with the prospect of another immediate meeting, and Sean never heard again. Thereupon *Within the Gates* became solely a play, the first composed in Woronzow Road.

Our close friend, Evan Walters, the Welsh artist who did some powerful paintings of Welsh miners, had just held an exhibition that John praised generously. Evan was an entrancing character. On Breon's birth someone had brought me a pot of blue hydrangeas; Evan, when he saw them, raced back to the studio for his things and returned to paint for me a swift and exquisite flower-study. Several evenings he came for a meal. Once, he told us, having fallen in love with a good-looking girl, a really hard nut, he called at his bank on a Saturday morning to draw out two of the three pounds in his account. Leaving her to click her heels outside, he joined a long queue to the cashier; impatiently, she kept glancing in at the door until Evan, terrified that she might clear off, pushed to the front of the queue, waved his cheque at the cashier, and said loudly, 'If you don't let me have my two pounds immediately, I will take my account to another bank.' He reported this to us gravely, seeing nothing funny in it. Another time, when he called after a visit to his mother in Wales, Sean observed how well he looked. Smiling broadly, Evan patted himself: 'You think I'm very fat, Sean? My mother sent me back with seven shirts that had just been laundered, but I don't like to carry baggage, so I put them all on. Much easier too. When the top one gets dirty, I take it off and there's a clean one underneath. I can go on until they're all used.' 'But,' said Sean, 'the last shirt is going to be the dirtiest.' Suddenly Evan shouted with laughter: 'Ah, I never thought of that!' He was fond of telling us that if he were Prime Minister the country would be entirely different, and I dare say it would have been. Anyway, he was great company. Cochran, who admired Evan's drawings at Woronzow Road, invited him later to paint the large figure of the Madonna, hung on the stark white wall of the hospital in the *Tassie's* third Act. His charcoal sketch of Sean was the frontispiece to the first edition.

III

This was a good time in our lives. We were happy with the baby and had Mrs Earle as housekeeper. Sean, delightfully affectionate as a father, thought the world of Breon and was with him whenever he could. I had engaged a middle-aged nannie, a simple country woman, tiny, rather plain, but kindness itself. Since she was fourteen she had looked after other people's children, staying eight or nine years with one family and keeping in touch with most of her charges after she had left; I found it sad that she had never had a child of her own. Quickly she grew devoted to Breon. When he was about four months old the question arose of getting him out of London in a surprisingly hot summer. Nanny Trim, who mentioned it, was obviously longing to go away, so early in September we chose a pleasant little hotel at Angmering-on-Sea in Sussex. Sean, I discovered, hated both the hotel and Angmering. Dinner at night was torture for him; sitting in the lounge for coffee was even worse; probably it was the stuffy atmosphere, for talk hardly flowed. Anyhow, Sean was never a man for hotels; he would have to go to one where he could lose himself. Like most people who have achieved anything in the arts or sciences, he had a conspicuous personality. As with John or Epstein, or anybody comparable – doubtless today such an actor as Olivier – he could not enter a hotel foyer without somebody saying: 'I wonder who that is?'

Sean did not care for Angmering's rather desolate beach, just a few huts, sand and sea. The weather being so fine, Breon and I were content; I would sit him in the sea – he loved the water – while I lazed in the sun. Sean would have been better on a more crowded beach where he could have strolled round listening to the conversations and watching the minor family dramas. Neither of us had ever had an annual summer holiday; it was an experience Sean wearied of after two days. As we returned from the beach at tea-time, he saw desperately that he could not face another dinner. Pleading with me to check the next train to London – it was somewhere round six and also the last – he thrust his belongings in his case and dashed for the station, brighter than he had been since his arrival. During the rest of the stay I had daily telephone calls from him, and letters telling me of his loneliness. This is one soon after he had got back to St John's Wood:

> The first time since we came together that you have been away from me for some days, and my heart, darling and beautiful Eily, is heavier than I wished to be. Curious quietness about the house today and now tonight quieter still – quiet and not a little sad. Strange sense of calm restlessness, not of the body but of the spirit – yes, of the body too, really; a curiously quiet, uneasy restlessness that nothing will remove but the clasping in my arms again of my darling Eileen. I look at the things in your room and in my room, and they, too, seem to have gathered into them some of the patient resentment of your absence.
>
> I miss you, Eily; I miss you very much indeed. Your going away has shaken an uneasy silence over everything that I see, and over everything that I touch. Everything is the same, yet nothing is as it was. Eileen Carey – beautiful, brown-haired, white-breasted Eileen Carey is very, very, very dear to Sean.

Hardly for a moment have you been out of my mind; I am always thinking of you, trying to get away in thought and finding myself in a moment again looking at your image. Seeing you in your pink dress, in your black dress, in your white and brown and gold dress, your black hat, your grey hat, your blue and grey hat – in all the charming things that frame your lovely face. I have thought of you the first time I saw you when you came down to the Fortune Theatre, and of that visit to St Andrews Mansions to bring you to the theatre, that gave me the first opportunity of feeling that in you there was something more than the beauty of your face and the charm of your form. And I have thought of the time when in your dressing room I used to hold you tightly and roughly, and tell you that I would make you love me. And even then, patient and indifferent as you were, thoughts of Sean O'Casey were finding a place in your heart and in your mind. I have visioned again the day you came to Clareville Street to tell me you loved me, and I have seen again the tears in your eyes because of the fear born in your mind through that admission of your love for me. And of the first sad frightened night we spent together in St. Andrews Mansions, when I gathered and gathered all my energy and determination to go, and could not, could not leave you.

How glad I am to remember that I saw so much in you from the start to knowing each other; that there was breadth and depth in that beautiful girlish form of Eileen Carey, that a lovely face and beautiful figure were veil to something deeper still, that behind the loveliness was a personality and a power. That this loveliness was to be desired, but it was to be honoured too.

You are more to me than anything in the world. I love you deeply, intensely, passionately, my own beautiful, adorable, and desirable darling Eily.

SEAN

A second, and more matter-of-fact, letter begins with a plain statement about the *Tassie* contract:

I signed the contract that came yesterday from C.B.

Pussy's quite safe, and flits about the house in such a way, easy and self-contained, as to show that to her our absence or presence is neither loss nor gain. The bath has been enamelled, and I have spent hours sponging my trousers with violent solutions of ammonia. Took dinner last night with Billy and Tom Berry [bank manager]. Of course I'll meet you at Victoria and bring you home. And on Sunday we'll go to the Queen's and have dinner there, though perhaps it might be better for you to stop where you are a little longer. I am really longing for you to come back to me. Curious this restless, annoying, ever-present sense of missing you from me. There's only one thing to do – to go away from you for a year or two – and I can't do that. Billy's going to suggest to C.B. that you could play the part of Jessie [in *The Silver Tassie*], and if that happens, well we'll –

It would be really a great thing if you were chosen for the part of Jessie, for then you would be keeping yourself fit to battle for Breon if anything happened to me. Even if nothing should happen, I'm not going to be, apparently, of very much use to you or him.

My dearest love to you, my darling Eily.

SEAN

Sean's main work continued to be *Within the Gates*. On some Sunday afternoons we would go to listen to the speakers at Hyde Park Corner. One, an atheist, Sean persuaded back to the house for a meal: a first-class talker, he had a room in Edgware Road, and Sean called on him there once or twice. Obviously he must have helped the play. Sean would talk also to speakers outside the Park and watch shrewdly the chair attendants and other persons he might meet. The hypocritical mother in the play may have been drawn partly from a woman known as Red Biddy; the prostitute could have been suggested by an intelligent and good-looking girl whom a friend of Sean's brought to Clareville Street several times, and who described how she had drifted into the life as an easy way of existence. But, after all, Sean had already drawn one prostitute, Rosie Redmond in *The Plough and the Stars*, though Rosie was a rough, good-natured type and the other one more delicate and educated. Most of Sean's characters were a mingling of various people.

It was at this time that he missed a meeting with James Joyce whom he revered. Joyce, on a visit to London, rang up, suggesting a drink and a talk at the hotel; but Sean, who had a heavy cold, could not go out, and they had instead a prolonged and excited conversation on the telephone, each sure that there would be some other chance of getting together. The chance never came. At a party given by Sidney Bernstein we did meet Liam O'Flaherty, the Irish novelist. Sidney was a man of expansive and kindly personality that meant a lot to his parties; at one I recall, in 1929, after his showing of the Russian film, *Battleship Potemkin* at the Tivoli, we met the Russian producer, Eisenstein. On the evening when we were introduced to O'Flaherty, handsome, immaculate, and surrounded by admirers, I could not feel attracted to him; though a witty talker and attentive and flattering to me, I felt he was conceited. Possibly I was struck by the contrast between him and his wife who was at the other end of the room among her own friends, a woman of distinction in no way conscious of her appearance or dressed for effect, but, I thought, worried and harassed. I liked her, and did years afterwards when I ran into her in Totnes with her daughter.

IV

Charles Cochran, having marshalled his backers, was getting ahead with the casting of *The Silver Tassie*. He had decided upon the director, the Canadian-born actor Raymond Massey, who had been in charge of several London productions; Sean praised his 'strange patience'. Cochran had leased a country cottage – I think it was at Cookham in the Thames Valley – set in a garden with the richest herbaceous border I had seen. We used to go down on Sundays so that Sean could discuss the details of the play; often various girls were there from the London Pavilion revue. On a final visit, when most of the casting had been done, C.B. pulled me aside just before we left and asked what I intended to do. 'What do you mean?' I said.

'Well,' he replied, 'are you returning to work, Eileen? You must, you know, because you will find it hard to settle to the quiet life. You are accustomed to going out in the evenings. Sean is older than you are; he is a wonderful person, and I have grown very fond of him; it would be terrible if you hurt him, but that might happen easily if you were not occupied. You are naturally ambitious, and I am convinced that you do want to go back to the stage.'

I answered that I had not considered it; indeed I had had no time to think of anything but Breon; we appeared to be completely happy as we were. C.B. told me then of auditions due in about a month for a musical play by Noël Coward, entitled *Bitter-Sweet*; it had a number of small singing parts, and he would ensure that I had a card.

Cochran was an undemonstrative man, solidly built but dapper; though most sympathetic to me, I am sure that he could have been stubborn and difficult. His love of the theatre was extraordinary; when he began on a production he could not stem his extravagance, for he was a perfectionist able to see only the picture as a whole. He brought to us the best from many worlds. Photographs on his grand piano were signed by the stars of opera, ballet, musical comedy and the boxing-ring; he loved the mastery of a major artist in any field. He appreciated beautiful women. He was a connoisseur of painting, and his collection included one of the most enviable Renoirs I have known, a picture that hung in his dining-room and was sold, I think, when he was bankrupt, to Edward G. Robinson, the film actor, also a collector. Sean said memorably of Cochran: 'The clowns were always on one side of him, the tragedians on the other, and he had the imaginative eye and cunning hand to weave lovely patterns round the pair of them.'

Presently I received Cochran's card for the *Bitter-Sweet* audition at His Majesty's Theatre: a singing audition and an ordeal for anybody who had broken temporarily with the stage, as I had. I tried for the part of Jane, one of six bridesmaids. Many other girls were there, and that day I heard nothing. Evidently Noël Coward had not been at the audition, and three or four of us who were thought suitable had to sing for him again a week later. After this I was instructed to come to rehearsal and entered briskly into the whole thing. In spite of the utter dissimilarity between Sean and Noël, I had genuine respect for Noël as a director; at rehearsal he never showed any feelings he might have had about my position as Sean's wife.

We were an odd household in Woronzow Road. Mrs Earle appeared every day to cook and look after us. Her husband was a stage doorkeeper; and her children, a boy and a girl, twelve and thirteen years old, came up every evening after school to have their meal and to stay with her. Our kitchen, looking into the garden and next to the little dining-room in the semi-basement, was both largeish and snug, with an old-fashioned range that during the winter would have a bright fire burning; we were never short of fuel, for Billy McElroy, a coal merchant, would not let our cellar run short. The kitchen had comfortable armchairs, and Mrs Earle kept on the window-sill several of the plants she admired. When the baby was in bed, Nanny Trim would go down to have supper, often joined by a neighbouring friend. Sean would be writing in his room beside Breon's, so that he could hear any cry; and when he came to meet me at the theatre, as he did on most evenings, Nannie would have gone to bed. About Breon, then, my mind was fully at ease.

I ought not to forget an unofficial member of the household, a man who turned up once a month to help with the garden. Because he worked in Regent's Park, he was with us on Saturday afternoons for the most part, bringing all kinds of plants and bulbs. Usually he was a little tight; one day, I remember, during a steady downpour, he stood in the rain with the hose full on, watering the garden. He was reluctant, for some reason, to take money; though Mrs Earle paid him, he told her regularly that he had not done anything. In effect, all of us would tend the flower-beds; Mrs Earle liked gardening, and Nanny was from the country. The man simply cut the grass and watered the garden – in the rain or otherwise.

Cochran, as I knew, was right; I was glad to be at work in the evenings while Sean was occupied with his writings and, at the time of *Bitter-Sweet*, closely involved with the production of *The Silver Tassie*. Daringly, Cochran had proposed to ask Augustus John for a set design. John often corresponded with Sean to whom he had written a few weeks earlier from Fryern Court, Fording-bridge, near Salisbury:

My dear Sean,

Thanks for your recent letter. I've been going through a non-writing period for months. So glad you liked the show so well.

Your suggestion that my hand is 'soiled' by contact with the World, the Flesh, and the Devil (three excellent things) is alone a little unwelcome. . . .

In your letter you commiserated with me on my election to the R.A. I assure you it won't make the slightest difference to me, unless by stimulating me to greater freedom of expression. As you know, I never sought this honour and am not likely to be overwhelmed by it. Perhaps at any rate it will be a useful disguise. Cezanne longed for official recognition and the Legion of Honour and didn't get either. I ignored the Academy consistently and got elected. Van Gogh dreamed of electric light, hot and cold water, w.c.s and general *confort anglais*. I have them all and remain unsatisfied.

I shall return to Town shortly when we must meet. Yesterday I found five Martigues pictures I had lost and am sending them to Tooths'. All the best wishes to you and Eileen from all of us.

Yours ever,

AUGUSTUS JOHN

P.S. Tell Billy I couldn't get off for a night with him but took the girls to *Porgy*.

C.B. wanted John for the important second-Act set of the *Tassie* which Sean had described in close detail: the War Zone, its 'jagged and lacerated ruin of what was once a monastery', the stained-glass window, the life-size crucifix, and the great howitzer 'with a long sinister barrel now pointing towards the front at an angle of forty-five degrees'. (Sean had the note: 'Every feature of the scene seems a little distorted from its original appearance.') Would I suggest this set to John? asked C.B. Though petrified at the task, I telephoned John, said roughly what the idea was, and wondered if I could see him. He answered: 'I have read the play. I think it is a fine one, but am not sure about the stage set. I have never done one before; I don't really think I could. Still, do come along and talk about it – why not this afternoon?' At tea in a

room off his studio he was extremely shy, though as ever courteous and complimentary, for he liked good-looking women. This
helped me to plead my cause. We talked of Sean and Breon and
his own pleasure in sketching children who were so rarely
awkward. At length, after many preliminaries, I got back to the
Tassie set. Would he? 'Well, yes, Eileen; you have won the battle.
I will do it for you and Sean – and I hope I manage it.' On 13 May
he wrote from Fordingbridge:

> My dear Sean,
> I have my notebooks and sketches of war scenes in London, and
> they will provide all I need for *The Silver Tassie*. I shall be up
> before long and will give you a ring.
> Billy sent me a book on Food which is so badly written it
> put me off my grub – which apparently was the desired result.
>   Yours, AUGUSTUS

Undoubtedly John lacked stage knowledge. His final work was
unforgettable, overpowering; but the set was built so heavily that
in performance the scene-shifters had trouble with it.

The first night of *The Silver Tassie* was still more than three
months distant when I had to leave for Manchester for the last
rehearsals of *Bitter-Sweet* and its production there, at the Palace
Theatre, two weeks before the London première. Angmering
apart, I had not been away from Sean since our marriage; and he
wrote many letters to me like this one on 2 July 1929, the date of
the Manchester opening:

> Darling Eily,
> Here I am writing to you again, and fighting bravely, if hope-
> lessly, in an effort to disassociate myself from a sense of loneli-
> ness and pain. I hear Breon inside – it is 6.15 – peevishly
> proclaiming his hunger. Your mother is there, too, with Nannie
> and with Breon. I hear him crying still. I go in and they say it is
> his teeth that are troubling him. He is pushing his fingers with
> irritable uneasiness in and out of his mouth. So I take him to
> my room, talk to him, play with him a little, and hand him
> back quieter. We must be careful not to let him feed too much
> on attention from women. I really don't like your mother

mixing too much with him; particularly when you aren't there. Got a letter yesterday from Peacock. He wants me to spend an evening with him to talk about the cast and the production of the *Tassie*. I will probably see him next week. Went last night to a revue in the Holborn and came away with a heartache and a headache.

I have tried hard to make myself send a telegram or a note to Noël Coward wishing him success, but I could not. How can I wish success to a thing I know not to be good or bad? I might as well pray success to an exhibition by Laszlo or Lavery or Brock. If it be good and from God, then shall it stand, though it fail; if it be bad, and come not from God, then, though it succeed, it shall fail. I hope Coward may do good work, which wish is greater than a wish that this should succeed. But now, darling, you mustn't lose heart because you are away from me. You will soon be back, and we shall kiss and fondle each other again, sit in the garden, play with Breon, and talk, walk in the park and talk.

SEAN

On 14 July, a few days before the London première, Sean gave to me, inscribed to 'My darling Eileen, with intense love and sincere admiration from her Sean', the prose poem that, with a few alterations, appeared during 1934, entitled 'Gold and Silver Will Not Do', in the collection *Windfalls*. The first verse of the original ran:

Eileen most fair; Eileen most desirable of women; Eileen whose personality tempers my thought, and whose loveliness brings pride to my pleasure; Eileen whose companionship I need; Eileen whose love I sought, claimed, and laid hold of in the frowning face of others, who, frightened, fled, and were scattered even as the dust scattereth before a wind that is strong.

My name is used throughout, though for publication Sean decided to make the poem impersonal.

Coward's operette, which he had directed as well as writing the book and music, shifted back in time from 1929 to three late nineteenth-century periods and then moved forward again. I played one of half-a-dozen young bridesmaids who reappear as

Society matrons. In spite of a few adverse criticisms, the production turned swiftly into a fashionable success, running for nearly
two years. Peggy Wood, the American actress who was our leading
lady, had a boy of much the same age as Breon.

V

By the end of July everything was prepared for *The Silver Tassie*, the
tragi-comedy in which Sean said that he tried to 'go into the
heart of war'. Sean was naturally anxious that Barry Fitzgerald,
creator of the Paycock, should play Sylvester who, throughout the
piece, has a double act with his buttie Simon. (Later, after one
curious oversight by Hitchcock, Barry would have a renowned
film career.) When Cochran agreed to the casting, Barry crossed
from Dublin and stayed with us in Woronzow Road before finding rooms for himself not far away. Beatrix Lehmann would be
magnificently right as Susie; Binnie Barnes was the other girl,
Jessie ('ever dancing round, in and between the world, the flesh,
and the devil'), a part I had wondered about before *Bitter-Sweet*.
Charles Laughton, advancing towards his crest in the theatre, was
Harry, the lusty Dublin footballer, who returns from the war
paralysed from the waist downward; Sean was uncertain about
this, but Cochran had to consider the box-office. Prickly in
rehearsal and needing a good deal of attention, Laughton could
express Harry imaginatively, though I did not believe myself he
was physically suited to the part.

Cochran, who detested any change in a play while it was running, had not wanted to let me off from *Bitter-Sweet* to attend
Sean's first night on 11 October. We both pleaded with him, and
at length my understudy took over at His Majesty's and I went up
to the Apollo for a night tingling with excitement, the climax of
an eighteen-months' dispute since Sean had read Yeats's letter.
Somebody, looking at the audience, quoted Byron, 'Bright the
lamps shone on fair women and brave men.' I sat in the stage-box
with Evelyn Cochran and C.B., the three of us desperately nervous. Lady Astor came with the Shaws. Far from being on edge,

G.B.S. was enthusiastic and eager; during the interval between
the second and third Acts he made a point of finding Sean who
had sat somewhere quietly on his own, far too wrought-up to
show himself. G.B.S. insisted again that it was a great play: an
emotional moment for Sean after so vital an Act. There had been
an uncanny hush when the curtain rose on the War Zone to show
Augustus John's setting, the outline of the shattered monastery
with a vivid stained-glass window, lit from within, that threw
across the scene its mosaic of subdued colour. Martin Shaw had
supervised the complex liturgical chanting that mounted to a final
litany to the gun:

> Guardian of our love and hate and fear,
> Speak for us to the inner ear of God!

It was a startling half-hour with one moment when Cochran must
have felt that his heart might stop. The young Welsh actor,
Emlyn Williams, arriving with a tremendous flourish to sound the
trumpet, was so nervous that we heard nothing until about the
third attempt. I doubt whether the audience noticed. In the box
the moment was tense.

Barry Fitzgerald, unexampled comedian, was certainly not at
his best on this opening night. Cochran knew it, and I did: we
were both worrying on his account. Still, the reception was tremendous; everybody in the cast seemed relieved and satisfied.
Next morning C.B. rang to ask Sean if he had read the notices.
Sean had not, for he took only the *Daily Worker*, though he would
see the *Observer* and the *Sunday Times* at the week-end. In any
event, he never pondered on his press-cuttings. Now Cochran told
his secretary to take the Apollo notices without delay from all the
papers, and to send them to Woronzow Road. After the acrimony
and unhappiness, it was a joy for Sean to know that the *Tassie* had
come to life, properly staged, and that, for example, the critic of
The Times (Charles Morgan) would applaud an experiment of
'absorbing interest, and not less interesting because he has not
perfected it. Of even greater value is his attempt to break free
from the bonds of naturalism by the bold use of verse.' For myself, I returned, contented, to my small part in *Bitter-Sweet*.

VI

Sean's post on the day after the première contained a letter from
Dublin. It was from Lady Gregory, at the Standard Hotel:

> Dear Sean,
> I have only just now realised that your play comes on tonight –
> and though I never send telegrams on such occasions I want you
> to be sure that you have all my good wishes for it – and its
> success. I hope to see it myself very soon for I cross to England
> on Monday – I shall be for some days with Mrs Phillimore –
> 1, Upper Phillimore Gardens. And I look forward very much
> to a visit one afternoon if you invite me – to see and make
> acquaintance with your wife and your son – and your garden –
> Now good bye – with affection –
>
> A. GREGORY

Sean had a stubborn side; often he would hurt himself rather than
give in, and here he was in a dilemma. In spite of his affection for
Lady Gregory, she had been with Yeats in the refusal of *The Silver
Tassie* and the memory rankled. He would not see her, though at
heart he longed for her to meet me and Breon. 'Eileen,' he said, 'I
wanted so much for Lady Gregory to see you; I'm sure you would
have liked each other, but I just couldn't do it now.' I fully
understood. Thereupon Sean wrote back:

> The production of *The Silver Tassie* in London has made my
> mind a flood again with thoughts about the play's rejection by
> the Abbey Directors and bitterness would certainly enter into
> things I would say about W. B. Yeats and L. Robinson, if we
> were to meet, bitterness that would hurt you, and I am deter-
> mined to avoid hurting you as much as possible. . . . So know-
> ing how I feel, and guessing what I would say about the many
> literary and artistic shams squatting in their high places in
> Dublin, I feel it would be much better to set aside for the
> present the honour and pleasure of seeing you and talking
> with you.

To this Lady Gregory replied from 1, Upper Phillimore Gardens, Kensington, on 15 October:

Dear Sean,
Your letter has grieved me – perhaps I deserve that – but I do ask you to change your mind and allow me to come and see your wife – and the boy – and the garden and the pictures and *yourself* – I do not feel that any word need be spoken on that grievous matter that has given me so much pain – I am here but for a few days (till Saturday) – Could go tomorrow afternoon – if you give me leave – as always affectionately,

A. GREGORY

Sean did not give way, and on 23 October he heard once more:

Dear Sean,
Although I have missed the pleasure of seeing you, I should like to tell you what I have just written to Yeats about the *Tassie* – 'I am troubled because having seen the play I believe we ought to have accepted it – We could not have done the chanted scene as it is done here, it is very fine indeed and impressive' – But I say, and think, we could have done the other acts better – Barry Fitzgerald was of course very fine.

I leave for Dublin tomorrow, just passing through London. I have had some pleasant days with old friends but am sorry not to have made the acquaintance of that 'kid' whose father shows such splendid vitality, and of his mother. I have done a little work about the Lane pictures and have great hopes of them now.

As always affectionately,

A. GREGORY

We could not know that this was the last opportunity we had of seeing Lady Gregory, one of the people Sean really loved and called 'a gracious gallant woman'. She died in 1932.

CHAPTER SIX

19, Woronzow Road, N.W.8

A GUEST of ours at Woronzow Road, shortly after *The Silver Tassie* had opened its two months' run, was Sean's Dublin friend, Gabriel Fallon. In a book* published during 1965, not long after Sean's death, Gaby opened a chapter with the words: 'If I harboured any suspicion (I didn't) that the Sean O'Casey I knew had suffered a sea-change in coming to London, if I thought (as many did) that he had, as we say, lost the run of himself as the result of fortune, fame, and the friendship of the great, such suspicions and such thoughts would have been dispelled the very moment I crossed the threshold of 19, Woronzow Road, St John's Wood. For here was a welcome that *was* a welcome, with Eileen, calmly radiant, helping him to reinforce it.' To me this seems obliquely expressed. How many people did think that Sean had 'lost the run of himself'? Where was his fortune? He had none. Fame? He had struggled for nearly eighteen months against the rejection of the *Tassie*. Friendship of the great? In Dublin he had had Lady Gregory's friendship; in London G.B.S. had realised Sean's genius and there was a common regard; Lady Londonderry he liked, obviously not because of her political opinions, but because of her attraction to Celtic culture. But Sean made his own friends; at that period Gabriel Fallon, with his witty and astringent mind, was one of them. Gaby's memories of our household across thirty-six years are a little garbled. We did not live in 'a large double house'. Sean described it properly in *Rose and Crown*: 'The little house was one of two stuck together, as if the one wouldn't stand alone; so were they all on their side of the road.' And what of the

* Gabriel Fallon, *Sean O'Casey: the Man I Knew* (Routledge, 1965).

'housekeeper and a staff of three' we were supposed to have? There
were Mrs Earle, who came daily, and Nanny Trim.

In Dublin, Sean, Gaby and Barry Fitzgerald had always been
around together – 'butties', as they say over there. Gaby, Civil
Servant and part-time actor, was well read, particularly in the
theatre, and spent hours talking and arguing with Sean in a
manner far more serious than Barry's would have been. At the
time of his visit I got on with him pleasantly, though I did feel
more affection for Barry who, when he came to London first, lived
with us before finding a bed-sitting room in Baker Street. Sean,
who thought that Gaby's talent lay more in writing or direction
than in acting, had asked Cochran to see him and talk about a
possible engagement to direct. Sean accompanied him round
London; and Gaby also visited the *Tassie* and admired it, going on
a second occasion with Evan Walters and Augustus John.

Barry, cast so precisely as Sylvester, was a most amusing person,
given to worrying himself silly about his financial prospects. He,
too, had doubled the Abbey with a Civil Service job, and he was
gravely concerned about the risk of acting permanently. Sean,
aware of his immense talent and knowing that, unlike Gaby, he
was a bachelor, could not understand why an artist of his gifts
should fail to accept the risk. I think I am right in saying that he
had an ageing mother whom he was helping to support. Most
Irish people, except the very rich, appear to have an ageing
mother somewhere, and Barry was in the mode. When Irish children go abroad their weekly postal orders return so regularly that
I have always believed that the country must be flooded with
them – tributes sent by the young to keep the old. Barry, if
worried about the spending of money, had a nature as kind as his
humour was inimitable: it was grand for Sean to have him for a
while as a neighbour. We grieved that he had not a more testing
part in the Hitchcock film of *Juno and the Paycock* which was shown
in 1930, directed largely as a stage-set film and having the benefit
of Sara Allgood and Maire O'Neill. The mistake was Barry's
relegation from the Paycock: an unpardonable Hitchcock blunder
as the actor cast for the part was in no way comparable to the
other players.

An Abbey actress, a pretty girl named Shelah Richards, called at Woronzow Road to talk about the theatre and herself. She realised Sean was fond of her; he told me that, though Barry had loved Shelah very much, she had chosen the dramatist Denis Johnston. In later years she directed in Dublin Sean's *Red Roses for Me*, the play Ria Mooney would do in London at the Embassy.

Regularly I would ask the girls who were with me in *Bitter-Sweet* to come to see us, especially the three with whom I shared a dressing-room, Maie Drage, Mary Pounds and Rose Hignell, all of them playing bridesmaids. Sean, exhilarated by young company, enjoyed chatting to them. But normally we would be in with Breon, and on Nanny's day out one or other of the girls would often come to run round with us in Regent's Park. Breon's nursery was busy then. He would have various children to tea: Peggy Wood's David, who was of the same age, and Ian Hunter's son – his father acted Teddy in *The Silver Tassie* – adored Breon; they would play together as a team, imaginatively and almost in silence.

II

Dr Waller had asked Sean many times if he could meet Augustus John, and one evening after dinner John duly arrived. I fancy he had wined and dined already, for he fell firmly asleep in his chair which, though it amused us, seemed sad for the doctor, Anyway, about ten o'clock, John revived, grew fresh and lively, talked volubly with all of us, and Dr Waller's evening was made. During our talk the leonine figure sprang up suddenly, cried, 'I must see Breon', and discovered him sound asleep in his cot – 'a beautiful child'. (In later life the great painter and the young artist were friends.) Breon was not in the least impressed when G.B.S. and Mrs Shaw came to tea: he screamed his head off, and G.B.S. thought him thoroughly sensible in rejecting an old gentleman with a white beard. So I took Charlotte to the nursery where she soon got on with Breon and Nannie, and G.B.S. and Sean were glad to be left to talk on their own.

Generally we found invigorating fellow-guests when the Shaws invited us to lunch at Whitehall Court. Once T. E. Lawrence was there. As he sat at table he had so wonderful a head and eyes so compelling that I was amazed, when he stood up, to see how short he was. A shy man, he said little until after lunch when he and Sean – who called him a quiet tiger – began a sustained talk. We knew he praised *The Silver Tassie*; Sean had heard from Augustus John, 'Your play has moved people profoundly: Lawrence (of Arabia), who has been sitting for me, finds it the greatest thing of our time.' (There was a typical postscript, 'I don't see why you need attach yourself to any *class*. A poet, or artist, is really no class at all.') That day in Whitehall Court, Lawrence and Sean got on to G.B.S.'s plays; their author, who never minded discussing his work, accepted their judgement that *Saint Joan* and *Heartbreak House* were the best. They went on to writing in general and the fearfully hard task it could be. On Sean's confession that often he would be incapable of thinking another thought or of writing another line, G.B.S. said cheerfully that as a rule this would be followed by ideas in an overwhelming torrent and he did not know which was worse.

At another lunch, talk turned to the work of George Russell, the Irish poet and philosopher known as 'A.E.'. Helen Waddell, a fashionable writer of the period, and author of *The Desert Fathers* and *Héloïse and Abélard*, was a guest that day, with her publisher who was also Shaw's. She and Charlotte grew rhapsodic about 'A.E.', but Sean, though always courteous to Charlotte, would not humour her: he never cared for the mystic unreality of the man's work, and Charlotte, who disliked contradiction, was very cross. Sean would not yield; it was left to G.B.S. to get round it in his tactful way.

Invariably G.B.S. was loyal to Sean. Not long before the *Tassie* closed, he wrote (23 November 1929) a letter to Cochran which began:

> I really must congratulate you on *The Silver Tassie* before it passes into the classical repertory. It is a magnificent play; and it was a magnificent gesture of yours to produce it. The High-brows *should* have produced it: you, the Unpretentious Show-man, *did*, as you have done so many other noble and rash

things on your Sundays. This, I think, will rank as the best of them.

He ended:

If only someone would build you a huge Woolworth theatre (all seats sixpence) to start with O'Casey and O'Neill, and no plays by men who had ever seen a five-pound note before they were thirty or been inside a school after they were thirteen, you would be buried in Westminster Abbey.
Bravo!

III

Woronzow Road had a placid atmosphere. Sean, living his own life, did not have to bother with us unless he wished; when he was not writing he was reading, and if he knew that Breon and myself were around he was wholly content. Not a fast worker, he wrote everything in longhand in his notebook and transferred it to his typewriter, an old, heavy machine from his Dublin years. Typing in the way Americans term 'hunt and peck', he could work up a good speed. A first draft was rough; he read, altered, changed or deleted entire passages before starting on a final copy. It needed much physical energy, but he could not dictate, even when his sight deteriorated. Though his typing was scarcely flawless, it could always be translated; if it were a play he had it redone by a professional typist before sending it off to his publisher. Articles he posted to newspapers or magazines just as he had typed them himself.

Not a man for holidays, he did go in two successive summers to Margate. The first of these was in the August before the production of *The Silver Tassie*. I was doubtful, for I realised we could not afford a hotel; moreover, having had the previous year's experience at Angmering, I could not hope for real serenity. Nanny Trim told me then of lodgings where she had been with other children, and I hurried down to Margate during the day to see her addresses. One provided a large bedroom with a sitting-room, use of bathroom, and a landlady who would cook your food when you had bought it, and who would allow Nanny to do the washing; the house had also a second bedroom to let. As I was in *Bitter-Sweet*, we arranged to fix things up one Sunday. It was all homely and easy-going; once Nanny and Breon had settled, Sean decided himself that Margate was sympathetic. On its big sandy beach, crowded – unlike Angmering – at low tide, he could roam unnoticed among the people and listen to their talk and the odd family argument. We booked a beach hut for tea, and for shelter when wet. Undeniably one snag was the landlady's habit of locking the kitchen after lunch and going out, so that we were unable to get in until about six. But that was a minor problem; Breon gloried in the sand and the freedom and the chance to tear along the beach in the early mornings when it was practically desolate.

Sean approved so heartily that he was prepared to travel down with me on the second Sunday and stay for a week or so; I had to return on the Monday afternoon in time for the performance at night. If, as frequently, it became a cold evening, the landlady would give Sean a coal fire in the sitting-room, and she put in a table where he could write while Nanny was in the kitchen washing or ironing. Every evening I telephoned to a hotel where Sean would await the call. Presently three weeks had grown to five; Breon had made a swarm of friends on the beach and his father would play with him by the hour.

It was at Margate that I discovered Sean's unsuspected interest in cricket and football. At the end of the road where we had our digs, lunch-time scores in the Test Match were flashed upon an electric indicator in front of a big hotel; Sean would be found invariably among a crowd waiting on the green. I learned, too, that he would listen on a Saturday to the football results. Horse-racing never affected him, though sometimes if I put on a small bet he would join in the jubilation of a win.

We repeated the holiday in 1930, Breon (then two and a half) and Nanny living in Margate, and Sean there during most of the visit; I went at week-ends. In Sean's absence I sometimes had supper with friends after the show; with Dr Waller once or twice, and the throat specialist, Geoffrey Carte. An evening arrived when Lee, who was seeing a girl about a part in one of his future shows, called at the stage door of His Majesty's. I went to supper with him; he still attracted me greatly, and, acting without any thought, I did not consider the pain I might give to Sean. After dancing, Lee drove me into the country on a glorious moonlit night. He must have deeply resented my marriage; I was sure that in a way he remained extremely fond of me. I dare say it was inevitable that we should make love.

In time, knowing that I was pregnant, I felt acutely miserable and was most reserved and conscience-stricken with Sean. His was the only child I had wanted; now, in attempting to get rid of this one I had made myself ill: a situation in which I was both trapped and appalled. The truth had to be known, so I went to Sean and said, 'I am going to have a child.' Without giving him time to answer, I went on: 'Dearest, it is not yours.'

Turning dead white, he said, 'If it is not mine, I know who the father is.'

I just replied: 'Yes.'

'Please leave me alone, Eileen,' he answered. In my knowledge he had never been so upset; trembling, he was nearly in tears. I felt almost crazy. That evening I went off to the theatre without speaking to him. Somehow I got through the show; the girls in the dressing-room understood that it must be an emotional crisis, for during the eighteen months we had dressed together we were responsive to each others' problems. At the end I was about to ask the stage doorkeeper for a taxi when he spoke first: 'Mr O'Casey is waiting in a taxi for you.'

As I climbed into it, Sean embraced me. 'Dearest Eileen,' he exclaimed, 'you will get over it somehow. You must not make yourself ill. Mostly it's my fault.' I sobbed in his arms. We had supper together at home, and all that night I was ill. Sean got from Billy McElroy the name of a Harley Street specialist whom I went to see next day; already I had done so much to lose the child that it was easy for the specialist to say that I must have an operation. On the Saturday, after the performance, I drove straight from His Majesty's to the nursing-home and an operation at midnight: a horrible and saddening psychological upset. Sean never spoke to me about the abortion. Visiting me daily, he endeavoured to make me forget, indeed to make me feel it was part of our life together, and that he was concerned only with my health. In the end I arrived home to festivity at Woronzow Road with Breon in a state of excitement and Nanny and Mrs Earle pleased to have me back. At the theatre the girls brought flowers to welcome me. Lee had gone to America for a show; I bore no resentment, and there was no reason why I should; I never wrote to him or mentioned it. The whole incident seemed to fortify our marriage; I recognised Sean's full qualities, and he appeared to love me more than ever.

IV

After Christmas and early in the New Year I was able to go with Sean, who was much moved by them, to the famous Habima Players, presented by Sidney Bernstein for a brief season at the new Phoenix Theatre. I still remember their eerie mask-like make-up, the intensity of *The Dybbuk*, the gaiety of *Twelfth Night*. By this time my long engagement was nearly over. *Bitter-Sweet* approached its last months when it was moved for short periods to other theatres, and it closed finally in the late spring of 1931. Sean had had nothing on in London since *The Silver Tassie*. We were not well off. The decoration of the house had cost more than it should; like most artists, we had let the money go as it came in; I had no idea of its value. G.B.S. had insisted to me that it was impossible for a writer or artist not to be financially erratic, he was paid so irregularly. If he received a large cheque, he would spend it, not asking when the next might arrive, if at all. Rather he would look forward to the sale of a film or to the production of a play. It had, obviously, to be a matter of individual temperament; but here, by ill chance, both Sean and myself were alike. Years later, when he was corresponding with an American, I happened to glance at the typewriter. He had written: 'As regards money, my dear chap, I am particularly bad at managing it, but Eileen doesn't even know where the damned stuff comes from.'

In the circumstances, we agreed that we must sell the lease of

Woronzow Road which we had taken for seven years with the option of renewing it for another period; we had been there for only three years and could sell the balance. In this period of uncertainty Billy McElroy told us of a furnished cottage his daughter had in Buckinghamshire, at Chalfont St Giles, nineteen miles from London. Seeing that we had no sort of plan, he asked why we should not go to stay in this rented cottage, paying the rent to Evelyn McElroy until we discovered somewhere of our own to live. It sounded right, so sadly we left a house we had loved, the only one either of us had ever owned, and had its furniture stored away in Harrods' Repository. In later years, when we went into rented places, the curtains, carpets and furniture would somehow have to be fitted in as best they could.

Nanny Trim, who had longed for me to have a second baby in order that she could remain, was distressed to leave Breon, though at the age of three he had grown far too energetic for her, running at speed in the park where she had no hope of catching him. I had again to think of those occasions in her life when it must have dismayed her to say goodbye to her charges after watching them grow. Mrs Earle left us also. True, she had to care for her family who lived in London, but we could not have afforded her; I got a young girl, who would help in the house, and with Breon, to accompany us to Chalfont. There it was. We had had to sell our lease to get the capital we needed; the offer of the cottage made us accept the easy way out, flying, said Sean, 'from the frying-pan of city poverty to the furnace of poverty in the glad green country'.

I believe now that we made a foolish decision to take Billy McElroy's advice and to leave London. At the time we recognised that we had grown closer in understanding and love; we would have to see what a country life might yield.

CHAPTER SEVEN

Hillcrest, Chalfont St Giles

WE had not moved long before we heard from Charlotte Shaw:

> I rejoice to think of you both [she wrote on 15 November] in
> your own home with the garden and peace and quiet. Only I
> wish you were a little nearer. We know Chalfont St Giles quite
> well. We had a friend there once we used to drive over to see,
> only we were younger then and there were not so many cars on
> the road. Now I find it very hard to get G.B.S. to go out on
> winter afternoons. Summer, yes – he likes it; but in the winter
> he says, 'Wait until the days are longer.' So I'm afraid we'll
> have to wait! It is because he hates these lanes after dark, and
> meeting cars with blazing lights in fogs round corners.
> I am longing to hear you have a new play ready. Has the move
> interfered with one? G.B.S. has just finished his new one. It is
> called *Too True To Be Good*, and I call it a 'Super Farce'; I think
> you will like it.

The place we had rented from Evelyn McElroy was less idyllic
than Charlotte imagined: an ordinary workman's cottage on the
estate of Misbourne House. Evelyn had decorated it pleasantly;
but it was fairly primitive: no electric light, only oil lamps, and
an outside lavatory. In plan it was a doll's house: a door in the
middle, a room on each side. On the left one went through the
room to a scullery and kitchen (cooking by oil-stove) and out to
the yard. On the right was a small sitting-room. A steep staircase
went straight up the doll's-house centre to the first floor which
also had a room on each side, and a bathroom in the middle. Even
though he knew we were just bridging things over, Sean was
unhappy. With no windows at the back, the cottage was extremely

dark. No matter how the outside lavatory was whitewashed, one had to face on the wall beside it the colony of snails that Sean was still recollecting when he wrote *Rose and Crown*: 'A mass of wriggling, twisting slime. Hundreds of thick-bodied snails, oozing their phosphorescent sweat out of them, and as many more corpulent slugs, were sliding damply up and down the wall. . . . A Walpurgis Night of vermin.'

Sean, who wrote of 'the horrible cottage', disliked it far more than I did – because, I believe, its sanitation would remind him unconsciously of his Dublin slum life and the conditions his mother had to endure. On seeing the place and realising we could not be there long, we had resolved to try to manage in it. Sean used one tiny room on the first floor; I shared the other with Breon and the girl Tessa, who lived with us. In the evenings I sat mostly in the room where we ate; Sean, at work on the earliest of his autobiographies, *I Knock at the Door*, describing his Dublin boyhood, once more became involved in writing and had to have the other small room for himself and his papers.

It was a most awkward time for him. The sitting-room had one big oil lamp. Even when we added another, the light was dismal. Finally Sean discovered, by trial and error, that while writing in his notebook he could get on best if he put a lamp on the floor and leant upon his elbow; typing he could manage at the table in the other room. One morning he called to me in alarm, showing that his right elbow had developed an enormous swelling; the doctor told him that, instead of housemaid's knee, he had housemaid's elbow, caused simply by friction upon the floor. Thereafter he resolved that he must write in the other room.

II

We used to walk a great deal in the Chiltern country near Chalfont: genuine rural England with magnificent trees. Going off in mid-morning, we could ramble for hours, find a light lunch somewhere – Sean did not drink, and I did not care then whether I did or not – and get back to the cottage during the early afternoon.

Occasionally we took Breon in a push-chair; he was company for us both. All the while the weather was serene; the gardener of the big house looked after our patch of lawn, and on the hotter afternoons we could have our tea there while Breon splashed round in a tub of water. Sean, his book possessing him, would recall a lot about his early life; he had an acute memory that would evoke a scene in detail while he talked and I listened.

Admiring the area, if not the cottage, we searched for a small house that we could rent. At last, a quarter of an hour's walk away, we hit upon a bungalow called Hillcrest, set back from the road at the far end of Chalfont St Giles village and practically opposite John Milton's former home. Its rent was low and we had a three-year lease. Altogether, there was some half an acre, with a fairly long drive, a fruit and vegetable garden, flower-beds, a small orchard, a splendid lawn, and a lily-pond that we cleared later for a sand-pit. Within, we had a big hall, a french-windowed room that gave upon the lawn, a bathroom, and a kitchen where Billy McElroy's supplies of coal kept up the old-fashioned stove. Sean worked and slept in a room at the back; I had a tiny one beside it, and Breon and Tessa a much larger one in front that was also a playroom. We drew as much furniture from store as we needed, sorted out curtains and carpets and books, and settled in: the change seemed hopeful.

We had, even so, to realise that Chalfont St Giles was not a friendly neighbourhood in our sense of the term. On our walks through the village people stood at their gates and stared, scarcely nodding the time of the day. Our landlords, the Lanes, were builders, amiable enough; Mrs Lane's father, Mr Nash, who owned a large village store besides bakeries at Gerrards Cross, lived in a house across from us, and also set far back, that was full of solid Victorian furniture, highly polished. When he went to London on business he travelled in his chauffeur-driven Rolls; otherwise he lived an extremely cautious life. At first he talked to Sean on the rare occasions he went out; but, as Sean put it later: 'When the name of Milton smote his ear, he went silent and went away, never speaking a word to me again.'

On the other side of the main road were expensive modern

houses and bungalows. Their owners, I am sure, would have belonged to the local golf club: agreeable people, no doubt, but having nothing in common with us. Breon, now and then, would have one of the children to tea, or would be asked to tea himself; with the children's nannies present, it had to be a bit stilted and starchy. Though I had Tessa, this never meant that I kept apart from my child as some of the Chalfont mothers did. Because there were too few children for Breon, we began to look for a nursery school; and being a semi-Catholic still, and thinking fondly that I would like him to be brought up in the faith, I fixed upon a convent at Gerrards Cross – one that accepted boys as well as girls when very young. Even knowing the fees to be expensive, I argued that for such a mixed marriage as ours, with Sean a well-known Irish author, they might very well be reduced. So we went along; I took Breon in, leaving Sean at the gate. The convent stood in its own parkland, and its classrooms were airy, though I wondered at the lack of modern play-equipment. Our tour over, the nun brought me to a reception room where I told her my trouble with the fees; after all, I had been myself at a convent and had relatives who were nuns. Might there not be some chance of a reduction? The nun, tight-mouthed and frozen now, said she would call another Sister; and an older nun arrived, explained that no reduction was possible, and ended the interview. No longer smiling at Breon, they showed us to the door with a curt goodbye, clearly feeling they had wasted their time. It had begun to drench with rain; Sean was hiding in a telephone box near the gate. I burst out indignantly, then we raced for the bus; I was in a terrible temper, while Sean, who had never had the faintest belief that the nuns would reduce their fees by one penny, tried hard not to smile.

I heard next of a Quaker school in Jordans village that took children from three to nine years, and was run by a Miss Clarke, a relative of Dame Elizabeth Cadbury, of the cocoa firm. Equipped with climbing frames and the modern toys children needed, it was what I could have wished for Breon: a place where a child would have the freedom of his imagination. I was happy we had not been accepted at the convent. At once Breon started at Jordans, leaving us at half-past nine and not returning as a rule until late in the afternoon when one of us would meet him.

Sean enjoyed playing with him imaginary games of workmen or firemen, engine-drivers or policemen; more especially a game in which he could sit calmly while Breon trundled a barrow of sand round the garden and back again before tipping it into the sand-pit where it was to be delivered. On wet days he would sketch amusingly; they were the liveliest of companions. Breon had, too, a friend Sean was fond of, a sturdy boy, Johnny Grayburn, whose parents lived in Gerrards Cross and who needed a playmate. Often his smart Nanny would leave him at Hillcrest for the afternoon, bringing him in a carefully frilled shirt which we hastened to replace by a jersey so that he could go back as spick-and-span as he came. Nothing would make him other than a real toughie. More than a dozen years later, when we read that the same boy had been killed in the war, Sean dedicated the play of *Oak Leaves and Lavender* to 'Little Johnny Grayburn who, in his sailor suit, played football with me on a Chalfont lawn and afterwards gallantly fell in the battle of Arnhem.'

III

Our funds were low. Sean was beginning to be depressed; more-over, the Chalfont stuffiness was getting us both down. Hope flickered momentarily when Arthur Sinclair, managing now for the Irish Players, arrived to ask Sean for a brief one-act play, with not more than four characters, that might be done on the music-halls: it was increasingly hard to get work for the full Irish com-pany. Sean responded with *A Pound on Demand*, a brisk slapdash comedy based on a story Gaby Fallon had once told him about a drunk man trying to draw a pound out of the Post Office to get more drink, and being quite incapable of writing his name. A friend takes charge of the adventure and the form-filling:

> . . . only one double ell, only one double ell, man! You're not listenin' to me, Sammy. There's nothin' to prevent you doin' it right, if you'll only listen. You've nearly a dozen of ells down. . . .

Sean also wrote *The End of the Beginning*, a one-act kitchen-comedy from an old folk-story. But Sinclair never got *A Pound on Demand* upon the halls, and Sean made no effort to send *The End of the Beginning* to anybody, though Cochran would later ask to read it.

In July 1932 Sean wrote to the local tax-collector:

Dear Sir,

I have now only Twenty pounds in the whole world, but I send you, as ordered Five pounds to keep the wolf from the door, leaving myself with Fifteen to keep myself, wife and kid, and help to promulgate the Gospel in foreign parts.

I appreciate your point that my debt to the Inland Revenue is now £236 odd, but it won't be higher on account of last year's income, for there was none, for which I cannot thank God. With your permission, I should like to make a point myself, and it is this: when we poor devils of Artists get anything, we get it all at once, and not regularly, as others do, so that we have to pay more in taxation than most persons. There seems to be a core of injustice in that. I'm not referring, of course, to the official personnel of the Inland Revenue, for, from Commissioners to Collectors, I have been treated with courtesy, and, in many instances, kindness.

I have just finished a little one-act play, which I hope to see on the Halls; this may make things a little easier, and allow me to get down that £236 a little lower.

I hope, too, within the next three or four months, to finish my big play which I'm sure will be anything but popular, but may, I hope, add to the honour of drama written in the English tongue. So in this way, I will bless them that curse me, and be praying for them that despitefully use me.

I hope the Conversion Scheme will be a success, for everybody seems to think that this is much more important than the conversion of the heathen.

Sincerely yours, SEAN O'CASEY

Not having seen much of my mother since we left Woronzow Road, I tried to put her up for a week at the bungalow, only to see after a few hours what a fool I had been. She would disrupt the whole place in trying to tidy it. Though she might offer to do the washing-up, her clattering and moaning and remarks about the

dust and disorder in the kitchen were both exasperating and un-
true; the whole place was quite normally tidy and clean. At
night, when Sean was in his room, writing, I would sit to talk
with her, but she was so restless and critical – she just could not
help it – that everything she said irritated me. I could not tell her
my problems. Perhaps she was right in a way to tell me that I had
brought trouble on myself by my mismanagement and extravagance, but it was hardly comforting. We were pleased when the
week was over; had she been reasonable she could have helped
with Breon, made herself happier, and aided us financially, but it
was hopeless. The country she detested, preferring London where
at least she could look at the shops or go for the occasional bus-ride
to see a friend. When I was back in London on the stage, I would
often go to see her; Sean put up a gallant effort during that week
at Chalfont, yet by the end it was everything he could do to be
reasonably polite.

Luckily, Barry Jackson asked me to do an audition for the
fourth revival of Rutland Boughton's opera, *The Immortal Hour*,
founded on 'Fiona Macleod's' play about the fairy princess who
weds the High King of Ireland, and who must be wooed back to
her own people. Gwen Ffrangcon-Davies again played the lead
during a six weeks' run at the Queen's Theatre; I was to sing in
the chorus. It meant riding up daily in the bus from Chalfont. If
I were to continue to work in the theatre it would be impossible to
return every night after the show; instead I searched for a furnished room in London and found two unfurnished (thanks to
Mrs Earle, who worked opposite) upon the top floor over a tailor's
in Baker Street: one room and a kitchen, extremely cheap because
the lavatory was downstairs and outside. I rented them on a
monthly basis at a pound a week; they were painted white
throughout; and I used some of the furniture which had not been
fitted into the bungalow. The owners of the shop did not live on
the premises; one woman, whom I seldom met, had a room on
the other floor. In a block of flats over the way, Mrs Earle worked
for some rich Jewish people, going in every evening to cook their
meal; it was fortunate for me, because on matinée days I could
bring two or three girls from the show back to eat, and she would

have a meal for us, usually left-overs from her other job, chicken mousse, veal-and-ham pie, cold lobster, elaborate sweets. A good cook, she soothed our consciences by telling us that if the food were not eaten it would be thrown away. Now, too, she was able to be with me during the day; altogether it was a great arrangement.

IV

Frequently, if there was not a matinée, I could travel to Chalfont, an hour and a half's bus ride, arrive for lunch, and return to the theatre in the evening. My luck continued. Immediately *The Immortal Hour* closed, Cochran had me auditioned for a singing part in his Lyceum Theatre revival of *The Miracle*, the Max Reinhardt 'wordless spectacle' that had been staged twenty years earlier at Olympia; it was founded on the legend of a nun who ran away from her convent and who returned to it many years later to discover that the Madonna had filled her place. Now it opened in the great Lyceum which could hold 3000 and was made to look like a church. During the first half, as nuns, we walked, singing round the stage; the second Act was the banquet in which we were part of the crowd; and during the last Act we sang from high up in the gallery. There seemed to be hundreds in the cast of *The Miracle*: professionals aside, many society girls took part. Tilly Losch and Lady Diana Duff Cooper, who played the Madonna, were the leads.

Sean naturally missed me while I was in London during the week. Though, out of nursery-school hours, he played a lot with Breon, the hushed loneliness of the country at night must have depressed him; essentially he was a town man. He was glad that Gabriel Fallon, on an English visit, could stay for a couple of days at Chalfont while I was away. They were still warm friends; Gaby has related how Sean, anxious for his comfort, crept in early one morning to clean out the grate and to make and light the fire, hoping not to disturb his guest who tactfully feigned sleep. But such visits as these were few, and the Chalfont atmosphere was not inspiring. When Sean was not working, indeed, he had nothing to stimulate him; the villagers lived largely behind closed doors and one could not count on a friendly gossip. I remember one or two exceptions. On our walks from the first cottage we had got to know the owner of a small farm and hand laundry that impressed Sean because it was kept so well in so modern a style. Its owner, who preserved his standards by paying his workers a little above the average, was a bachelor with a housekeeper to look after him; an uncommon man, between sixty-five and seventy, who had run his business for six years. He could discuss the theatre, for in London he had been a violinist in the orchestra of the St James's; his hobby was the collection of violins, his joy a Stradivarius that he handled with proper reverence. Annual holidays he spent always in Vienna, or in Germany, or wherever he thought he could find another violin and go to good concerts. Certainly he was unlike the normal residents of Chalfont, and sometimes Sean would go over to tea with him, or he would call on us.

Sean's other friend, a Catholic lay brother from Gerrards Cross, was an Irishman, really wild; whenever he was free, he would be with us for supper. Often, when it was raining, he would have to discard his rust-red habit and blue girdle, and sit, while it was drying, in a sweater and trousers of Sean's. He is the subject of the chapter in *Rose and Crown* entitled 'A Friar by the Fireside' in which he appears as Father Clematis of the Cuneiform Order of Unimpassionate Canons Irregular, 'a pleasant, chatty young man', though 'a thought outside the thought of the Community would leave him almost lost'. At length a day came when he tore up the path to report that he was being transferred as he could not bear the district any longer. Sean, who saw him to the bus, told me afterwards that he was hurrahing and waving from the window in sheer joy at going.

My next play, six months after *The Miracle*, which had only a brief life, had ended, was a Cochran musical, *Mother of Pearl*, written by A. P. Herbert, with music by Oscar Straus; Alice Delysia in the lead. A young girl, Sepha Treble, would get her first important West End chance as Pearl Moon, though she had been in two of Cochran's Pavilion revues and had had a small part in

Helen! Once more I had just a little to do and understudied the
French maid; Jane Carr understudied Sepha who – by curious
chance – lived with her mother in a house on the corner of
Woronzow Road that Sean and I had admired without knowing
its residents. Sepha was fascinating: she had a good figure and a
vivacious face, though I would not have called it beautiful, and she
was invariably sunny and smiling, as if life treated her rightly; her
clothes showed that she had no financial problems. Struggling up
myself, I was in no position to criticise her acting. I recall that on
the final night in London, when Cochran gave a party on the
Gaiety Theatre stage, she was there with a man, wealthy, Jewish
and alert, who had something to do with the art world and whom
I would have found excellent company. Though I believe she had
half a dozen further West End parts until 1939, I never met
Sepha once *Mother of Pearl* had ended. Years afterwards, when
Cochran was unwell and I was visiting him, he liked to talk of
the girls who had acted in his shows. I told him that two I
remembered especially were Sepha and Isla Bevan. Sepha's control over affairs of the heart had astonished me; Cochran had met
her once in New York where finally, he said, she had married a
rich man whom undoubtedly she loved. I would like to see her
again. Isla, who had been with me in *Bitter-Sweet*, was another girl
of much personality and decision; Cochran told me that she had
married a wealthy businessman in the North of England.

After we had rehearsed *Mother of Pearl* in London, the play
opened in Manchester at Christmas 1932; sometimes I walked
round the town with its author, A. P. Herbert, looking at bookshops where he could buy for me a few of his works and sign them.
After we had been in Manchester for nearly a week, Sean telephoned me on a Friday to say that Breon was ill with bronchitis.
How I worked that night, and through the two shows on Saturday, I cannot imagine; but I kept in touch with Sean who told me
that, though Breon had had so bad a turn, he was not in danger.
Alice Delysia was extremely thoughtful; learning that one of the
violinists in our band lived near Chalfont and motored home on
Saturday nights, she got him to give me a lift. We drove through
the small hours and arrived home about five o'clock; Mr Green

would call for me again on Monday morning. Breon, who was very sick, had missed me; I was able to stay with him all that Sunday, and by next morning his temperature was down. We had only one more week in Manchester before London; gratefully I contemplated returning home. I must have been mad to have chased my ambition to act instead of settling down, as I should have done, with Sean and Breon whom I loved dearly; as it was, I occupied my Baker Street room but went to Chalfont all I could during a two-months' London run. I appeared several times as the maid, a fairly good small part; Eve, the girl who was cast for it, but who had been engaged mainly as an understudy for Delysia, was off a great deal.

At Chalfont things were at sixes and sevens. Sean believed that Tessa was unreliable; if Breon had gone to bed in time to nurse his cold, he might not have contracted bronchitis. Once Sean had turned against anybody, he would never look back; understanding this, I had to tell Tessa to go, and have Breon with me in London where he slept on a sofa in my room. Mrs Earle, who had given up her other job, looked after the flat; having known Breon since he was a baby, she could watch him while I was at the theatre. We were beside Regent's Park, and close to the Zoo; it was like the old days of Woronzow Road. For a time, splendid; then, when *Mother of Pearl* closed, I discovered an older person, a widow, to come down to Chalfont to look after Breon and to help generally. To Sean's great delight, I was back at home, the family together; I did not act again, realising that, as a married woman, I had been foolish in trying to preserve a career which, more than anything, I had used as a personal indulgence, an outlet.

v

In London we had tried to go to the theatre when we could. It was a pleasure we missed in the country; but we began to make a weekly trip to a small cinema at Chalfont St Peter – rather than to the bigger one at Gerrards Cross because Chalfont St Peter showed older films which were more fun. It was an ancient cinema, with the noisiest music – we could almost hear the film rolling round – but we did see some grand old movies, especially cowboy stuff in which we delighted. To get to the five-thirty house, we had to start after tea, and we looked forward to it as a weekly excitement. Otherwise, our amusement was to visit the local market-towns on market-days. Though, when the fair reached Chalfont twice a year, we took Breon to it, barely anyone spoke to us: the stray word, no more, unless we happened to be with the parents of a child Breon knew: nothing at all of the lovable atmosphere we met years ahead in Devon when everybody on a Totnes market-day chatted to everybody else. The two counties were utterly different in mood.

Sean, one morning, got a frantic telephone-call from the critic, Desmond MacCarthy, whom he had never seen. MacCarthy was in a fearful state; Sean could get little from him except that it was a matter he must come down to talk about at once, a terrible problem in which only Sean could help. MacCarthy was speaking from London. Could he come to Chalfont on the next train? Sean, leaving the telephone, asked me what we ought to do; the poor man, who seemed to be at his wits' end, would hint only that it was about Sean's work. I said: 'You'll just have to ask him to come.' We waited and speculated. When Desmond did arrive, tall, thin, drooping, apparently distracted, but with a personality rather childlike and disarming, he practically burst out with his problem in the hall. Putting his hand on Sean's shoulder, he exclaimed, 'My dear man, I was going on a train to the north. Macmillans had given me your manuscript to read, the manuscript of *Windfalls*, and to my horror, when I got home, I found that I had left half of it on the train. I have hunted everywhere. Have you got a second copy?' Apparently much sorrier for Desmond than himself, Sean attempted to console him, sat him down in the front room, and came to search for another copy. Here he did show his own panic to me. 'I don't know what in the name of God, Eileen, I've done with the thing I wrote. It's at least five or six weeks since it was sent away. Which drawer can it be in? Where can it have been put?' He grew panicky; and it took him half an hour to find what had been the rough copy of his two missing stories, and to see that they could be typed again. He rushed into Desmond, crying, 'I'm saved. But let me tell you that I didn't feel as calm as I pretended to be.' They both cheered up, Desmond in particular; he stayed for an hour or so and had a meal while he and Sean who had taken to each other – which in the circumstances was lucky – gossiped about everything but the lost manuscript. Macmillans published *Windfalls* in the following year. Besides the short stories, written, Sean said, 'to get rid of some of the bitterness that swept into me when the Abbey Theatre rejected *The Silver Tassie*', the book contained some poems and the two short plays, *The End of the Beginning* and *A Pound on Demand*.

We seemed at Chalfont to be continually in money difficulties. Samuel French, the play publishers, had asked often if they could buy the world amateur rights of *Juno and the Paycock*, *The Plough and the Stars*, and *The Shadow of a Gunman* for £300 and a half-share of all royalties for evermore. Sean hated to part with this property; equally, he hated to borrow. If we had been wise, we would have asked G.B.S. or Macmillans to give us a bank guarantee. Two friends Sean tried could not lend him the money, and though we suggested to Billy McElroy that the Augustus John pictures would be his security Billy just then had his money tied up. Anyway, we were resolved not to sell John's portrait of Sean.

Unwillingly, we accepted the offer for the play rights; and Samuel French asked us to do prompt-copies, with a series of stage plans that I produced with great labour after we had taken hours and hours to draw and measure them, a task we loathed. G.B.S. disapproved of the bargain. He wrote: 'Three hundred pounds for half-rights for your lifetime plus fifty years is an absurdly bad bargain for you. My advice is to let wife and child perish and lay bricks for your last crust, sooner than part with an iota of your rights.' Nevertheless, Sean felt he had to agree. On an afternoon while we were struggling with the dreary task for French's, the door-bell rang and in walked H. G. Wells, the last person on earth I had expected. Suddenly I remembered. Lady Keeble, the actress Lillah McCarthy, had written to ask Sean to go to her house in Oxford to listen to verse-speaking by some eminent English players, and though Sean had written back to tell her it was impossible, she next sent a telegram to say that H. G. Wells would call for him; she would not hear of a refusal. Hence Wells's arrival at a moment when we were thoroughly unhappy over our prompt-books. I had never met him. A dapper little man, neatly dressed, he greeted me affably, and I quite liked him, though Sean described him afterwards as 'a rather stout, shortish figure, looking like a classic undertaker whose services were given only to the distinguished or very wealthy'. Wells was bustling. 'I've come to take Sean to Oxford. Isn't he ready?' 'No,' I said, 'we're in the middle of working together; I thought Sean told Lady Keeble he wouldn't be coming.' Both of us had forgotten the telegram.

Wells talked for a few minutes with Sean before urging him to go; Lillah McCarthy herself was to read poems that day, and they particularly wanted Sean's presence. Sean remained firm, 'I'll stick to what I'm at until the job is done'; and at length Wells, exceedingly cross now, left us with the curtest of goodbyes. Obviously he was a man accustomed to getting his own way; but not this time. We never saw him afterwards.

VI

Life moved quietly until Sean began to get such agonising pain round his heart that the local doctor told him to consult a specialist. Lady Londonderry had asked us both to see her if we were in town. When I told her of Sean's illness she sent her chauffeur to Chalfont to drive us to Harley Street. On the journey we hardly spoke. I had a vision of Sean completely helpless for the rest of his life and myself as the wonderfully brave wife who wheeled him about. Sean himself had dramatic pictures of his death and of leaving me unprovided for, with Breon to bring up. He hinted at this before we reached Bertram Nissé's consulting-room. We had only to wait ten minutes during which neither of us said a word. Sean went to be examined, and for the next three-quarters of an hour I got more and more worked up. Eventually Nissé emerged alone, saying cheerfully, 'Your husband's dressing: I wanted to tell you there's no cause for worry.' He turned to Sean who had entered: 'Your heart is all right, but you need careful treatment and dieting. I've written a prescription to ease the pain, and I will send you a diet-sheet.' We looked almost disappointed. 'Well,' said Nissé, 'what's wrong? You ought to be very happy.' At length we could laugh and tell him: we had been deep in our wheel-chair drama. The hardest part, I found, was to follow: Sean, who was a chain-smoker, getting through sixty or seventy cigarettes a day, must cut it down. Gradually, he did; the only way he could manage it was to reduce daily the number he smoked and to write this number on the back of the packet. He got to fifteen, and then to ten; but it was so obvious that he missed his constant smoking that I suggested he should try a pipe.

Soon afterwards we reached the sixth anniversary of our wedding. That day he gave me this:

Hillcrest, Chalfont St Giles, Bucks
23 September, 1933

To Eileen,
On the Sixth Anniversary of our Wedding.

Six years of life, each like a room immeasurably small in the tiny house of life.

So small, that entering one, we pass into another, till the last and smallest room of all is reached, and then pass out alone, each in his own way to gain or loss; or, maybe, neither gain nor loss to know, leaving behind a sigh or two in several breasts, when it's time to go, go out, and leave behind the supreme sighs in breasts a step behind.

Six rooms passed through, and feet upon the threshold, another!

Well, we have glimpsed the shadows of bright flowers;
Have heard in drowsy ways the song of birds;
Seen slips of colour in the evening skies;
Felt fleeting touches from the hands of friends, as we went on from room to room;
And bred a child of fair lady and a quickening mind, who follows on, and will, we hope, push life's narrow circle further out when we are gone.

Six years of life, each like a room immeasurably small!
A little tired we are, but droop not, and pass on into
With steady steps all spans still before us
Till we reach the last.

With love
SEAN

For some time now he had finished *Within the Gates*, his 'play of four scenes in a London park', the work which he had told the tax-collector in the previous year 'will be anything but popular but may, I hope, add to the honour of drama written in the English tongue'. In a preliminary note Sean said:

If possible, the Curtain intervening between the opening of the play and the scenes following, should be one showing the Park Gates, stiff and formal, dignified and insolent. The bars should shine with the silver gleam of aluminium paint, and cross or diagonal bars should be a deep and sombre black. All space between the bars should be dark – but not too dark – green. The gates proper are flanked by generous panels of a vivid yellow, representing the piers, lower than the bars, and topped by copings of orange-coloured panels. This curtain, when it is pulled back, represents the opening of the gates, and, when it falls back into its place, represents the closing of the gates: or, the outline of the gates may be suggested on the curtain.

The above idea of a front curtain was derived from Eugene O'Neill's suggestion of a front curtain for his great play, *Mourning Becomes Electra*.

Macmillans published *Within the Gates* in December 1933. During the summer he had sent a copy of the script to Cochran. C.B., sympathetic but unable to venture, wrote on 1 August 1933 from his Old Bond Street offices:

My dear Sean,
I am worried about *Within the Gates*. I don't believe I could produce it without financial loss. It is true that I might incur this with less worthy material.
You have written some grand stuff and I am intrigued by your manner of introducing the singing, although you have created another difficulty for the producing manager who must

Courtesy W. Suschitzky

Sean

Eileen's mother and father, Kathleen and Edward Reynolds, photographed in Johannesburg when first married

Eileen Carey, photographed while a member of the D'Oyly Carte Opera Company, 1923

Eileen Carey, photographed in London before meeting Sean
O'Casey

Eileen Carey modeling hats, 1925

This picture appeared in a weekly illustrated journal in 1927 with the caption "Beauty and the 'Black and Tans': Miss Eileen Carey hides a bag of Mills bombs during a raid by the 'Black and Tans' in Mr. Sean O'Casey's *The Shadow of a Gunman* at the Court"

Sean and Eileen O'Casey are married at the Church of the
Holy Redeemer in Chelsea on September 23, 1927

19 Woronzow Road, St.
John's Wood, N.W. 8

49 Overstrand Mansions,
Battersea, S.W. 11

Tingrith, Station Road,
Totnes

40 Trumlands Road, St.
Marychurch, Torquay

Sean and Eileen O'Casey leaving the Church of the Holy
Redeemer, Chelsea, after their marriage on September 23,
1927

The family at Totnes outside Tingrith: left to right, Niall, Breon, Sean, Shivaun, Eileen

find an actress who can sing. The non-singing actress is difficult enough to find – the combination is very rare. I wish I could see my way to risk the production, but frankly I can't.

I am glad you are changing the Bishop's wife to the Bishop's sister. I read your play before your letter and I felt that you were limiting what the Bishop stood for by giving him a wife.

Please send me your sketch, *End of the Beginning*, and I might be able to place it for you, although I shan't have use for it as I am not contemplating any more revue productions.

I hope ever so much that I am all wrong about your play and that somebody will do it and earn royalties for you. You can't go on writing fine things, Sean, unless they bring some material reward. I suppose you are tired of people advising you to get back to the method of *Juno*. I wish you would.

Yours as ever, CHARLES B. COCHRAN

To which Sean replied at once:

My dear C.B.,

Thanks for your kind letter telling me what you thought about *Within the Gates* and, alas, telling me that you couldn't take the risk of its production. Although I hadn't asked you, I, of course, had a hope that the play would appear under your name. But I clearly understand your fear, and though I have a feeling that this play stands a far better chance than stood *The Silver Tassie*, I realise that a 'feeling' is a poor thing to put before any sensible Manager. But I can't see why the play, being at least above the average, should be cluttered with costly accessories, and that, since a risk must be taken, why that risk shouldn't be as simple a risk as possible, with a simple scene, and a group of actors ready to act in a good play – a play that gives each a good part – for a reasonable salary.

As regards the sketch [*The End of the Beginning*] I have the air of a song to get, and when I have this I shall send it on. It wouldn't be suitable for any revue that you might put on, for it was written for Sinclair – who pestered me into doing it when he was out of work – and then didn't do anything with it.

I have been able to afford only two elaborately-typed copies of the play, and I should be glad if you could let me have back the copy I sent to you.

Your advice to go back to the genius of *Juno* might be good for me, but bad for my conception of the drama. And the fault of finding it almost impossible to get a good play produced is not in us, neither in you nor in me, but in an ignorant public that have nothing, and who, eventually, shall lose even that which they have.

Please give my best wishes to Mrs Cochran; and good luck to you till you are in a position to do any damn thing you like.

Yours as ever,

SEAN

There seemed to be more hope in America. George Jean Nathan, the major drama critic, who had read the manuscript, wrote to Sean from New York in November:

I read it last evening and want to tell you, in all and heartfelt critical sincerity that it is one of the most beautiful plays I have read in a long, long time. I am thoroughly delighted with it. It has an *overwhelming* beauty.

Nathan gave *Within the Gates* to Eugene O'Neill's agent, Richard Madden, to negotiate. At the end of November Sean heard from him again: 'O'Neill is so deeply interested that he tells me he is writing to you. . . . At the moment three different producers are angling for the the play. I am holding off until the very best offer is presented.' On 14 December he was worrying a little:

The Theatre Guild, to both O'Neill's and my own profound disgust, have decided against *Within the Gates*. Both O'Neill and I used all the pressure we could, but to no avail. I am now having the manuscript read by three other producers, and should have some news for you very shortly. O'Neill tells me that he wrote you yesterday.

I still believe that your play is one of the true masterpieces of the modern theatre, and have so written in the three American publications which I serve as dramatic critic. I shall leave no stone unturned to get it the best hearing here possible.

Immediately, Sean was cheered by the letter from Eugene O'Neill, which was actually dated from New York on 15 December:

My dear Sean O'Casey,

I have been meaning to drop you a grateful line since I finished reading your *Within the Gates*. It is a splendid piece of work. My enthusiastic congratulations to you! I was especially moved – and greenly envious, I confess – by its rare and sensitive poetic beauty. I wish to God I could write like that.

All who admire your work here – and there are a lot of us – are hoping that the play may be placed with the right management to give it the New York production it deserves. And when it is produced I hope you may come to this country, and that while you are here you and Mrs O'Casey will find time to visit Mrs O'Neill and me in our home in Georgia.

I have just seen the English edition of *Within the Gates*, and I deeply appreciate your generous reference to *Mourning Becomes Electra*. If anything about that play has suggested anything which was of the slightest service to *Within the Gates*, I am only too flattered, and I like my trilogy all the better for it.

Good luck to you. My admiration for your work – and all personal good wishes.

EUGENE O'NEILL

P.S. For years every time I've read a new play of yours I've meant to write you to this same effect, and my only excuse for not having done so is that where letters are concerned I'm the laziest man on earth.

(Sean answered this letter on 2 March 1934.)

Still, nobody in Britain offered to stage the play. Sean, ever aware that we needed the money, was much troubled. In the end a letter came from Norman Macdermott about whom Sean knew nothing except that he had directed the Everyman Theatre in Hampstead where, ten years earlier, he had put on Coward's first true success, *The Vortex*. He was prepared to offer an advance on a production of *Within the Gates* at the Royalty Theatre; but some of this had to be shared with the musician, Herbert Hughes, who would arrange the simple tunes Sean had included. When we went to London for the rehearsal period, it was hard to decide where to stay. Kindly, Lady Astor invited us to 4, St James's Square; she gave us a large room at the top of the house, a coal fire on chilly evenings, and the first American-type bathroom I had come across, with under-floor heating and a sunken bath; everything unostentatiously perfect. I soon made friends with the downright Nancy Astor; she used to tease Sean, calling him 'an old Red'. Bill, the eldest son, took me out to dinner once or twice while rehearsals were on; the second son, David, who at that time was interested in the theatre, would always keep up a correspondence with Sean. Nancy was a generous woman; one morning, after telling me of a sudden windfall, she asked me to accept a gift of money to get something I really liked. In the end she sent me to a fur company that made me a beautiful nutria coat; I valued it greatly, but it had to be sold, when we were living in Totnes, to help to pay for the hire of the car that we needed greatly at the time.

Ramsay MacDonald, then Coalition Prime Minister, wrote to Sean (10 January 1934) while we were living at St James's Square:

10, Downing Street, Whitehall.

My dear Sean,

I was very glad to have your letter. Nothing would give me greater pleasure than to see your play, but I have almost had to forget that there is such a thing as a theatre in existence, as my work continues late into the evening and, at best, is so uncertain in its calls from day to day that I can rarely make engagements ahead unless imposed by necessity.

I have read [Lord] Macmillan's book and find in it many echoes of what I myself have been saying and writing for years. . . . The gap between an idea and the working it out in detail is very wide and contains really all the difficult problems, as I am sure you know when you first get hold of a play and then sit down and work it out in its stage situations.

I wish I saw you oftener, but life seems to be taken up with an endless stream of 'concerns'.

Yours always,

J. RAMSAY MacDONALD

On the next day Sean had a letter from Augustus John, who had been reading the text of *Within the Gates* at his Chelsea studio:

28, Mallord Street.

Dear Sean,

Many thanks for so kindly sending me your new Play. I am studying it with the greatest interest and hope soon to see it produced. A very different thing from reading it. I read a very good thing of yours in *Life and Letters*. I've only just got your address from Billy [McElroy] or would have written you before. I am pleased to know you like the old Galway cartoon. I have a tenderness for it myself in spite of all its faults. I was rather puzzled with your summary treatment of the Cockney dialect which is really pretty subtle and complicated with its numerous sub-dialects, but it would require an expert phonetician to deal with that subject adequately. I don't know enough about Bishops and their sisters to be in a position to appreciate your rendering with any authority, but whores I do know something about, so much indeed that I am unable to generalise with confidence as you have done. In any case that good old word has lost its pristine kick except as an expletive, and like 'Sin' and 'Virtue' belongs to an obsolete theological vocabulary. Such verbal jewels adorn with lustre the back pages of one's memory, but are used now either in an antiquarian or an ironical spirit – preferably both.

Did you see my rendering of Billy?

Yours ever,
AUGUSTUS

Rehearsals, Sean's principal concern, were wearing. Norman Macdermott, who directed the play himself, had two rooms in the Royalty as offices, and one always noticed a social element, with people drifting in for sherry. It was a complex play; Sean thought that it would be wiser to discuss its difficulties than to hold small sherry-parties. This was all so different from the Cochran method where, if there was anything to talk about, we did so at length, over coffee. But Macdermott, whose wife designed the attractive front gauze curtain of the Park gates, did strive for an honest production; much of the play came over, even if it was nothing like Sean's hope; in his view, the night 'reduced whatever lustiness there was to an agitated and timid tinkle'. Sir Basil Bartlett was the Dreamer; Marjorie Mars, the Young Whore; Douglas

Jefferies, the Bishop. The première on 7 February brought the usual smart audience – with the Shaws, the Cochrans, Lady Londonderry, Lady Rhondda – and we went on to St James's Square for Lady Astor's supper-party to the cast. Though we did not believe the occasion had been a success, everybody tried to forget and to enjoy the rest of the evening.

VII

Notices were indifferent. *Within the Gates* lingered for only three or four weeks, but we had some cheering letters. One was from Martin Shaw, who had directed the chanting in *The Silver Tassie*, and who now wrote: 'I saw the play on Friday. I took T. S. Eliot. We both thought it rare. I thought you'd like to know.' Then remarkably, an American impresario saw the production and bought the play for New York; Sean was asked to go over.

As neither of us was happy at Chalfont, we resolved not to renew the lease of the bungalow; I went flat-hunting in London and found a large one among the mansion blocks of Prince of Wales Road, Battersea, overlooking the park. Sean completed all his travelling arrangements from Chalfont; our furniture had barely been shifted into Overstrand Mansions before it was time for him to leave. Having little ready cash, we divided what we had, fifteen pounds each; rent was paid for a quarter in advance; Sean had money due to him from Samuel French and one or two other sources, and we were hopeful enough to expect more from America. Lady Londonderry asked Sean to spend a week at Mountstewart in County Down on his way to New York; later he described the estate as 'lovely and languid, embossed by beautiful gardens'. When at length he came back to Liverpool to begin the voyage for which he had been booked first-class, he realised that he was embarrassingly short of cash. Pondering on the number of tips he had to give, he wished he had left me with five pounds and given himself another ten; as it was, he must have been the poorest first-class passenger.

Alone now in the Battersea flat, I read for hours on end, going through Sean's bookshelves, passing from Zola to Maupassant and Balzac, and generally soaking myself in depressing literature. The new child I was now expecting would be born, I was told, soon after Christmas. Breon was staying as a boarder at Jordans where there were only two others with him, children of a teacher; I went down for week-ends, longer sometimes, getting a room in a cottage and occasionally taking the children to Gerrards Cross for a whacking tea. I saw my mother fairly often; she had settled temporarily and quite contentedly in Brighton; and this year, with the baby on the way, my annual problem with her would not arise. Simply, how should she spend Christmas? Highly sentimental about it, she usually wanted to be with us. The first Christmas after my marriage was no difficulty because Sean did not bother with it and I went down to the country on Boxing Day for a short visit to Mona Hilliam whom I had known in *Rose Marie*, and who had married 'Flotsam'. At the next Christmas, in Woronzow Road when Breon was a small baby, we did try asking Mother; it was a quiet time, but I had the hopeless sense again that I could not get on with her. In following years it would have been terribly awkward if an old Irish friend of hers, Mrs Cavanagh (mother of John Cavanagh, the dress designer), who also came from Ballina, had not invited her to their home in Bayswater. There Mother could relax; she and Mrs Cavanagh had known each other as girls, and I was glad that she could have the Christmas she wanted; it eased my conscience. Over the period I would have her for a day or take her out. But, though I felt horrible about it, she simply did not fit in with the family.

VIII

All through the autumn of 1934 I was receiving Sean's glowing letters about the New York progress of *Within the Gates*. He loved America; it seemed odd to me that he should have taken to New York as he did. After a day or so he had moved into the same hotel as George Jean Nathan who had met him at the docks, in the Customs' shed, a prominent figure with his 'luminous, wine-

coloured eyes, a thick crop of dark hair slightly tinged with grey',
and 'a curving wrinkle of humour, now in repose, trimming the
corners of a full, sensuous, handsome mouth'. Sean also en-
countered, for the first time, Brooks Atkinson, Richard Watts,
Junior, and Eugene O'Neill, all of whom would become his life-
long friends. Daily he met his agent, Richard Madden, and one
of the play's backers, George Bushar Markell. I doubt whether he
would have returned to London if I had not been having a child;
it was in his nature to stay where he was contented, and he could
easily have remained in New York. He had a good week-end at
Markell's Pennsylvania home with John Tuerk, the other backer,
whom he called 'one of the most good-natured and amiable men'.
On the way they passed through country with the finest autum-
nally hued trees and woods Sean had known since a visit to
Burnham Beeches; on Markell's estate he walked among acres of
tomatoes, 'so hard to come by at home; as plentiful here as
blackberries on a bramble-covered English common'. During
rehearsals he was often in the National Theatre dressing-room of
Lillian Gish, who played the Young Whore. Once he told her,
gesturing towards the lobby, 'I can't stay out there. They keep
asking me what my play is about, and I don't know what to tell
them.'

Extracts from Sean's letters to me show his New York progress:

[*On arrival:*] I am in New York at last, and my first im-
pression is as usual a feeling of resentment; it goes its way too
quick and I have to try to keep up with it. Nathan lives in this
hotel and I am to be his guest for a week. . . . One thing I
notice, America seems to be the country of the loud voice. I
haven't got into personal touch with the company yet, though
I heard them reading the first act and they read it very well.*
. . . Heaven grant that the play may be a success of some kind
so that we may be able to jog along quietly for a little while.

[*Later:*] Rehearsals are going well. I think the cast fine, and
the producers are certainly sparing no expense, so the first night
should be a fine one. . . . So far since coming here I have spent

* In the company were Lillian Gish as the Young Whore, Bramwell Fletcher
as the Dreamer, and Moffat Johnston as the Bishop.

one dollar. I am writing an article that may bring me fifty dollars, but I may have to spend 250 dollars for the music.

[*4 October 1934:*] Two more weeks, and we shall know how the play will be received. George Jean Nathan still thinks it is the finest play written for many years. . . . I am still stopping with Nathan, but George Markell wants me to change to his hotel. . . . I have been to see three plays, but none were very good. George J. invariably leaves after the second act; I don't blame him.

He moved now from the Royalton Hotel to another called the Devon:

Here I am now in the Devon, close up to the producer, Mr Tuerk, and the patron, Mr Markell. They were a little hurt because I was so far away from them. No one comes near George Jean unless he asks them, and so, George arguing, I left him, and am here now. However, no pair of mortal men could be friendlier and nicer and more childlike than John Tuerk and George Markell. Markell has none of the impudence that often goes with money alone, and is a shy, kind gentleman. A fine suite of sitting-room, bedroom, and bathroom, and a man to wait on me hand and foot. Rehearsals are going along finely, and I have spent no sleepless nights here over the play as I have spent in London. Melvyn Douglas is a fine young producer, and he and I get on splendidly together. In spite of the ease of mind over the play, in spite of the comfort I experience here, in spite of the friendliness I meet everywhere, I'd much rather be having breakfast with my Eily, walking in the park with her, fondling her lovely body, and kissing her sensitive mouth in the night-time and in the morning too. George Jean thinks the article I wrote for the *New York Times* a fine one and it is to be published on Sunday. I will send it on to you. We have a fine and friendly cast. . . . I pray God the play may go well. They are to review *Windfalls* in the *American Spectator*, and George Jean and Ernest Boyd are stirring up Macmillans about the sale and advertising of the book of the play and *Windfalls*.

[*21 October:*] By the time you get this the play will have had its presentation and we all hope for a success. I am going down to the theatre for one more run-through to-day (Sunday). . . . I think there is a hope of far better criticism than in London.

[Sean, in his *New York Times* article, published that day, said: 'These English critics have become old and doddering minds in the theatre acclaiming an ageing and withering form, and the marching drama is leaving them behind with their dead hope and their dead faith.']

[*26 October: Cable:*] O'Casey, 49, Overstrand Mansions, Battersea Park, London, S.W. Everything going splendidly. All expect success. Love. Sean.

[*31 October:*] Just a line, my darling, to follow the cable. We took in the first week nearly 14,000 dollars, but this included £600 for the first night. This week Monday was £360 and Tuesday £240, which would be magnificent in London, but the running costs here are high. However, all seems almost certain of a success, and the company is on its toes, certain of a success too, so everything is hopeful. We got record notices from the best papers, and just two or three of the critics couldn't see anything in the play. Yesterday I attended a luncheon where 300 were present. I spoke for twenty-five minutes and cut the bowels out of one of the critics. The audience laughed and applauded, and I was in fine form. I was very nervous at first. When I saw the crowd my heart nearly stood still, but I had something to say, I felt like a fight, and I held them all from beginning to end. The poor devil of a critic was there, but when I began to speak – I am told – he got up, sneaked out, and listened in the hall, half in and half out of the room. It was fine, and I felt much better after I had had my say.

The book of the play is going into its third edition. . . . The company gave on my first night a dead performance. The play didn't come over at all, though happily the audience thought it did, and I, Melvyn, and John Tuerk were miserable. The company were too afraid of the dialogue and the new form and went through the play in a dream. It was terrible, but now they are used to the swing of it and one wouldn't know the play. It is very moving. George Jean Nathan on the first night, too, was sad, and none of us knew what to say. However, all's much better now; nothing could be done until the company themselves got used to the new style. We were fortunate to get such grand notices. All this for yourself only, darling.

[*14 November:*] I have arranged with Mr Madden to pay the Dramatists' Guild from my royalty. I should be able to let you have over £100 this week. Things haven't been so good at the beginning of this week, but they tell me that New York is moving into the height of the season and they expect good business. I hope they'll get it. . . . I haven't had time yet to see much of New York. My time is filled up for me, and any quiet time I spend with George Jean Nathan. His book, dedicated to me, will soon be out. I am preparing my notes now for Harvard tomorrow. On Saturday I dine with Atkinson and Nathan, and on Sunday I speak at the American Drama League. Some going!

[*21 November*]: I am still not sure of *Within the Gates*. The receipts so far this week are down and there is no chance of a smash hit now, but it may go on, if it covers running expenses, for some weeks longer. Nathan thinks it will go altogether for ten weeks and then it may go for a few weeks to Boston and Philadelphia, but it's all problematical. We may get £500 or £700 out of it, not a lot but better than nothing, and it will keep us going for a little while anyhow. Lecturing here isn't what it used to be. There's very little money here now, and the fees are low. For instance, I got 75 dollars for a lecture in Boston, but had to pay my own expenses, rail and hotel, and afterwards had 20 dollars only left, about £4, so the reward isn't worth the trouble. . . .

A strange thing has happened here. Lots of young men are beginning to wear turtle-necked jerseys, and I am told it is hard to find one now in any New York shop, so I have set a fashion anyway. I am feeling grand and fit, and that's something too; and as you and Breon are well – well, what more can we ask for the time being?

I am busy today and have to rush off to rehearsal to watch a new man playing the First Chair Attendant. The man who originally played it fell dead last night from a heart attack. He was a fool. After playing in my play he ran off to play over the radio, and as he was playing, he just fell down and died. He knew he had a bad heart, and yet he couldn't resist the urge to make more money, though he was getting grand pay for the work he did in my play. So he dies and gives us all a hell of a lot of trouble. . . . I have settled on a date in December to sail for England, but if the play needs it I may have to postpone it.

[*28 November:*] Well, love, I spoke yesterday in Bronx to three hundred businessmen and their wives and did very well. Now they want me to speak to the students of New York University. I hardly know whether all this is worth-while. Business in the theatre isn't very good, and to me it hardly appears that things will get better, However, Tuerk is anxious to keep things going until he can get the play to Philadelphia, Boston, Washington, etc., where he thinks the going will be good. He thinks it will be necessary to go to these places with the play to stir up interest. I hate the idea, but it may mean some more money for us. Curse on this blasted money, but we can't live without it, and our expenses in future will be more instead of less, so I suppose I shall have to agree. What do you think of it? Are you brave enough to do without me a little while longer? Tell me actually how you feel about the matter, and how you feel yourself. It's rotten to be separated from you at all, but more rotten still to be from you when you are having a baby. Of course, if the play comes off, I'll come back in quick time. But if they decide to keep it on and chance it, they'll want me to stop and help. It wouldn't have done so much if I had not been here. I'm puzzled and anxious as to what may be the best to do. . . . I have just learnt that the takings tonight are down, and I fear the week's results will be bad. . . . I should have welcomed a success, but a failure isn't going to torment me. I have a calm mind over it all.

Within the Gates closed soon after this. The company was to go on tour; but Sean decided that he must come home. In consequence, he missed the final banning of his play in Boston and the scandal that so peremptory an action caused. 'Wesleyan and Jesuit have joined hands to down it,' he wrote later. Other towns, frightened by the news, followed the Boston ruling and disrupted the whole plan of the tour which had to be abandoned. From London Sean wrote to Lillian Gish:

The last performance must have been a strange experience and I should have given a lot to be there, though not so much as I should have given to be present when the ban was declared in Boston. I got a whole pile of correspondence about it, and a lot of press-cuttings, but these couldn't give the thrill I'd have got from standing and hitting out in the centre of the fight.

Though the ban caused some excitement and a lot of talk, I should have preferred the tour and it is a pity that the Jesuits of Boston were able to stop it.

Let me thank you, Lillian, for a grand, a great performance; for your gentle patience throughout the rehearsals and for the grand way you dived into the long and strenuous part of the Young Whore.

He had given to her a finely bound copy of *Within the Gates*, inscribed:

> In Remembrance of Things Past,
> of this play's production and performance
> When we all, at least, battled
> together for the return of some
> of the great things that belong to Drama.
> A bad thing well done can never feel success;
> A good thing well done can never feel failure.
> With love,
>
> SEAN O'CASEY

Lillian, a lovely and vital woman who was in George Jean Nathan's circle, visited us when she was in London.

IX

Just before Christmas, and before the Boston news, Sean had arrived home laden with gifts for me, a dressing-jacket from Sylvia Sidney, the film actress who would also visit us; a scarf from George Jean Nathan; lots of silk stockings from everyone, including Lillian Gish; and many children's books for Breon. I discovered that Sean had never properly unpacked his suitcase; at the bottom of it were jerseys and shirts that had obviously been left untouched.

Christmas was strange. I went back and forth between the nursing-home in Sloane Street, where the child was to be born, and the Battersea flat. For hours Sean walked with me while I tried to help the baby on. It was a long wait. Then, one afternoon just as we were leaving the home, I said to the nurse, 'I don't think I ought to go very far, do you? I really feel it is about to happen.' She answered briskly, 'No, no, you can go wherever you like. Get back for supper.' We went out; but while sitting in a Sloane Street teashop I suddenly told Sean that we should leave our tea and hurry back; I was certain now that the birth might be at any minute. The moment I entered the hall of the nursing-home I felt agonising labour-pains and could scarcely move. Sean yelled to a nurse to get the matron; unperturbed, she replied that Matron was out. Fortunately, my room was on the ground floor; I told Sean to go away, almost pushing him; the main thing was somehow to get the nurse to help me, and I had just managed to reach my room and to scramble upon the bed when Niall's birth began. To my intense relief the doctor came towards its end. Sean never liked the place, doubting its efficiency; but I was not un-comfortable there, even if I wished I had been able to arrange for a hospital.

On the day of Breon's birth Sean had known of the Abbey Theatre's rejection of *The Silver Tassie*. Now, on the day Niall was born, he had a cable with the news that *Within the Gates* had been banned in Boston.

CHAPTER EIGHT

49, Overstrand Mansions, S.W.11

BOSTON'S ban, harshly disappointing to Sean, had meant the end of the run in America. Lillian Gish, Melvyn Douglas, and others wrote to say how grieved they were about the whole foolish business. Boston had always been a Puritanical city; and its authorities were alarmed at the idea that a character described bluntly as a Young Whore might be seen on the local stage. They kept their fears secret until the twelfth hour; members of the *Within the Gates* company did not know of the decision until the night before the planned opening. Nathan, who had been ill, preferred – in a letter Sean received a few weeks after getting home – to remember the New York success:

> I have been having a terrible time. My old neuralgic pains have laid me low, and for the last two weeks I have been able to do hardly anything. They have two more weeks to go, and then, by God, I shall be able to raise hell again.
>
> All the news about *Within the Gates* you have heard from Madden. Its run of four months is infinitely pleasing to me. Those two managerial boys did a commendable job. The last few days of the engagement, I understand, played to very big audiences. And the whole enterprise remains, to my mind, the one completely distinguished thing of the New York theatrical year.

Sean, glad to be with me and with the children, was naturally missing people he had grown so fond of in New York. It must have been as hard for him to adjust again in London, after his months of theatre life and companionship, as it was for me, when first married, to adjust to a new existence. From now on he was sent the American literature of the theatre, something he could not have afforded himself. His affection for such a man as Nathan, G.B.S.'s 'Intelligent Playgoer Number One', grew from a profound respect for a theatre critic of bravery and truth. I am certain that to go round with Nathan, and to talk with him, reminded Sean of early days in Dublin and that companionship with Barry Fitzgerald and Gabriel Fallon; after all, he needed a man on his own level to argue with, and in London he must have missed Nathan more than he showed. Then, too, there was Brooks Atkinson, of the *New York Times*; gentle, charming, and another staunch friend, whom I was to meet later with Oriana, his wife. Brooks, in a letter to me, has recalled his first evening with Sean to whom Nathan had introduced him:

> Sean and George came to our apartment at 299 West Twelfth Street for dinner, and we had a noisy and gay evening. I remember our coloured maid the next day made a disapproving remark about a guest wearing a sweater. It offended her sense of propriety.

Sean, obviously, was the guest; he generally wore a turtle-neck sweater in New York. With Brooks I think also of Richard (Dickie) Watts, Junior, whom a friend of his, a political columnist, Joseph Alsop, had taken along to the Harvard Club when preparing to interview Sean: Dickie has a warmth of personality and a quick humour that Sean recognised immediately.

Within the Gates, in spite of its American adventure, was not done again for any major production in England, though Sean continued to hope and had an idea once that Michel Saint-Denis might direct it at the Old Vic. Shaw wrote to him about this in May 1936:

> There is no reason on earth why *W.T.G.* should not go on at the O.V. if Lilian Baylis wants it. But as she has a competent producer (Guthrie) on her staff there is equally no reason why you impose St D. on her unless his qualifications are extraordinary and indispensable. An author can pick and choose his cast and even his staff for a West End production at a theatre hired ad hoc; but repertory theatres must be taken as they are,

lock, stock (especially stock) and barrel. As to rehearsing, all an author can do is to produce the original performance so as to establish a tradition as far as possible; but beyond that he cannot go without ruining himself.

We are still in arrears and confusion after our 11 weeks at sea, and very old at that, Heaven help us; but we shall get straight presently and see something of you twain.

G.B.S.

II

After Niall's birth, early in 1935, we got down to everyday life in Overstrand Mansions. Sean's big room, overlooking Battersea Park, was again a near-copy of his other rooms, the desk so placed that he could pull round his chair to the fire. Because it was a larger room than some, he had far more in it, including a sofa from Dublin, a well-made piece if cumbersome to move, that he was proud of because he had known its maker. The room had only one disadvantage, shared with the rest of the flat: we had no coal fires, and Sean had for once to make do with gas.

We had soon to decide on a school for Breon: not a simple decision for I was eager for him to carry on, as he had begun, in a method co-educational and, I suppose, modern. At lunch with the Shaws I talked of this; and G.B.S., invariably wise in his advice on children and advanced in his outlook, described a small 'co-ed' school in Wimbledon to which he contributed. Beltane School, in a big house on the edge of Wimbledon Common, was not rich but what equipment it had was right; and an Austrian teacher, who looked after the five-to-seven group, made life as happy as it could be, with geography and arithmetic on the most direct and imaginative lines. A bus called for children daily and took them home in the afternoons. Breon, when at length he moved from Jordans, quickly flourished at Beltane.

One fright I remember. Niall, at about three months old, got whooping cough which Breon caught; and for two weeks we had an all-night drama with both the children choking; Sean, always patient with the young, would calm Breon miraculously. Niall, being so small, had to be taken every day to the hospital where a young research doctor named Waller – no relative of our old friend – performed a miracle with him. Waller came on many evenings to see Sean whom he admired and who was astonished by the work the young man did on so small a salary.

Earlier, Lady Rhondda, who owned and edited *Time and Tide*, had written to Sean for a monthly article: those he would collect one day, with others, and publish as *The Flying Wasp*. The magazine held periodical luncheon parties for its writers – such celebrated feminists as Winifred Holtby and Vera Brittain contributed regularly – but I remember Sean going to only one of them. G.B.S. came over to me that day, asking if I would sit by him while Sean talked away to other people. Next to me I found a rather frightening woman who asked at once, 'Are *you* Mrs Sean O'Casey? . . . What do you do?' When I told her that I had been an actress and had worked for C. B. Cochran, she said, 'How often it is that amazingly intelligent men marry very good-looking girls who have very little brain!' G.B.S. touched my arm and smiled. Within a minute or so, she turned to me again: 'Have you, by any chance, read such-and-such?' naming a popular book of the moment. I answered: 'No; I've heard of it, but not read it.' Whereupon G.B.S. leant across and said to her, 'Now I found that a most interesting book. What did you think of the scene where Harold and his wife have that long discussion in the orchard?' 'Oh!' she cried, almost in ecstasy, 'that was magnificent!' 'Ah!' responded Shaw, 'but it is not in the book we have been talking about.' A brief silence; then the conversation went on. G.B.S. said to me softly, 'You are quite right, Eileen, to be so truthful about what you have read and not read.'

Once or twice Lady Rhondda invited us to dinner, mostly to discuss her magazine. These were never really lively occasions, and I do not think Sean himself enjoyed them; Lady Rhondda could be a formidable woman. What he did enjoy was a visit to her, on his own, for tea; he told me afterwards that he began genuinely to know her, she was so completely relaxed, talking to him freely about her life, politics and everything else.

In Battersea Sean adopted a regular routine. Getting up about eight-thirty in the morning, he would run through his letters, smoke, read the papers, and carry on with his writing. I would know if he were engaged on anything creative, a play perhaps, for during the day and out walking he would constantly make notes on scraps of paper or in a small book. When considering an idea for a new play, he had a trick of singing a good deal; I imagine that by lilting folk-airs he probably got an unconscious rhythm into the whole of his work. An article he would tackle otherwise, walking to his room as wearily as I dare say a bank clerk might walk to the bank. He never liked writing these articles, but being obliged to do so for money, he approached them as a task. Unable to dash them off as a journalist is popularly supposed to do, he took infinite pains, sighing with relief when at last his finished pages were in the envelope.

III

Still curiously wistful for the stage, and not knowing whether, even now, I might return to it, I engaged a young girl for Niall. Nanny Trim, reading of his birth, had come to see if it were possible for her to return to us. Unluckily, we were in a flat, with five flights of stairs and no lift, that at her age would have been too much. Lady Londonderry had proposed that a former old Nanny of theirs should help me: a generous thought, but in our flat impossible. Helen, the girl I did get, was from Violet Melchett's day nursery in Chelsea; about twenty, country-bred, and a lover of children. Though my budget was higher than it should have been, I never considered doing everything myself; I was able to be continually with the children and also to spend hours with Sean. It was good for him and for his work; when not employed he liked to have company.

All said, life in Overstrand Mansions was easy. Sean made rapid progress with *I Knock at the Door* and talked to me frequently of his Dublin life, his mother and sister and his friends. Though at one point the agonising pains round his heart recurred, Bertram Nissé assured us that it was not angina, simply general health and a chest weakness that meant he must watch his diet and avoid getting cold; I did not try to search for work, aware that my job was to look after him. When he had recovered, we planned a holiday in Dublin; he travelled over by himself while I made the necessary arrangements at home.

Though he went third-class himself, he was concerned about my own journey, knowing me to be so poor a sailor. In a letter he said:

> Don't forget to book a cabin on the boat and travel *first-class*. It will enable you to get a porter more easily and a taxi when you get to Westland Row, the railway station in Dublin. I had a job to get one when I came, they took no notice of third-class passengers, so go first-class. Don't bother about changing money into Irish money; it isn't necessary. English money is current here. . . . I shall be very glad to hold you in my arms again, and to kiss you often and with love. I will arrange for a double room. I have sent the cheque to your mother. With fondest love.
>
> SEAN

Actually the crossing was not unpleasant; it was grand to be with him again. Just before this *The Plough and the Stars* had been revived at the Abbey; *The Silver Tassie* (notably) had also had a week, and we collected some of the royalties for use on our holiday. Now an odd thing happened. Solicitors in Athlone had been trying to track me. My father, as a young man, had left his father's farm; my grandfather died without making a will; in the event, the property came to me as daughter of the eldest son, and we had to go out to Athlone to see my two aunts who ran the farm and who had always lived on it. The train journey from Dublin was so slow that one could have jumped out, picked a bunch of flowers, and climbed back without thinking twice about it. Anyway, we arrived and lunched at a comfortable country hotel popular with fishing visitors from England. It was a good meal, but something had gone wrong with the fire which enveloped us all in a cloud of smoke; Sean, whose weak eyes were smarting, was about to leave, having had no lunch at all, when a waiter hurried along, gave him a bowl of chicken soup, and said, 'Sure, sir, you'll feel a lot better when you get this down you. What's a bit of smoke? Come on now!' Sean, starting on the soup reluctantly, felt better when he had finished, and by then the smoke had dispersed. We asked for a car; a pleasant young man of twenty or so arrived, dishevelled and dirty, studied us for a moment, and said he must really get back to wash and put on a clean shirt before he could drive the lady to the Reynolds' farm. Having waited patiently until he was spruced up, off we went in the big old car.

We reached the farm around three o'clock: a marvellous place, Elizabethan-style, with a staircase that led to a surrounding gallery. In the ancient chimney of one room a ham was smoking on a chain. The aunts had a vast meal ready for us, wine, chicken, cake; not to have eaten it would have given mortal offence, so we had to have a second lunch which was harder for Sean than for me. He was much taken with the aunts, eighty-year-old Kate, upright and strong and agile, and her sister, five years older, small and plump and just as active. On the wall, and in the place of honour, as I was Edward's daughter, there hung a large photograph of me, blown up from a small one taken when I was a convent girl of thirteen or fourteen, looking very sombre and wearing a dress with a lace collar and a medal.

While we talked business, I was relieved to have Sean at hand; clearly he agreed with me that the farm was morally the aunts', for they had given their lives to it. That evening we sought out the solicitor in Athlone town; he occupied an office in which he was entirely encircled by books, with room for one seat in the middle of them. From this cavern he explained to us that he had let the aunts have a little bit of the money, and that they had made with it their first, and very gay, excursion to Dublin. He offered sherry; then, after foraging round for a long time under God knows what, he produced for our signatures a paper that would give over the house, and most of the money, to the aunts, while letting me have five hundred pounds. I thought this would be fair; it would help to keep my mother. Periodically, she had drinking-bouts which I realised were merely a form of sickness; and I knew it would be foolish to let her have the whole sum to spend outright. Instead, on getting home, I gave her about £100 to put in the Post Office so that it would be by her in an emergency.

Our train did not leave for Dublin until late. We walked through Athlone, watching the people going to Benediction at the Catholic cathedral in the centre of the town; most of them seemed so poor that I could not help thinking about the pennies they had probably contributed to the Cathedral building-fund, and wondering whether the money might not have been spent far better in improving their lives. The only other thing we could do before going to the station was to watch a cowboy film while sitting on rickety chairs in a small church hall described by courtesy as a cinema.

In Dublin again, I was worried about going to see my Aunt Alice, Mrs Cleary, who was in hospital. Her daughter, a Sister of Charity at St Patrick's Roman Catholic College in Maynooth, where young men were trained for the priesthood, was another relative I knew and liked. The son, who lived in Ballycroy, Mayo, my mother's home, I had not seen; he was coming up to Dublin to meet me, but we never did meet as one or the other of us was late for the appointment. Sean hired a car to take me to the Royal Hospital at Donnybrook, where Aunt Alice was dying of cancer; he could not face going in himself, but I was glad I did, for she had always loved me and, more broad-minded than my mother, would listen to my talk. That day she was under morphia, and I could not say much, but I know that the visit gave her happiness. Sean went with me also to Maynooth in County Kildare to see my cousin Molly (Sister Catherine); there he allowed her and the Reverend Mother, who put themselves out to entertain us in true Irish fashion, to take him all over the College, including the library of theological books that deeply interested him. (I wondered myself how so much could have been written on the subject.) Sean's interest in the College perplexed me; I did not feel in the least happy that all these fine young Irishmen were to be priests, even if at the time I was still half-heartedly practising my religion. I could not reconcile myself to the thought of young men leading so unnatural a life. But then in Ireland a poorer family that has a son in the priesthood feels it has been especially blessed. I asked Molly what a boy from such a family would do if he found that he had no vocation; and though she dismissed this, saying it occurred rarely, she did point out a window in the College from which one boy had flung himself. Why (I reflected) had he done it?

Sean that afternoon must have been thinking of Dr Walter McDonald, Professor of Theology at Maynooth for forty years. In his youth, when at first he had not the money to pay for it outright, he had bought from a second-hand shop, on Aston's Quay in Dublin, *Reminiscences of a Maynooth Professor*, a posthumous work in which McDonald, a man of courage unafraid of the unpopular opinion, had shown the Catholic faith with all its faults and all its blessings. Sean dedicated *Inishfallen, Fare Thee Well* to 'a great man gone, and almost forgotten; but not quite forgotten'; and he wrote in the book of McDonald's work:

> Here were the cold, sober thoughts of no renegade Catholic nor the criticisms of a Protestant and impatient unionist. . . . No. Here were the spear-like criticisms of a flower of the flock; of one writing from the very core of the Catholic fortress, Maynooth; of a rebel confined to the bed of allegiance. By God! here was a show-down of the mitred oracle of Maynooth.

My cousin and all my Catholic relatives, my mother in particular, were convinced that Sean, in some way, was responsible later on for my failure to practise my religion. That is not true. Marriage to a Catholic was no problem for Sean. He had lived with Catholics all his life; if I had wanted to bring up the children in the faith, he would not have objected; he did not object when I went, originally, to a convent to ask about a nursery school for Breon. He was naturally curious about religions; especially Catholicism among which he had been bred; there are few Protestants in the slums of Dublin. Many other major writers, Anatole France and Joyce and Mauriac, have been passionately involved in a debate upon religion, the problem of retaining the faith into which, through no fault of one's own, one has been born.

Sean had great respect for the old Reverend Mother at Maynooth; and he would not have dreamed of hurting my sweet and good-looking cousin, Sister Catherine, by beginning to argue with her. Our minds were much occupied while we were driving back to Dublin, Sean thinking of these matters straightforwardly, myself more puzzled than muddled. A year later, when the Reverend Mother died, my cousin succeeded her.

While we were in Dublin the dramatist, Lennox Robinson, long and lean, with his small head and his far-away drawling tones, entertained us at his home outside the city: Sorrento Cottage with its own little beach, and a view of the sea as you sat at the dining-table. I remember that Hugh Hunt, about to direct at the Abbey for the first time, was there with his mother. Gaby and Rose Fallon also asked us to dine at their house on the outskirts; their little girl stayed up to see us, an attractive child, shy and highly strung, who appealed at once to Sean. Rose was most welcoming. We noticed that since Gaby had last seen us, his Catholicism had grown much more rigid, a change that obviously puzzled Sean, though our talk was good-humoured – better, of course, when it slipped from religion to theatre and personalities, and the old Gaby, with his sarcastic humour, returned. (Years afterwards he wrote in his book, *Sean O'Casey: the Man I Knew*: 'Sean and Eileen both looked well on their return from the U.S.A.' But I never went to the States with Sean; I was having Niall and it would have been impossible to have afforded the trip and to have left Breon.) I think of another Dublin interlude, an evening with the Garnetts, long known to Sean, who kept a famous fishing-tackle shop above which the family lived spaciously and comfortably. Here I saw Sean in a quite different light. After the meal, while Mrs Garnett played the piano, various people – there must have been about fourteen or so there – got up and sang. I sang. Sean sang. It ended with everyone singing together round the piano while the young son of the house calmly went on playing chess in the corner with an elderly visitor. Sean told me that chess was a great game in Dublin, though after marriage he had no chance to return to it until the children were older, when he could play with Breon and Niall. Because of his fantastic memory he was good at bridge as well, but here there was seldom anyone to join him.

IV

In Battersea he began again on his work: he was writing a play called *The Star Turns Red* which, as it happened, would not be staged for some years. His book, *The Flying Wasp*, a collection of his essays, some from *Time and Tide*, some from other journals, went to the publishers: a book with stinging views upon drama criticism and the conduct and material of the contemporary stage. Harold Macmillan, worried by this downright expression, came over to Battersea one day to ask Sean whether he might not feel like reconsidering the chapters entitled 'Coward Codology' and 'The Cutting of an Agate'. Did Sean want to say these things about these people quite so emphatically? Sean did. When he had formed an opinion he would never change it or milk it down. Harold Macmillan, being the man he was, agreed to publish the book as it stood. It could have been a dangerous half-hour; but, thanks to Harold's tact and graciousness, it was just a sensible talk.

Some time before this, Lady Dorothy Macmillan had invited us to bring down Breon, who was seven, and Niall, who was only seven or eight months, to a long week-end at Chelwood Gate. Sean had never been in Sussex, and I had not been since I was a girl; Helen came with us to mind the children. After the country drive from Haywards Heath, we had the friendliest greeting at Chelwood Gate, a square, late-Victorian building, not beautiful externally but most comfortable and unfussed within. Harold Macmillan's brother-in-law, Lord Hartington, and his wife, were staying at the house; Maurice Macmillan was on holiday from Eton, and there were Harold's three daughters, the youngest about Breon's age, the others nearer their teens. Breon, from his modern school, would have felt stranger than any of us, for here were children whose outlook must have been quite different from his. I dare say, in spite of their good nature, they criticised him as children do, but we realised, when he came to our bedroom where he was to sleep, that he could hold his own and was not at all envious. Once he had settled, he cheerfully spent most of his time with the others.

Lady Dorothy, whose directness and consideration Sean appreciated, told him to do what he wished, so as usual he rested his eyes in the afternoon and spent the morning quietly, joining us at tea. We admired Lady Dorothy's garden, its rock plants and its lupins. You walked through the main garden to the foot of a hill, passed through a gap in the hedge, and saw before you a long, long slope of lupins, mauve, pink, white, red, light shades and dark; they had been planted originally in colour-blocks, but because lupins seed themselves they had mingled in a quilt of every conceivable hue round which the bees hummed madly. It was an extraordinary sight in those days; several times we walked down to it. The trees on the estate were particularly fine, one especially which Sean admired, an ilex or holm-oak, with its branches to the ground. There were other impressive trees near the lake where we had a picnic.

On Sunday, after lunch, Harold Macmillan proposed that everyone should join in chopping and gathering logs. Feeling awkward, I merely stood watching. Sean was not a bit awkward. He discussed the way to chop the wood, applauded Lord Hartington's almost professional efficiency, and asked where in the name of God he had learned to be in any way useful. Evenings at dinner, with their talk about theatre and books, I enjoyed; Macmillans had just had a big success with Margaret Mitchell's romance, *Gone with the Wind*, and I was reading it. Sean was in rare form; though he and Harold were so opposite politically, each respected the other's honesty of purpose. And after dinner Sean could keep the company gay with his flow of Irish anecdote.

V

Since our move to Battersea, I had seen my mother far more than in Chalfont. When she left hospital after an operation, she had returned to lodgings in her usual fashion; I had hoped she might find somewhere lasting. It was now that we heard of a Bayswater convent where the nuns, who had several boarders of her type, would allow her to bring furniture of her own and settle permanently, taking her meals in the dining-hall. I went to the sympathetic Reverend Mother, explained my problem, and fixed the room up with some of the stored furniture from Chalfont, bed, wardrobe, sofa, table. Mother appeared to approve of it and I thought for a moment that troubles were over. If she had wanted, she could have come to us several times a week to see the children. But, though we had a good afternoon now and again, Breon disliked her coming to tea; she insisted on fussing and tidying him, making him wash hands that were perfectly clean, and brushing his hair flat. I had to persuade him to be nice to her. It was principally her own fault, even if I do wonder now whether I helped to make it easy for her: she must have been lonely.

Sean was asked to lecture at St Catharine's College, Cambridge, a type of invitation he had often refused. He was nervous about lecturing; indeed I had heard him only once, in a small and crowded room at the Irish Club in Eaton Square, with people standing at the back. When he rose I was petrified with nerves myself; he looked so white that I expected him to faint, and his opening words were practically inaudible. Then, his composure returning, he spoke finely and often wittily on Ireland and Irish literature. His listeners loved it; but he would never repeat the ordeal. However, young students at St Catharine's had persuaded him to visit Cambridge, though when they heard his proposed title, 'The Holy Ghost Leaves England', they were more than a little scared, assuming that it must be something atheistic. Not at all. To Sean the Holy Ghost implied the gifts God gave to anyone, writing, painting, sculpture, any talent; the only sin that upset him was what he called the sin against the Holy Ghost, knowingly betraying a talent, selling it for a false purpose. Worried about his lecture – which came across splendidly – he was appalled also by the discomfort and chill of his College guest-room: in the chapter of *Sunset and Evening Star*, entitled 'Cambridge', he describes how he was shivering all night with cold and had to get up and put on his clothes, even to his overcoat. He had never been so cold. Whatever else was missing in his Dublin slum, the tenement would have had a fire; warmth meant more than food.

Several of these Cambridge students later called on Sean in Battersea; one especially, Peter Newmark, who had begun already to study the theatre; he would be most helpful in getting *The Star Turns Red* put on in London at Unity of which he and John Allen were keen members. Sean had other visitors. A handsome, idealistic young Irishman, Frank Ryan, suffered from deafness caused by a serious injury to his ear during the Spanish Civil War. With Sean he spent two days explaining his intentions; he was resolved to go back to Spain, but Sean, realising that Ryan's health was broken, appealed to him to change his mind. Would it not be far better to fight for his ideals at home than to risk being killed? Nothing would persuade Ryan; he went back. Sean tried later to find what had happened to him, but nobody knew; it was thought that he had died in Spain. Sean, of course, was anxiously concerned with the Civil War and the fight against Fascism; he watched every development and wrote an occasional article. Though I was not in the least politically minded, he would talk to me and I would listen; obviously my sympathies would be with the Spanish Communists. Sean's ardent belief in the working class shows through all his writing; he would express his feelings to me without reserve. Later in life, after I had said something to the effect that I was not really a Communist or politically inclined, G.B.S. said to me: 'A Communist is born a Communist, Eileen. It's in your everyday life. It's in your attitude to people. It's in your obvious desire for everybody to have a fair share, especially in education.'

Jack Carney, who also arrived at Overstrand Mansions, had been a Dublin friend of Sean; they had both worked with Jim Larkin, the great Irish trade unionist. Now Jack brought with him Barney Conway, a docker known well in Dublin, a huge man whose voice was beery and husky, and who certainly loved his pint; he and his frail, small friend made a remarkable pair, and with Sean they talked far into the night of the days with Larkin.

Frequently Sean would take his visitors over to walk in Battersea Park which was opposite the flats. Daily he went himself, loving the grand mixture of games, schoolchildren playing cricket or football, or roller-skating on the wide paths. The Park always had a medley of working-class and middle-class children; Battersea, at the back of Overstrand Mansions, was entirely a working-class neighbourhood, with plenty of the variety in it that Sean liked.

VI

As it chanced, we were there less than five years. Twice during the period we travelled to Wales for summer holidays, first in 1935, because Evan Walters had spoken of his country with so much patriotic pride. We chose Penmaenmawr, near Llandudno in North Wales, finding bedrooms and the use of a sitting-room in a small boarding-house where we were the only family, did our own shopping, and left cooking to the landlady. She made us perfectly at home; Sean liked it so much that, though he had left his typewriter behind, he managed to make copious notes for the final part of *I Knock at the Door*. The sands here were fine; moreover, we had a solid little chalet, with an electric fire and ring that added comfort on wet and miserable days. A Welsh boy, who got on with Breon, would often have tea with us; alert, and good at drawing, he was a railwayman's son; you had to be careful if you gave him anything, for he was proud and sensitive. When it got about that Sean was in Penmaenmawr, several Welsh Nationalists, ardent folk, called to see him; sometimes he would have supper in the hut with them, talking in Gaelic, discussing their national problems, and comparing Wales with Ireland. They even asked him on their annual coach outing to a distant part; doubtful at first, he yielded to their eagerness. His worry had been the knowledge that on a trip of this sort the men would have to get off every so often to drink beer; drinking seldom himself, he felt – though he was wrong – that his presence might be a slight damper.

The day, with its drive through magnificent country, proved to be a real success. Welshmen, on such trips as these, sing a lot and in true harmony; Sean told me that, far from being in any sense raucous, they grew steadily sentimental; he found himself getting to know them and their problems, much like those of the Irish.

On reaching home, late and exhausted, his mind was still full of the day's talk. I have seen it written that he spoke at Welsh Nationalist gatherings and sang at their concerts. This is not so; once or twice he was approached to speak, but never did; and, even if he sang a great deal in the privacy of his home, he would never have done so at a concert.

Next year, Mrs Roberts at Penmaenmawr welcomed us as old friends. I recall one occasion, a moonlit night when we were asked to go into the mountains. I suppose forty or fifty cars drove up to a large, flat field, right at the top of the hills, where a platform had been raised for singing, piano and harp playing, and the performance of sketches by a locally renowned company from the mountain sheep-farms. Chairs were arranged, and drivers parked some of the cars in a semi-circle at the back so that their headlamps could floodlight the platform. After the performance, various people from the audience were invited to do something. They picked on Sean; nervously he climbed on the platform and soon found his form in those amusing Dublin stories. When picked on myself, I had to sing 'Danny Boy', the only song whose words I could remember. The group of farming players so impressed Sean that in London he attempted to get Cochran to commission them, in some manner, for a stage show. Nothing came of it, or of another effort later when I approached Dorothy Elmhirst who had a small theatre on her Devon estate: I doubt whether the Welsh people would ever have left their farms.

VII

G.B.S., at lunch one day, was talking excitedly about the Devon school, Dartington Hall, near the market town of Totnes. Having inquired about most of the modern co-educational schools, I naturally knew of it, but Dartington seemed to be far too expensive for us. Shaw waved this aside, saying lightly, 'Well, you could pay for it somehow. If not, don't worry too much. The higher the standard for the young, the better, so long as it is good and simple. They will try all their lives to fight for better living for themselves and others.' He spoke of the excellence of Dartington music and art; the country was lovely, and it was where the O'Casey children should go. By a coincidence, Mrs Elmhirst asked Sean to Dartington to talk over the drama department conducted there by Chekhov's nephew, Michael. She showed us round the estate, its cider factory and its tweed looms, and we saw the schools which were in three sections: the nursery school in an old parsonage, among big gardens; the middle school, elsewhere on the estate, in modern buildings split into houses according to the ages of the children; and the senior school apart, each child having his own room. I longed to send our children there.

Dorothy Elmhirst told me that she hoped we would come to live near Dartington, so that Sean could work with Michael Chekhov: I took it that she wanted him to provide ideas, or to write short sketches, that the students might practise in their classes. Though nervous with such a person as Dorothy, I could generally be brave on Sean's behalf, and I told her at once that this would be a catastrophe. Sean would never do anything but his own creative work; it would be a sheer waste of anyone of his quality, and quite useless for him to take it on. Certainly Dorothy was not offering a fortune; even if she had been, the reply would have been the same. Appearing to understand thoroughly, she never asked him. She was an outstanding woman; one had to respect her appreciation and knowledge of music, and the use of her money to further art and education.

Something eerie occurred during this visit. We had two bedrooms, one on each side of a corridor. In the middle of the night, Sean, looking almost faint, came in to see me, saying that the supernatural atmosphere in his room had badly affected him. Invariably he was sensitive to atmosphere; he had felt like this in the bathroom at Battersea where he believed that either something evil had happened, or that somebody was seeking hard to communicate. Twice he complained of this; we had all felt strange and afterwards would leave the door slightly ajar. At Dartington I changed rooms with Sean. Though naturally apprehensive, I had no sensation at all. If he ever mentioned it to Dorothy and Leonard Elmhirst, it would probably have been in a joking fashion.

He did have sharp intuitions; if you took his advice about people who did not wish you well, he was usually right. And he held to the 'third time lucky' superstition that if an article, or indeed anything he wrote, had been refused once, it could not possibly be taken when offered again; the third time would be all right.

Now that we wanted the children to go to Dartington, and because I did not believe in boarding-schools, our next task was to contemplate a family move. Our Battersea lease had a year to go, so we talked to the agents who said that they were modernising the flats and would not mind taking the lease from us. When the head of the office came to tea, inspected the place, and agreed that it looked quite sound, we imagined that this was a form of gentleman's agreement. At the time we were busy; and though Helen Elliott said to me that we ought to have an agreement in writing, I never saw to it; events would prove how right she was.

Finally, in the early autumn of 1938, Sean went down to Devon with Helen Hover and the boys. Until we found somewhere permanent, we were to live with the gardener and his wife at Dartington Hall lodge: an old-style house that had been modernised and where our rooms were at least adequate. I joined the family about a week later, after packing the things in Battersea and having our furniture stored. For Sean it was an uneasy, frustrating period. He had to earn his living with *Time and Tide* articles and odd book-reviews; and he was continuing work on his play, *The Star Turns Red*, set 'Tomorrow, or the next day' during the last few hours of a Christmas Eve, and dramatising a 'turmoil between the Fascists, a Church with her eyes on the earth, and the claims of the militant Workers'. The light in his room was bad, his eyes were painful, and he seemed like a lost soul without any of his books and with the uncertainty of finding a house. First, the Elmhirsts showed us a bungalow, probably on their estate, low in rent but not big enough. Our final choice was an old Victorian house named Tingrith in Station Road, Totnes. It had large rooms, a garden in front and at the back, a garage, and an ample unused stable and loft; the rent, only eighty-five pounds a year, was extremely low compared with London costs.

So here was the house. We made several trips down to it from the lodge, taking Niall's push-chair to carry the stuff we had accumulated (as with children it must always accumulate). But, before we could do this, and before the house was really ours, we had to get a friend to supply references and to guarantee the rent: a precaution upon which the landlord, who was a dentist, insisted. We asked G.B.S., and I wonder now that we ever got the house; he told the landlord that, though he was ready to guarantee the rent, he was uncertain of acting as guarantor for Sean; there might be a minor revolution in Totnes any day. At the same time he wrote to Sean:

> 4, Whitehall Court, London, S.W.1.
> 17th October, 1938.
>
> Dear Sean,
> Your landlord, being a dentist, has developed an extraction complex. He proposed a lease in which I was not only to guarantee all your covenants, but indemnify him for all the consequences. I said I did not know his character, but knew enough of yours to know that the consequences might include anything from murder to a European war; so I re-drafted the agreement. The lawyers, knowing that their man was only too lucky to get a gilt-edged (so they thought) security, and that his demands were absurd, made no resistance. I mention it as you had better watch your step, not to say his, with the gentleman. Anyhow, I had a bit of fun with him. I seem to have picked up completely. The anaemia was not really pernicious. I am glad to learn that the two miniature O'Caseys are happy among the young criminals at Dartington and that their mother is now one of the Beauties of Devon. Charlotte sends all sorts of affectionate messages.
>
> G.B.S.

In fact, though completely humourless, the landlord was a very fair man. Both Sean and G.B.S. signed the lease; I do not know where it is today, but it should be an uncommon historical document. Sean wrote to Charlotte, saying that he felt the trek to Devon would be good for the children, and this was what mattered. He added:

I have been searching my conscience, since you spoke to me about my tendency towards quarrelling. But I don't think this tendency goes down deep in me. In all productions of my plays, I have had but one quarrel, and that's saying a lot. The 'quarrel' with the dentist landlord was just a flash rejecting the idea of 'references'. I can, and did, ask for a financial guarantee; but I'm not going to ask anyone to guarantee my morals. I can't say myself what sort I'll be a week from now. To be asked to get a moral guarantee from others, or one from myself, is, to me, stupid, and makes me mad. A long time ago I was asked to declare that a worker looking for the job of caretaker was sober, honest, truthful, reliable, and industrious. I replied saying that what was wanted was a saint, and not a worker. And the man got the job!

I think my *Flying Wasp* did a little good. Recently, Agate spoke at Toynbee Hall in favour of Government support of Music and Drama. Anyway, the book was just a continuation of what I said at a dinner given by the Critics' Circle in 1926, when I, foolishly, I suppose, told them my mind. They haven't asked me since.

I have always had to fight like the devil for life; but you must blame your husband, G.B.S., for whatever sharpness and wit that have come into my fighting qualities; and my young Dublin comrade, member of the Fourth Order of St Francis, who first put the green-covered copy of *John Bull's Other Island* into my then reluctant hand. I am a fighter as G.B.S. is a fighter; neither so great nor so amiable a fighter, to be sure. But then, Peter wasn't so great nor so lovable as his Master; but he was a forcible fellow, and I really believe that I am a forcible fellow, too.

With many thanks and affectionate regards.

Yours sincerely,
SEAN O'CASEY

All settled, we took possession of Tingrith: a new and surprising move in life for the O'Caseys from town to country, from urban Battersea to the very heart of Devon.

CHAPTER NINE

Tingrith, Totnes

TINGRITH, in which we would live for the next seventeen years, was a substantial Victorian house, good for a family, on the main road from Totnes to Plymouth. When the furniture vans turned up, our important task was to get Sean's own room straight, he was wandering about so helplessly, longing to carry on with his work. Through our life together he seemed to have this compulsive urge at the most awkward times imaginable; Christmas, say, or Easter, or any Bank Holiday, would certainly kindle in Sean an absolute fever to write. A move had the same effect; there was no doubt that he must be established quickly in a ground-floor room where the table was set out, the bookcases were set up, and desk, chairs and sofa conformed as closely as possible to the old Dublin pattern. After the Battersea gas fire he was glad to have in Totnes a coal fire in a large grate, able to take logs that were plentiful in the town. Immediately he was in, he started to write while the rest of the house was in turmoil around him.

Floor covering was our principal shortage. We had to varnish those parts not covered by rugs. Sean's room, the nursery, kitchen, and the boys' two rooms all had linoleum. When I knew we were to move I had bought yards and yards of curtain material at the London sales, and somehow I soon got it fixed. I had a spacious kitchen with a larder and built-in dresser; cooking I did on a gas stove in the scullery where we later painted the stone floor with a red stain that was always coming off. Here we had both a front and back staircase; the back one led to what in the old days would have been a maid's room, so there was opportunity to spread ourselves; a passage right across the house to the back stairs helped a lot in hide-and-seek and games for the children.

Tingrith was near the station. Though we felt we might never accustom ourselves to the noise of the trains, after a few weeks we hardly noticed it. Sean did not appear to miss London; but I did, and often longed to be on the train going back. When we lived in Battersea, we had had a way, if there was a promising bill, of going to the Chelsea Palace of Varieties – Sean enjoyed the music-hall – or, now and again, to the theatre; even today I still get restless in the evenings and seem about eight o'clock to come alive. During our first months at Tingrith damn all happened in the evenings; it would improve, of course, when Sean, who was such an original and lively talker, was not involved so deeply in his work, but at first it was a bad period; the boys were young enough to be in bed by eight o'clock, and for me after that the hours had to be long and dragging.

II

We were both pleased on knowing that I was to have another child; we hoped for a girl. War was talked of everywhere by now, and most thinking people realised that it was bound to happen. Sean and I had another kind of fight on our hands. The agents who had verbally freed us from our Battersea lease wrote suddenly to demand a year's rent in lieu of written notice; with the threat of war more people were moving from London, and the agents had decided to go by the letter of the law. Sean, on receiving the official demand, was horrified and helpless; then the injustice of it angered him, and putting his work aside, he appealed to D. N. Pritt, the barrister respected for fighting in so many worthy causes. Sean wrote in our defence at great length, seeking to show how wrong it was to demand money now, with the flat left un-rented; we had been away from Battersea for six months without receiving a demand, and it was obvious that if the war had not upset rents we would never have heard. We were not the only tenants caught; later we learned of another who had been similarly treated. These were dreadful weeks during which Sean sat by the hour, writing page on page, wasting himself on reams of explanation and argument to prove that we were in the right. It was quite impossible for me to persuade him that the fight was useless; in any event, my efforts were half-hearted because I felt the injustice so intensely myself.

When at length our case came up, I was about five or six months pregnant. I went to London with Sean while Helen stayed with Breon, who was at school all day, and Niall who had started at nursery school in the mornings. Breon cycled up, and a bus called at the door for the young children and delivered them home again, so here at least there were no worries. London, in its summer before the war, was crowded, hot and noisy; Sean and I took a room at the Strand Palace Hotel, near the Law Courts; we were hopelessly short of money, and I knew that the breakfast this hotel supplied would be ample to cover our lunch as well. Though hardly the place for Sean, it could not be helped; he was, anyway, in a highly nervous state, and in retrospect it seems horrible that he should ever have had to think about fighting such a case; he was so entirely sure that justice and right must prevail.

We were all acutely strained. It was a pity that D. N. Pritt could not appear for us personally. As it was, he had to entrust us to one of his juniors, a charming young man making his first appearance as an advocate. Though Pritt came round to tell us how sorry he was that he could not manage it, Sean at this stage was in such a haze of nerves – and they showed in the witness-box – that he was unable to take much in. My condition did get a certain sympathy in court. For some reason or other, I did not feel uneasy and tried to explain the situation as clearly as I could. The case, which appeared to be going well for us, had almost ended when the opposing counsel, an admirable lawyer, asked suddenly for some old law books, and such and such a page was turned up; there it stated clearly that, unless notice were given in writing, no other was legal, or words to that effect. The book, opened at this page, was handed to the Judge to read. After a pause he decided the case against us; Helen Elliott's words about the need to have everything in writing had come true. As far as I remember, the Judge did suggest that, morally, we were right, if not according to law; even so we had to pay (and could do it only bit by bit). Exhausted and depressed, we had not money enough for dinner at a hotel; instead we had a light lunch at a Lyons café in the Strand. Next day we returned to Totnes, and on this occasion I was glad to get back.

Somehow I persuaded Sean to try to forget the business and to throw himself into his work. He had practically ended *The Star Turns Red*, and he was also writing articles for the *Daily Worker* and for a Russian publication, *International Literature*. *I Knock at the Door* had already been published to splendid reviews and many cheering letters of congratulation; I had helped him to correct the proofs, something in which I did feel cheerfully occupied. Next, he was contemplating a play entitled *Red Roses for Me*, in which one of the Dublin characters was partly based on a figure familiar to us in Totnes.

On Fridays we looked forward to the big market in the town square; every farm in the region would have its own stall and bring to it cheese, butter, eggs and other produce, jam and honey, vegetables and fruit; and an auctioneer would stand upon his rostrum, shouting a farm's name and putting up its goods: 'Going . . . going . . . *gone!'* Down his hammer would come. We housewives would plan among ourselves to share the lots of butter, cream, eggs and so forth, as they were auctioned by the dozens or the gallons. I recall the noise, the bustle, the talking: all of it before the war; all of it, alas, vanished. Regularly, on these Fridays, we saw at the market an old man who was there not to buy, simply to walk round and chat; he buttonholed Sean, pouring out his troubles. His constant worry was his money in the bank. Was the bank to be trusted? Weekends must have tormented him, though he was all right on a week-day when he could go to watch the bank clerks keeping his money safe. Moreover, he had a few stocks and shares which meant a close study of the daily paper; and he also owned a small house which kept him everlastingly bothered for fear the woman who cleaned it might be robbing him. A little way out of Totnes he owned another cottage; wet or fine, hail or storm, he would go weekly for his rent, living in agony lest something might go wrong. I observed that all the time the old man was speaking to me Sean was taking notes. 'I am putting him in my play, Eileen,' he said. 'That's a wonderful character.' This is how Brennan o' the Moor in *Red Roses for Me* came to life. You find him described in Mrs Breydon's first lines: 'Oul' Brennan on the Moor. . . . He's got his rent for his oul' houses, an' he wants to be told again that the Bank of Ireland's a safe place to put it in.' And later: 'I've just a little consideration of stocks an' bonds nestin' in the Bank of Ireland at four per cent – just enough to guard a poor man from ill, eh? . . . Stony walls, steely doors, locks an' keys, bolts an' bars, an' all th' bonds warm an' dhry, an' shinin' safe behind them. . . . An' none of it sthrollin' into Peter's Pence. Wouldn't the Pope be mad if he knew what he was missin'.' The rest of Brennan belongs to an old man who played the fiddle in Dublin streets. Sean had a favourite story of him. All the little children would gather round the fiddler while he played and sang a hymn that used to go:

> To Jesus' heart all burning
> With fervent love of men. . . .

Then, aside, 'Go away, you little bastards!' Certainly, Brennan was there; but as yet *Red Roses* was only just forming in Sean's mind; he continued to put the last touches to *The Star Turns Red*.

This summer Jim Larkin, the great Irish trade unionist, travelled down to Devon for a single afternoon, arriving at midday and returning in the evening to London. Jim had always been Sean's hero; often he had told me of him and of how even his prison sentence had left him undaunted; they seldom come like Jim nowadays. Probably seventy at the time, he was a tall man, finely built, with a lovely head of hair and a compelling force. The children must have been at school; I remember that he and Sean, who was overcome by emotion at seeing him, sat in the kitchen to eat their meal and to talk over the past in a racing torrent of words. The writer, H. A. L. Craig, remembered the afternoon in an article for the *Irish Times* twenty-one years later, at Sean's eightieth birthday:

As a student I had crossed over to attend the Fabian Society

Summer School at Dartington Hall. Mr O'Casey lived in the
town of Totnes below. One afternoon I was told that I was
wanted at the door; I went down and there stood Larkin. He
had already attracted a crowd, for although he was an old man
then he was a great sight. He said that he had come over on the
spur of the moment to see O'Casey whom he had not met for
many years. But now, at the last mile, he didn't like to go in
alone – would I accompany him? O'Casey opened the door and
the two men stood for what seemed a long time without saying
a word. Then Larkin touched O'Casey's arm. O'Casey smiled,
and Larkin slouched past him into the hall. That August afternoon I will never forget.

Harry Pollitt, secretary of the Communist Party of Great Britain,
also called on Sean: another type of personality, smaller and
slacker, but with a sincerity of belief that showed itself mostly in
his eyes.

III

Sean described the old town of Totnes in an essay he wrote first
for the *West Country Magazine* and elaborated years later for the
final volume of his autobiography:

> Apart from the quiet hurry of market day, gentleness is the
> first quality to give it; gentleness in its buildings, and in the
> coming and going of its people; and in the slow, winding,
> winding of the River Dart from the moor to the sea. Oh, Lord,
> the natural lie of it is lovely. Except when visitors pour in
> during the brief summer, the town is so quiet that it looks like
> a grey-haired lady, with a young face, sitting calm, hands in
> lap, unmindful of time, in an orchard of ageing trees, drowsy
> with the scent of ripened apples about to fall, but which never
> do.

Life in the little town changed uncannily after the declaration
of war on 3 September 1939. We had to put black-out curtains
over every window. Evacuees from London arrived by the train-
load, a touching sight: hundreds of children, some unhappy,

others only dazed, all with labels round their necks. At centres in various parts of Totnes they were sorted out and sent to people who had volunteered to take them. Dartington Hall owned a spacious dance school which had been the English centre of the Ballets Jooss. Now the main hall, where lessons had been held, was filled with line upon line of small mattresses and blankets. Downstairs the children used as a refectory a room off the kitchen, with long tables and benches. These boys and girls from the slums of London were utterly bewildered; the deep country meant nothing to them; brought up among noise and bustle, here they had absolutely nothing to do, and it took them a few months to be acclimatised. Their first reaction, entirely natural, I dare say, was to destroy anything they came across. After all, they had been thrown into a strange world: nothing but green fields, no playing on the pavements, even their everyday companions gone. The chief trouble was with the ten-to-twelves: some of these, who discovered petrol pumps up on the Dartington estate, must have been delighted to see something they could pull or push, and before anybody got wind of it gallons of petrol were wasted.

In the end most of them did accept a new life. At Tingrith we offered to take three from the heart of the East End: a girl, Doris, aged about twelve; her younger sister, Zoe, who was five; and their brother, three-year-old Bobbie: nice-looking children, quite dazed, I thought, not weeping or unhappy, just lost. Doris was really excited about it all. We gave them three little beds in a big room at Tingrith; Doris, as the eldest in charge, had clearly had a tough time looking after the others. Mostly they had had their meals – fish and chips, eaten with the fingers – while sitting on a doorstep. They seldom used the lavatory, and the small ones, who never thought of getting up at nights, were quite used to sleeping in wet beds. Their heads were in a bad way with lice. Sean, in his own room and writing hard, saw less of them than we did. His mother, of course, had kept her tenement home spotless and their few clothes washed and ironed; she loved flowers, and he always spoke of her pots of geranium and fuchsia and musk. But the Dublin slums had lain all about them, and the appearance of these London children – from a very poor family indeed – would not have been new to him, though it was something I had never experienced. For Helen and myself the task was formidable; but Doris helped vigorously with the training of Zoe and Bobbie who did not take long to realise what was wanted. Like Helen, my young daily girl, Joy, who was about nineteen, worked hard with the children and became interested in them; it was not easy work, for everything they had brought in their small cases had to be turned out, washed, ironed and mended.

It was now, in the first month of the war – with the black-out strictly kept – that I was due to have my baby in Torbay Hospital, ten miles from Totnes; I had to go daily for injections and treatment. Once, as a girl, I had been given to sleepwalking, and here I was at it again, roaming round in my sleep, polishing the floor, putting polish everywhere it was not needed, and trying even to wash the floors and to make tea. Sean, worried lest I hurt myself, would put his bed against the door of our bedroom, so that before I could get out I had to disturb him. Somehow he would manage to lead me back to bed without waking me, and if I did wake he would hasten to make tea and talk to me with a patience and gentleness quite astonishing. He was sensitive and highly strung; the worry about me, and the whole upset of the war, must have been terrible for him.

Our evacuee children had been with us for only a week when the doctor proposed that I should stay in Torbay Hospital until the child arrived. I was there for two or three weeks, and somehow Sean managed to get in to see me, either on a bus or with a lift in somebody's car. It could happen that, between injections, I could meet him in Torquay town; but generally he would come to the hospital and we walked in its grounds. He could never stay long because he had to get home well before evening and the density of the black-out.

Shivaun, a lovely child with lots of black curls, was born on 29 September, and I soon recovered; within a fortnight I was at home. The doctor, who had grown friendly with Sean during my pregnancy, was delighted it was a girl; almost at once he had left me to rush to the telephone and ring Sean with the news: 'A girl; and both the baby and her mother are fine.' We had letters from everyone and flowers from many; and G.B.S. sent fifty pounds as a birthday gift, with a letter from his London home in Whitehall Court (4 October 1939):

My dear Eileen,
It is important that the boys should have a sister. Sisterless men are always afraid of women.

I enclose a birthday present for her. The next one will be only half-a-crown. The Budget – oh, the Budget! The end of the year will clean me out.

We take it that you are doing as well as can be expected.

G. BERNARD SHAW

Harold Macmillan wrote on 5 October from 90, Piccadilly, W.1.:

Dear Eileen,
I was so glad to get your letter and its very exciting news. I do congratulate you. If your daughter is born into a temporarily unhappy time, I am confident that she will grow up into a better age, which I believe will succeed these follies and horrors which now seem so terrible.

I am so glad to hear that you are both well. I am sure Sean will be delighted with his baby.

We have handed over our house at Birch Grove for a nursery school. We already have forty children and are expecting sixty more. We shall move into one of the cottages ourselves. My two daughters are at school and only Sarah at home. Maurice is in the Field Artillery – to which the Sussex Yeomanry have been converted – and is stationed at Brighton. This is quite nice for us, for he can get home alternate Sundays to see us. I hope they will be there for some time yet before going out to France.

For myself, I am at present looking after the business as well as going to the H. of C. I am trying to get back to the Grenadiers, but am not wanted at present.

Well, this is a long letter, all about ourselves. So I will end as I began, with all possible good wishes to you and all your family, with an especial extra blessing for your baby.

Yours,
HAROLD MACMILLAN

Niall and Helen came to see me in hospital one day; and four-year-old Niall whispered to me quietly that Helen had been really horrible to him. I asked why. He said, 'She wouldn't let me go to school because I had little animals in my head. But all the children loved looking at them.' I arrived home with Shivaun at a four o'clock tea-time. Breon had come down from Dartington; and, with the three evacuees who already looked far different and who had started at a village school, we were quite a family. Doris was eager about the new baby. I got to know her well, for she stayed up late, had supper with us, and grew thoroughly relaxed while she told us stories of her life in London. There was one, I remember, about the bag-wash. Laundries would send round for washing which was stuffed into one large bag, rough-washed, and returned for its owner to iron. Doris's aunt was in the trade, collecting for a laundry; when she had a chance she would call and empty out all the bags so that Doris's mother could choose some of the slightly better clothes and replace them with her own. 'We had very nice clothes,' Doris said proudly. I noticed that one of her ears was unpleasant. Though she said it did not hurt at all, there was a nasty cavity, still suppurating. When I asked dear Dr Varian about it, he surmised that it might well have been caused by a series of blows; for a full cure she would have to enter Torbay Hospital. Frightened at first, she let me persuade her, and in a week at the Torbay the whole thing was cleared up.

IV

Unexpectedly, on the way to her house by the Hoe in Plymouth, Lady Astor came in to see Sean of whom she was extremely fond. Witty, volatile and energetic, she was anxious to take us into Plymouth to see her nursery school at the Virginia House Settlement; and one day we did go with her: Sean went once only, but I made other visits. Nancy was always amusing about Dartington Hall School; during a call at the Elmhirsts, she got Dorothy to ask us up to lunch, and later during a drive round the estate she said playfully that it was dreadful of G.B.S. to recommend such a school as this. Sean took her up in a hot argument; but it was never at all satisfying to argue with Nancy; usually she would not let you get a word in, she simply went on talking. Through his life she continued to correspond with Sean, writing to him or telephoning, just to keep in touch with the old boy, as she put it.

Sean in this period had to split his time between his writing and a number of chores such as carrying wood for the fires and filling the coal-buckets. The evacuees had settled comfortably, and we received the Government allowance. This was all right; but there was little doubt that the children interfered with Sean's work; they had not been trained to keep out of his way, and one could not prevent them from tapping at his window or trying to get into his room. For all that, we would have gone on housing them if Sean had not become very ill with bronchitis. A good working-class family close by, which really needed the money, was prepared to take the children from us; knowing they would have the best kind of home, we let them go. I had enlisted my friends to help, so the trio were thoroughly stocked with clothes, and, sorry to leave us though they were, they quickly grew into fresh surroundings. Sometimes we would meet them in the park. If ever they were in any bother they would run round to us to find Helen.

They had not long left Tingrith when one of the Dartington staff approached me to ask if I would have a boy of twelve who was most unhappy, and who needed a different billet; I said I would, and Peter came, a sensitive child, frightfully over-mothered in every way. He did not get on with our own children, not that it affected any of them because he went off daily to Totnes Grammar School. His mother had a job at Dartington, helping with the evacuees; he saw her at week-ends before going, I fancy, to stay in a billet nearer to her after he had been at Tingrith for some months. In later life he was an actor.

A visitor that fortunately never reached us was a leopard from a privately owned zoo at Paignton. Escaping, it ate a few lambs from a farm, and a danger warning was issued. Sean decided it would be wise for Niall, who must have been about eight, not to go to school; but Niall, wondering what his friends would think, was desperate. I argued with Sean, saying I would see Niall upon the bus, that he had only a short walk at the other end, and that it was ridiculous to think of keeping him at home. Sean would not give in; I had practically to smuggle the boy on to the bus, and when I returned I felt that Sean was glad, in an odd way, that I had acted for myself. He could get highly imaginative, and I believe that if he had been given his head he would have barricaded the windows; it was not a question of bravery, merely one of dramatisation. Niall got home safely from school, and that evening the leopard was caught.

V

Before Breon was a boarder at Dartington, he would be back at five. Sean had started to read to him *Moby Dick* and other stories, acting them out with a gusto that Breon (quite old enough to read the books himself) fully shared. Mark Twain was popular as well; and they worked steadily through *Tom Sawyer, Huckleberry Finn* and *The Prince and the Pauper*. Sean also played a lot with Shivaun as a small child. When the boys were at school and I could get ahead with the housework, he and Shivaun would be together most of a morning, either in the conservatory or the nursery-playroom. Their game called 'Little Boy' meant simply that Sean was the small child to be looked after, put to bed in a chair with an old blanket over him, and given big cups of tea. When he wanted to be quiet he would pretend to be unwell so that he could sit calmly while they played at doctors and nurses, Shivaun racing round him, taking his temperature, and seeing the blanket was in place. They would repeat this by the hour. On wet winter days they turned the kitchen table upside down and transformed it into either a train or a boat, with teacloths for sails and Sean and Shivaun rocking from side to side in a rough sea. All Sean's games had to be full of acting and imagination.

Shivaun, too, as time passed, would often make up plays with her little friends, a business that called for dressing up from an old trunk packed with my discarded chiffon evening dresses, high-heeled shoes, and frilly nightgowns which I had never looked at after moving to Totnes. The children spent hours with these, wafting about in the fashions of the nineteen twenties. Then they would think of a play and one would have to go in to sit through it, finding perhaps five or six children there on a Saturday morning when none of them need be at school. Breon and Niall generally had Saturday games. Each of them found, in turn, that by the time he was at the Senior School life was so all-involving that he did not want to remain a weekly boarder with its inevitable gap.

VI

I have gone ahead a little. The play, begun in Battersea, that Sean finished early in the war was his anti-Fascist parable, *The Star Turns Red*, its allegorical action taking place on Christmas Eve. Peter Newmark and John Allen asked if it could be staged at Unity, the thriving left-wing theatre in King's Cross, and ultimately it was done during the late spring of 1940. I took Breon to London; we stayed at the Cumberland Hotel – a grand change for us both – and Harold Waller, who had been my doctor at Breon's birth, accompanied us to Unity: a fine production, we thought, and especially Lawrence Gowing's sets, scenes which Sean, as always, had described with such care. Thus for the first Act:

> The walls are a vivid black, contrasting with the dark blue of the sky outside, seen through the windows. These windows (two of them), one to the right, the other to the left, at the back, are long, reaching almost to the ceiling and beginning a foot or so from the floor. Through the window on the right can be seen the silhouette of a towering church spire, and to the left of this spire is a large, shining, silver star. Through the window on the left can be seen the silhouettes of two towering chimneys, one shorter than the other; from these chimneys smoke is pouring, and an occasional tongue of flame shoots out. To the left of the window on the right is a sketch of a bishop's mitred head; to the right of the window on the left, a sketch of Lenin, with his name underneath in Russian characters. Underneath these

sketches, a cupboard on the top of which is a white teapot, symbol of life's necessities (the cupboard is black). In the centre of the room, a table, black, covered with a yellow cloth bordered with white – the papal colours. Several kitchen chairs, painted white, give an indication of occasional rest. The hearth, with a cosy fire, is to the right. . . .

After the play Dr Waller took us for supper to the Café Royal where Breon, though looking incongruous there late at night, sat on the sofa beside me and enjoyed his meal. The doctor went on talking, and Breon fell asleep. I remember the evening, too, because I noticed a woman in an immaculately tailored suit, with a flower in her buttonhole and hair in a mannish cut, talking with happy animation to a beautifully dressed and most feminine girl. I could not help asking Harold Waller to look at them. 'Oh, Eileen,' he said, 'that is Radclyffe Hall. She wrote *The Well of Loneliness*.' (I read it later; but the novel of hers I like best is that simple narrative, *The Unlit Lamp*.) We could stay in London for only three days; before we returned to Devon Breon saw *The Star Turns Red* for a second time, on a night when an alternative cast was appearing. Before the play ended – at a period of crisis in the war – Sean received, on 9 June 1940, a letter signed by every member of the two companies:

Dear Comrade,
Your play closes on 23rd June. In these very difficult times it will have been running continuously for over 85 performances. That Unity has been able to do this is due to the greatness of your play, and the two casts wish to tell you how much they have enjoyed performing it.

It has given them a great opportunity to take part in the production of a poetic masterpiece which represents a new step forward in the development of our drama, and which has widened our understanding and quickened our enthusiasm at a time when so many other means of expression are closed to us.

We are under no illusion that we amateurs can do full justice to the quality of this magnificent play, but we have done everything that hard work, enthusiasm, and sincerity can do; and we feel that John Allen's production, Lawrence Gowing's settings and costumes, Alan Bush's music, and Louise Soelberg's choreography have helped to make theatrical history with *Star*. Will you come and see us before the final night?

Earlier, G.B.S. had sent a card from Ayot St Lawrence (22 April 1940):

Never heard of Mayokowski.*
All well here.
I havent been in a theatre for years; and I cant think of a new play, though the continuance of the Malvern Theatre Festival depends on my producing one. Can you oblige?
I should have gone to The Red Star, black-out or no blackout if I hadnt read it. It shewed up the illiteracy of the critics†who didnt know that like a good Protestant you had brought the language of the Authorised Version back to life.
Splendid!

G.B.S.

Although in deep sympathy with the production, and knowing how much we liked it, Sean resolved not to journey to London. He rarely visited London from Totnes. Only one thing would have made it imperative, a visit to his eye specialist; but Bishop Harman had recommended one in Plymouth whom we visited regularly. When I was in London, Harman had told me how to take out Sean's lashes, necessary now and then because they were in-grown and had become tough enough to scratch the eyeball. Though electrolysis removed most of them, a few remained, and Harman gave me special tweezers and a pair of magnifying glasses like those he used himself. After that, unless Sean's eyes were particularly ulcerated, I managed to remove the lashes; Breon and Shivaun took it on later when my own sight was middle-aged and less acute. At this period Sean could see fairly well with one eye, and he was continually reading books and newspapers. Books were his special joy; being so careful a writer, he looked up words and definitions until he had perfected what he wished to say. He

* Vladimir Mayakovsky, the Russian poet and dramatist, author of *The Bed Bug*.
† But it had an enthusiastic review from (of all people) James Agate, a critic with whom Sean was at odds.

would turn a passage or a sentence over and over in his mind, re-casting it on paper until he was satisfied. And every word he wrote in longhand. At this stage he had finished the 'wayward comedy' of *Purple Dust* which had occupied him for some time (and which preceded *Red Roses for Me*): Macmillan published it in 1940. More-over, he was reviewing books for the *Sunday Times* and writing articles for the *Daily Worker* whose editorial board he had joined just after the publication, also in 1940, of *The Star Turns Red*.

Our Irish Dr Varian was a Dubliner, bred there as Sean had been, though in different circumstances, and knowing the city inside out: a real comfort to Sean, he was one of our closest Totnes friends. The Catholic priest, the fine and broad-minded Father Russell, was another Dublin man. He and Sean would spend ages in the late evening endeavouring to get 'Lord Haw-Haw' on the radio: it was tricky but they did it quite often, chuckling delightedly when the voice came through. I suppose it amused them that he was Irish.

Though, naturally, we talked about them, Sean had never interfered in the slightest with my religious views or the chil-dren's education. About this, luckily, we agreed; knowing I was keen on what was then styled modern education, he wanted me to choose what I liked, giving the children as much room as possible to express themselves. Anyway, in the matter of educa-tion, G.B.S. seemed to have offered me all the advice. I had not quite abandoned the Catholic faith and would go to Mass at Totnes Church on most Sundays, taking Breon with me. (There was no formal religious instruction at Dartington Hall.) At this period I was in doubt, trying to decide what to do. Sean never mentioned it; practising no religion himself, he had been used to Catholics in Dublin, and he would help me to get ready for Mass when I was late. Shivaun was duly baptised and had one local and one proxy godfather; Breon would go to Father Russell's after Mass on Sunday to learn his Catechism while the priest was at breakfast. Trudging up the hill every week, I grew less and less certain, and on the road back one Sunday I realised that I was merely carrying on a routine, without any deep feeling. So I said to Breon: 'I've decided I will not go to church any more, and you needn't go to Catechism unless you want to. When you are older you can decide your religion for yourself.' Breon, I am sure, had gone only to please me. He was much relieved.

VII

Everybody in war-time Totnes tried to squeeze a full day and a half's work into one day. Tingrith was a lively place; and Sean, his writing apart, still found himself doing a variety of household jobs. Joy, who worked for me, had married; Helen went for a while to the short-staffed Dartington day-nursery, taking Shivaun with her. I would go to help with the evacuees at Dartington, hurrying up and down the hill as one could not use the car for this kind of journey; after cutting bread and butter by the plateful and serving meals, I would dash home to get on with my own house-work. We had a car because when we reached Totnes I had seen that if I could drive life would be far easier; in spite of so many opportunities with my boy friends, it was something I had never attempted. Then at Totnes, in a frenzy of nerves, I got through the provisional test and bought, to begin with, an old Morris that dropped to bits, and later a Ford. Sean's eyes had been so painful that I applied for permission to take him to and from Plymouth for his treatment, and sometimes to bring the children from school. Petrol was rigidly rationed and one had to have a good reason for using it. We had another worry. When we had first met, a London specialist was treating Sean for ear trouble; now this flared up again, and weekly, for a long time, he had to go to a specialist in Torquay, another journey for which I was allowed the car.

My mother, at the beginning of the war and just before Shivaun's birth, had left London; after illness she asked to be sent to a convalescent home in Torquay, and when I was out of hospital she called sometimes at Tingrith. Presently, with Peter as our sole lodger, we agreed that it might be reasonable financially if Mother would live with us. It was the same story. She did not like Totnes, and we saw that the idea was hopeless; she stayed in Tingrith about a week. Finally, getting a room in Paignton between Totnes and Torquay, she rested for a while: unhappy because I was doing nothing at all she wished. The children were at a school she considered appalling; I taught them no religion – though actually they were being brought up well. Because she was incapable of giving or taking, maybe one could not blame her for being so miserable about her religion.

In Totnes, full of emergency war-efforts, several of us, working on a rota, had a busy shop for Mrs Churchill's Aid to Russia Fund. As the Fund's local organiser, and resolved to be unpolitical and unsectarian, I approached Mr Edwards, Rector of Dartington and an advanced thinker, a teacher from the County School, another from Torquay, two housewives, and a carpenter: all said yes. Opening a bank account, we met at Tingrith every month to make our plans, and, whenever we had raised £100, sent it to the office of the Fund in London. Artists from London and Bristol came down to a concert I arranged at the cinema. With so many soldiers billeted in Totnes, dances were extremely popular; we had various whist drives, and the shop was a permanent source. I persuaded people to make voluntarily such things as children's clothes which were very scarce during the war, and to give dolls they had dressed. Some of the local shopkeepers presented their goods.

That was one side of the war at home. Another was less pleasant; we had to guard against air attack. At Tingrith, though our cellar was damp and earth-floored – 'moist and maggoty', Sean said – we turned it into a dug-out, cutting a hatch in the kitchen floor and lowering a step-ladder. At first it was fun to paint the cellar white and red, to cover its floor, to sling a hammock for Shivaun, and to instal camp-beds and orange-boxes; we had a gas ring so that we could easily make tea. Then, during the spring of 1941, Plymouth, centre of the south-west, was raided fiercely night after night; the sirens would rouse us as the German aircraft, after dropping their bombs, returned above Totnes with a frightening roar. Our cellar proved to be drearily damp; we were relieved when the Government issued special shelters, steel-meshed like a big cage, and with iron or sheet-steel tops and iron bottoms; after the war you saw them everywhere as hen-houses. In war-time they held two adults; when one end was opened you crawled in and lay or sat until the All Clear. Shivaun and Niall used to squeeze in with me and with Helen until she left us to join the A.T.S. Shivaun, who was so small, enjoyed the raids thoroughly; not knowing what it was about, she found it exciting to get up in the middle of the night. Niall was old enough now to be really affected. Breon was calm and a great help; as a rule, he and Sean sat round, trying to judge how near or far the raiders were. Sometimes, after going thankfully to bed at the All Clear, we were roused again; it could happen twice or thrice in a night. Sean often wrote on and on, making up his sleep during the day. At this period of the war, adults, up late and early, were always tired.

We did have a few daylight raids, mostly by aircraft that came from an attack on Plymouth (which had been badly smashed) and were likely to drop an odd bomb on the way back. One morning I had returned from seeing the children to school. Sean and I were washing up in the scullery when the noise of an aircraft deafened us; we looked from the window, and there was a German bomber flying low above our garage, with one of our own aircraft in chase. Within seconds a fearful crash shook the house; it did seem for a moment as though the whole place would fall. We ran through the kitchen into the front room. 'Come on,' Sean cried, 'we're better in the open,' and, thrusting up the window, we scrambled out and raced on to the lawn. Sean was still holding a plate, and I was clutching a dishcloth. The bomb, which struck a bridge about four minutes away from us, near the station, had damaged the station, wounded several people and demolished the windows of a grocer's shop, scattering the goods. Back in the front room of Tingrith, we saw that the glass and china on the sideboard had been broken, as well as a lovely bowl Dr Cummins had given to us as a wedding present. Somehow, during the war, these things did not seem to matter; lives did. The children, who had heard the explosion at Dartington, cycled down immediately to see if we were all right, and found us perfectly well.

One other experience, away from Totnes. Early in the war, and when Shivaun was a young baby, Sidney Bernstein had come to see us with his charming wife, Zoe. Twice later, when I was briefly in London, Zoe invited me to stay at her flat in Arlington House, off Piccadilly. Once, when I was there alone, a bad raid began about midnight. With the few other residents left in the flats, I went down to the hall; but nobody was anxious to go into the shelter somewhere beneath the block. Several times before daybreak the bombers thundered over; and, really frightened, I understood what it was like to live in war-time London.

VIII

At the end of 1941, to our enthusiasm, America entered the war; soon the G.I.s were familiar. In Totnes they took over the small town park and erected tents in it. From now onwards, several Americans, newly in England and admirers of Sean, were eager to meet him: one of them was Thomas Quinn (Tom) Curtiss, formerly a New York drama critic, a friend of Nathan, and at the time a young sergeant in the Intelligence Service, stationed in London at SHAEF, the Allied headquarters: before the war he had lived and studied in Europe and he spoke several languages. Nathan had given him a batch of letters of introduction to English friends, Ivor Brown, Desmond MacCarthy, James Agate, among them; and Tom said that the one he most treasured was that to Sean. At first there was a delay because after Tom had written to Totnes, enclosing Nathan's letter, Sean answered that, unluckily, he did not see how they could meet; while he was held in the country by his work and the care of a young family, Tom was held by his military duties in London. It was not much encouragement; but presently, having a few days' leave, Tom wrote again to say that he was travelling to Devon. Sean replied to this that he and Mrs O'Casey would 'try to be polite', on the face of it a cool welcome though I am certain Sean intended it as a joke. Anyway, Tom, who was determined, took the risk, arranging to lodge at a Red Cross hostel for soldiers and to telephone from there.

His train was late, so he drove straight to us, hoping that he might be able to meet Sean during the evening. To his astonishment, when he got to Tingrith, Sean greeted him warmly, telling him that we wanted him to stay and were indeed waiting dinner: a shock for Tom who had not meant to intrude, but who now found Sean so insistent that he dismissed the cab. Once together, as Tom has reminded me, he and Sean started to talk of everything from the New York *Within the Gates* in 1934 to the latest news of Nathan. It was obvious how well the two men got on; after dinner they talked into the small hours of Yeats and Lady Gregory, the turbulent opening of *The Plough and the Stars*, the rejection of the *Tassie*, and Cochran's production in London. Sean (with *Red Roses for Me* finished and published) was writing at the time the play that would appear afterwards as *Oak Leaves and Lavender*, a war-time fantasy of the West Country (Cornish dialect and all). Its original working title was 'A Warld on Wallpaper', in ironical allusion to the phrase in W. B. Yeats's letter, rejecting the *Tassie*: 'The whole history of the world must be reduced to wallpaper in front of which the characters must pose and speak.' Sean gave the script to Tom who, before he left at six in the morning, sat up most of the remainder of the night, reading it. 'It's been a great privilege to come and talk with you,' he had told Sean. Whereupon Sean had answered swiftly, 'That's a silly thing to say. Never say it's a great privilege to meet anyone.'

Tom had been impressed by the easiness of our relations with Breon and Niall; Sean told him they were at a progressive school and encouraged to give their own views. Now, at breakfast, Tom met Shivaun, who was not yet three and of whom he had had only a glimpse; we saw him off at the station in the grey morning, and she won him completely with her parting hug. She was an active child; when we rose early she kept me on the go until nine o'clock and time for school. She gained; but I did not. For years, when she was small, I was practically half asleep; in fact, during the war I never properly opened my eyes but felt that I was squinting round at everyone.

We had many other guests from the U.S.A. Dave Green, a University teacher, and his friend who directed an American art gallery, were billeted near Plymouth; often they drove to Totnes in their jeep and stayed talking until late. Food, in American rations, was not scarce; and they would bring plenty for us to share with others, as well as the bubble-gum, box upon box of it, that the children carried proudly to school as a piece of one-upmanship. Apart from the pleasure of being in a house with children, several of the college-trained Americans loved to talk over literature with Sean. I remember an evening when Dave Green and some others were with us and the telephone rang: a call from a firm, representing a Hollywood company, who asked if Sean would adapt Wolfe's novel, *Look Homeward, Angel*, for the cinema at what seemed to be, in the shaky state of our finances, a very large sum. Knowing the book, I wondered at once how Sean would fare without his own highly personal tragi-comic method; whether he could adapt this to anyone else's text; whether indeed the strain was worth it. . . . All of this was in my mind when I went to him. Why should he not carry on, heart and soul, with his own work in which he was so intimately involved? Still, I had to let him decide.

'Oh, dear God, Eileen,' he said, 'I don't want to do it; I don't even know if I could. But it's a lot of money, and we need it.'

'Well,' I replied, 'if you don't think you'd be happy doing it, say so.'

He nodded; so off I went to the telephone. I was sorry, but Sean was in the middle of his work, editing the second volume of his autobiography, *Pictures in the Hallway*, and the play, *Oak Leaves and Lavender*, and he could not break off: also he was not certain of his competence for this particular job. The voice at the other end of the line was not pleased with me: 'Are you *sure*, Mrs O'Casey?' 'Yes,' I said, 'I am sure.' That was all. Dave and his friends had heard my side of the conversation, and my talk with Sean, and one of them said, awed, 'Gee, Sean and Eileen, you've turned down a load of hay there!'

Another film company telephoned to ask whether Sean would make a script from a novel: the story of a man who told a priest, under the seal of confession, that he had committed a murder. The priest, bound to silence, could say nothing even when the wrong man was hanged. Sean knew instinctively that he would not want to tackle it; and the caller, a friend who knew our financial position, said crossly, 'But, Eileen, I thought you were hard up.' Yes, I said; but couldn't he see that a writer of Sean's special distinction should not, and very probably could not, recast another man's work? We left the answer at No; and we did not break a friendship.

Numerous Russian journals, *International Literature* and others, had commissioned articles on such subjects as Shakespeare, Tolstoy and the Soviet Army. One asked Sean to do an appreciation of Chekhov, and to get other authors to join. He approached several without success, including John Masefield, the Poet Laureate, who wrote in courteous regret from Abingdon that, pressed with other work, he could not quickly do something that needed much time and thought and care. Sean himself sent a fine article that was published in Russia during 1943. 'Chekhov', he said in it, 'is one of the unmitred bishops of men.' G.B.S., too, sent what he called 'a Chekhov blurb'. Intermittently, he and Sean corresponded. Early in 1942, when Sean was looking for a picture of Lady Gregory that might – he thought then – go into a later volume of his autobiography, he asked G.B.S. about the Epstein bust and had this reply on a postcard:

> The Epstein bust was a failure because E changed his plan when he was half-way through and ended with a muddle of the two. Besides, he was always seeking to reveal the aboriginal savage beneath the civilised sitter; and nothing could change Augusta into a Brooklyn washerwoman, much less into a half humanized lizard.
>
> If I can find the negatives, I shall try to get some better prints for you.
>
> G.B.S.

Towards the end of the same year, answering another letter from Sean, G.B.S. wrote from Ayot St Lawrence:

14th November 1942.

My dear Sean,
Dont on your life bring up your boy as that most despicable of all shams, a stage Irishman. A man's country is the one whose

air he breathes and whose people he knows. Breon is an Englishman, born in British Battersea,* bred in British Devon, singing Drake's Drum and not Let Erin Remember, having Raleigh for his local hero. To him his dad must always be a funny sort of fellow, let us hope beloved and admired, but still a curiosity. O'Flaherty, whom he calls O'Flayerty, is a native of a savage island, who seems to take it as a matter of course that his mother should be a thief and a liar who, by way of being patriotic, claims that all great Englishmen were Irish. Like Queen Victoria he is 'not amused'. Why should he be? And arnt you glad he isnt? Why do you add 'strangely enough'? The air has made an honest English lad of him: that is all. Sixty six years of English air have not made an Englishman of me because I started with 20 years of Irish air. Battersea and Devon have by this time marked Breon for their own; and nothing could be more wicked than to rob him of his birthright.

By the way, he will be greatly hampered by his father's fame if he does not change his name. Think of Mozart's son! of Wagner's son! of that unlucky Mendelssohn who said 'I have been son of my famous father and the father of my famous son, but never myself.' If he intends to become famous he had better call himself O. K. C. Totneson or Devonson.

Charlotte is an invalid now; and we are both damnably old.

Pearson's book is all right as to the facts, and very readable. I helped him all I could.

Thats all for today. I am sorry I wasnt in London when your consort came up. It is pleasanter to see her than it is to see me in decrepitude.

G.B.S.

It would have been impossible to pay anything like the children's school bills with what Sean was earning from his books and articles. I used to write to Daniel Macmillan, setting out my troubles, and he would advance money to me without telling Sean; I had explained how upset Sean would be if he knew. The money was not deducted from the royalty sheets, but treated as a separate loan to me that could be repaid years later when times

* Actually St John's Wood.

had improved; nobody could have lent more graciously. Because of this I had funds for my personal extravagances in clothes, or for any money I had to give to my mother. Sean, unaware, would be left with a little more for the Dartington fees; it would worry him when the bills came in for a second time and he had no funds to meet them. He absolutely hated borrowing.

IX

The food problem in war-time was not so bad if you lived in the country. People mostly grew vegetables. Some kept chickens. As a family we were fortunate at Tingrith. Though the Government took the bulk of the eggs, butter and vegetables collected from the farms, Totnes retained a small Friday market for vegetables and fruit, and some of the conversations there must have sounded decidedly odd. Having bought whatever else we needed, I would say, 'I wonder – do you have a few breakables today?' and Mrs B., the farmer's wife at the stall, would reply, 'Well . . . there are six here,' or nine, or whatever – never a large number, but always really fresh eggs. You would hand her your basket, and she would pack the breakables safely at the bottom. Even telephone calls could be curious: 'Hello, Mrs O'Casey, are you going into town today? . . . If you like to call in at my cousin's shop [he was a shoe repairer] I have left a few breakables there for you.' I revelled in it all.

Una Albery, wife of the manager Bronson Albery, who knew how much Sean loved tea, sent him most of her ration throughout the war: a truly Irish gesture. As I have said, too, the Americans were generous, though we did tire of Spam which was so plentiful with them. When I ran some dances at the Dartington hall, for the Aid to Russia Fund, I had to see the sergeant-major of the English soldiers, who were billeted there, to ask about the room and the catering. He took a shine to me, and we had a mild flirtation that was all to my good: he would give me sugar, raisins and bacon – not much, but it helped. Knowing he was fed up and lonely, a regular soldier and an oldish man, I invited him down on some evenings to talk to Sean, who liked to recall his own brother Tom's experiences in the Regular Army.

I thought now, on the suggestion of my cousin, the Reverend Mother at Maynooth, that I might get an Irish girl to help in the house; I had nobody at all with me, for Joy had married and Helen had joined the A.T.S. The girl had to be met in London, so I went up with Shivaun and her nursery-school teacher, Trudl Bearen, one of the most sympathetic people I have met with children; she brought her little girl Crystal, who was fond of me. Trudl was the only person Shivaun would ever stay with; thus we had no trouble with the children when one or the other of us wanted to go anywhere. I had a room with Shivaun at the Regent Palace where we also booked a single room for Kathleen, who was to join us on the evening we arrived. Though, when I met her, I did think she had a peculiar shape, like a small barrel, she looked so sick after a bad crossing that I just got her to her room where she went straight to bed. Next morning, when we met in the lobby, she was stones thinner. I was startled. Kathie explained: 'You see, I've brought some sheets over for you – four pairs. Your cousin thought you'd be short of them, but I knew I would be allowed only one pair, so I wrapped the other three around me.'

Shivaun promptly took to her; and, back in Totnes, Kathie, who lived as one of the family, proved to be as likeable and full of fun as she was pretty. She came from a large and poor family; after her stories I felt that I knew her sister and the children as if I had met them. Often quite a bit of smuggling went on between Dublin and Tingrith. Kathie's sister would send her the Irish papers. When they arrived first, she glanced through them and put them in the dustbin; but when she opened the second packet, she discovered, done up skilfully in grease-proof wrapping, rashers of bacon between the pages. Now and again there would be a pair of nylon stockings. My own cousin, the nun, sent me a length of tweed, bound at the edges with coloured braid; and another of the nuns from Maynooth carried it on to the boat as a rug. Later it was posted to me. It made a beautiful tweed coat.

x

At last the war that had seemed to be eternal ended. In Totnes the evening of that day was most memorable. Dartington village celebrated in its own fashion, with bonfires on top of the hill; but Totnes had a torchlight procession joined by all people able to walk, children as well, with some babies wheeled in prams. We started at the market-place where we collected our burning torches and then walked down the hill, right through the centre of Totnes Plains, up the hill, round the town, and back to the centre, a wide circuit, with everyone singing lustily the tunes that were popular in the years of war. Father Russell, who stood with Sean at our gate, told me afterwards how astonishing it had all looked: 'a truly moving picture,' Sean wrote himself, 'as the procession wended a flaming way down the hill of the town to the level of a green field'.

Niall and Breon were at Dartington. Shivaun, who was five, walked with me; and, after she had gone to bed, I went down once more to the Plains where everybody danced together into the small hours of the summer morning.

CHAPTER TEN

Tingrith after the War

Now we had to make an entirely different life, strange indeed to most people after the day-by-day turmoil of the war. Gradually rationing ceased, and slowly the evacuees returned home, though some stayed in Totnes which had been a good town for them. Devon people were kind and, as a whole, fond of children. A few of these, the older ones, now eighteen and over, had got work in the Dartington sawmills or at local builders; and occasionally, on the bus, you would feel you knew the conductor and remember that, of course, he had been one of the youths for whom, not long ago, you had cut the bread and butter.

I was sorry that our war-time comradeship had so little value when the war was over. If, instead of a return to party politics, there had been a coalition government, we might have been encouraged to use our energies as we had done before, but this time to straighten things out in our own districts. All those allotments, needed once to grow extra vegetables, were left untended. Though many of us still had this terrific urge to go on doing something constructive for the country, it had to die in us: a sad answer to the phrase, 'When the war is over', that had often seemed so magical. We had gone back to concentrating on our homes. The former friendly 'Good-morning' became just a polite and stilted greeting.

At first it appeared to be a time to do up one's house. I think the stuff we used then for decorating our Tingrith rooms was called Walpamur. With Kathie's help, after the children had gone to school, I energetically Walpamured every room, nearly smothering myself, especially when trying to do the ceilings. We managed to get through most of the rooms, Sean's omitted. Later, when he had to move upstairs, leaving the large room below for Shivaun and her friends to tear round in as they pleased, the place was in so grimy a state that we had to employ a professional decorator.

II

Christmas for the children was a great thing in our family. Sean, owing to his poverty in youth, had never had a Christmas celebration in the usual way; and, strangely, I had not had in my life a Christmas in anybody's home. After Father died, and my mother was working, I was left at school; only a little group of us, mostly foreign girls, remained at the convent during the holidays; though we had our parcels, it was rather a dreary time. Previously, at the orphanage, the day was slightly more exciting: we had at least a stocking at the end of the bed, and we would wake to find in it one of those lovely sugar mice and any small toy that our one parent or the nuns might have given to us.

Our Christmas at Tingrith after the war would be really far too extravagant. We would get an enormous tree, and I would go simply wild buying far too many presents for the children and putting myself in debt for another full year. The children themselves invariably got the same gifts for Sean, either a jersey or a shirt, some handkerchiefs, socks, pipe-cleaners and tobacco, done up in separate parcels. Generally I bought a book I knew he wanted; the cost would all be put down to some account or other. Sean, though he never bought presents himself, would give money to the children to get what they thought I needed. As a rule, again, it would be something quite extravagant; one spent most of the year paying for the previous Christmas. Sean particularly loved Christmas Eve, wrapping the children's parcels and doing funny little sketches on the labels. I am certain that, subconsciously, we were putting into this occasion all the excitement we had missed. As with every family, the unwrapping in the morning was a joy; the one different thing was that Sean and I, after so long a time, were having our first real Christmases.

In boyhood Sean could not have been unhappy at Christmas; everybody near him was equally poor, and the children, I imagine, would have got some small gift, a tin trumpet or a toy soldier, costing little. Later in Dublin, when he was writing, Christmas did not exist for him: he just continued his work, for these were his free days. He always hated the idea that children would get a good dinner from some institution or other on merely this one anniversary in the year. In his childhood every family about him would be on the same level. It was not so with me because, though I was contented at the orphanage where everyone shared alike, I was completely miserable and out of things at the convent where the children were so much richer. Not that Mother failed to give me the best gift she could, but having no family and nobody of my own to be with on Christmas Day I felt cheated.

After the war our children were fortunate to get so many parcels from their American friends. Thus I remember that, when dolls were scarce, Tom Curtiss sent to Shivaun the most beautiful creature – one that, though she is married and with her own child, she has kept to this day: she called it Daffodil Rose. There was, too, an American woman, Susan Goetz, who heard that Shivaun was collecting dolls, and who sent her every year one from a different country until they grew to a fine collection. Parcels came annually from Min and Jack Carney – once a projector with which the children could show a variety of films, Charlie Chaplin, Minnie Mouse or Donald Duck, at their parties.

Father Russell telephoned on a Boxing Day to tell us that John Dulanty, the High Commissioner for Eire, was spending Christmas with friends at Paignton, and would like to come across. So four Dublin men had a grand talk together, Dulanty topping Sean every time in tall stories. One he told us that night was about Con O'Leary, an Irishman and a character, a well-known Fleet Street journalist who had visited us at Chalfont St Giles: we would meet him also at St Patrick's Day functions in the Embassy. Con, though a fantastic talker with a swift brain, did drink too much and wasted his talent. It seemed that, about eleven-thirty p.m. on a Christmas Eve, Dulanty met him in the West End, utterly tight, and urged him – being a good Catholic – to go along to the midnight Mass at the church in Maiden Lane. When they arrived Dulanty buried his head in his hands and settled down to meditate; at the end of the service he could not see Con any-where. At length, giving it up, he went down to look at the Crib. There, among the asses and oxen, Con lay fast asleep.

Frequently Con was in and out of the police cells for a night. Dulanty gathered that he nursed a fierce resentment against the ABC Dairy Company which had done something unspecified to Ireland. In consequence, whenever he got drunk, he was apt to heave a brick through an ABC shop window and Dulanty had to bail him out at the police station. Once poor Dulanty was about to go to a big official function at Buckingham Palace when a frantic appeal reached him to bail out Con for the customary brick. He stopped at the station, paid the bail, secured Con, said that he was in a hurry and drove to the nearest cab-rank so that Con could get home without delay. During the short drive Con said simply, 'Honest to God, these Irish are just terrible – they never help each other.'

III

Sean's lyrical and very personal *Red Roses for Me*, dedicated to 'Dr J. D. Cummins in memory of the grand chats around his surgery fire', had been published in 1942,* the same year as the second volume of autobiography, *Pictures in the Hallway*, which inspired certain scenes in the play. Four years after this, in 1946, Bronson Albery, on the advice of his wife Una, was keen to do *Red Roses* at the Embrssy in Swiss Cottage – then one of the two most im-portant theatres (the other was the Lyric, Hammersmith) on the London fringe. When Sean suggested that I went to London for the rehearsals, I arranged for Shivaun to stay with Trudl and Crystal: it was never easy to leave her as a small child, and she hated to go away from home. I got up in time for the last rehear-sals, directed by Ria Mooney, who was over from Dublin; on the

* It was acted at the Olympia, Dublin, in 1943, Sean's first Irish première for seventeen years.

opening night, attended by most of theatrical London, the play had an overwhelming ovation. Eddie Byrne was grandly Sean's idea of Brennan, 'owner of a few oul' houses'; Maureen Pook, who would become Maureen Pryor, acted Sheila with an uncommon poetic sense; and I remember the haunting quality of the third Act, the Bridge of Vision, when Dublin is glorified in the sunset ('Our city's in th' grip o' God,' says Ayamonn). Mrs Breydon in *Red Roses* is based partly on Sean's mother whom he loved dearly and who influenced him throughout life. He said and wrote about her much that was wonderful. In the chapter of *Inishfallen, Fare Thee Well*, entitled 'Mrs Casside Takes a Holiday', he recalled her death-bed:

> Life would be chill for him when that warm heart had ceased to beat. . . . If ever a woman in this world had earned a rest from her labours, this was the one. He didn't wish her to live because of any pleasure death might take away from her. He wished it simply because she seemed to make life easier for him. Nay, not seemed; she did. To wish her to live was a great weakness that he couldn't shake aside. He was the one of her children who had been with her all the time. Thirty-five years or so she had cared for, and defended, him. Her works would follow her. What works? Attending to him. That wouldn't fetch her even a good-conduct medal from a local G.H.Q. of heaven! This woman's spiritual hardihood, her unshakable energy, her fine intelligence, had all been burned to unusable ashes in the tedious smokiness of a hapless life. Life had wasted all her fine possessions. None, save he, could recognise her for what she was; and he was powerless to yield her any words of praise, for if he spoke them, there was none to hear. She would die alone – unhonoured and unsung.

Sean's mother was not unhonoured. He honoured her in his autobiography and in his play: all who have read his work know how brave and noble she was. While, in *Red Roses*, Mrs Breydon is partly Susan Casey, Ayamonn has hints of Sean himself in youth; we recognise, too, his brother Archie's pleasure in the stage. Sheila, the girl frightened of Ayamonn's poverty and wild ideas, could well be a school-teacher with whom Sean was in love, but who could not escape from her religious upbringing and break the barrier of class. The scene on the bridge shows the passion Sean had for Ireland, his impatience and grief and scorn at the waste of such fine people: Finnoola, especially, is poignant in those moments of passing gaiety and warmth, all ugliness gone, when she cries of the transfigured Dublin, 'She's glowin' like a song sung be Osheen himself, with th' golden melody of his own harp helpin'.' The Rector is taken from the Reverend E. M. Griffin, a Protestant for whom Sean had great regard, and whom he put consciously or unconsciously into much of his work. Finally, the 'single shilling' is a symbol of what so many strikes and riots are about: any fight for the betterment of humanity which will offer 'th' shape of a new world'.

After *Red Roses for Me* had played to full houses at the Embassy through four weeks, Bronson Albery decided to transfer it to the West End. Until a theatre could be found for it, it had a week at Cambridge and a month at the Lyric, Hammersmith; then at last it opened at the New Theatre on 28 May, again to an outburst of enthusiasm. I persuaded Sean to leave Totnes for the first time in years; and Eddie Byrne's performance delighted him. Kevin O'Hanrahan, as he was called (he changed his name to Kieron Moore), was a good choice for Ayamonn; one thought less of his acting than of the fact that so strong and handsome a man could give to the part its needed virility. Unluckily, *Red Roses* had to make the short move to Wyndham's Theatre, and O'Hanrahan, who had a film offer for *Anna Karenina*, was replaced by Antony Stuart. I hardly think that its transfer and cast change helped the production, though it did run on until the second week in August.

A man I used to meet in London was that lovable figure, George Gilmore, Irish Republican and Socialist, one of the leaders of the Left Wing of the I.R.A. during the 1920s and 1930s. This gentle, quiet man had been a hero of the Irish Civil War; once, single-handed (as I was told the story) he contrived the rescue of a group of I.R.A. men from Mountjoy Prison in laundry baskets. George wrote a play about which he and Sean had corresponded; when I was in London he seemed often to be staying there – maybe for as long as two months – and he would have Shivaun for the day, or go to the theatre with Niall and Breon who, as youths, were very fond of him; they both spent a brief holiday in the isolated Irish cottage, off Howth, where later he lived almost as a recluse.

By 1946 conscription had started, and Breon was called up to do his two years' national service. Nobody could say that anyone in the O'Casey household was happy about this: it seemed so valueless, such a waste. But it was inevitable: I travelled to London with Breon on the night before he reported, and we saw a revue, *The Shephard Show*, with that hilarious comedian Richard Hearne, who did his one-man set of lancers. Next day, when Breon went down to the station to meet the other youths in his draft, I stayed in the distance, for it would have been ridiculous to see him off in the ordinary sense. He was posted to the Royal Artillery.

In Tingrith it seemed strange without him; he was the first to leave home. Still, he was stationed at Taunton, which meant that we could go to see him at week-ends. Later he applied for a short spell of farm work, possible then – he was on two farms, both of them in Sussex – and on returning to his unit he had various jobs, the best when he was in charge of the telephones and could ring us quite often. He did not want a commission which would have held him in the Army for another year. Before joining up he had been about to enter London University; but because the Army at this period gave grants to certain youths to continue their interrupted education wherever they wished, Breon decided not to go to University but instead to use his grant for a course at an art school.

IV

It was mainly owing to Una Albery, a devotee of Sean's work, that her husband Bronson had put on *Red Roses for Me*. She was the daughter of T. W. Rolleston, the Irish poet (he wrote 'The Dead at Clonmacnois'), a friend of Yeats and Lady Gregory; in its early days he had much to do with the Abbey. Now Una persuaded Bronson to do 'A Warld on Wallpaper', the Battle of

Britain fantasy that had been rechristened *Oak Leaves and Lavender*; Macmillan had published it in 1946. It was a play I never really knew, though I had read and liked Sean's typescript, especially his handling of the sets. In a prelude he described a room in 'a manorial house of long ago':

It is gorgeous, but has, architecturally, a chaste and pleasing beauty. Its broad and beaded panelling runs across the walls in simple lines and ovals, so that a dreamy engineer might see in them the rods and motionless shafts of machinery. Two high-up circular pieces of panelling . . . have whorling edges on them so that the same engineer might fancy them into germs of revolving cog-wheels. Three great chandeliers, at regular intervals, droop from the ceiling, and the dreamy engineer could see in them the possible beginnings of gigantic gantries. The three semicircular windows at the back, the centre much larger than those at either side, might become, in the far-away future, the head of a great machine, everlastingly turning out fantastic weapons of war. The big bureau might turn into a fine lathe turning out finely-formed tools. The columns round a wide doorway, on the right corner towards the back, might evolve into great ponderous hammers pounding shapes into hard and burnished steel. The wide floor-space below these columns might turn into a mighty coke oven to smelt the steel for the hammers. The end of a grand piano . . . might be the beginning of a monster table for the drawing of blue-prints. . . . A tall, gold-framed clock might in the future become a delicate wheel, turning the others, and setting the machinery going with zest and resolution. Above the clock is a circular glass bulb, shaped like the disk of a plain and simple monstrance. All this is hardly seen when the play begins, for the light playing on them seems to come from the ghosts of many candles.

Three couples, dressed mistily in the garb of the eighteenth century, come in dancing, forming a triangle of figures; they dance to a minuet, a little slowly and perhaps a little stiffly. The dancers move slowly and stiffly with the melody; indeed, they dance as if they found it hard to move, and did so in a dream. The wide-flowing skirts and high-powdered hair of the ladies are dimly grey. . . . The broad-skirted coats of the men and the wigs are of the same dim colour . . . while from each hip sticks out a shadow of a sword, slender as a needle, but black like the braid on the men's coats.

In production nothing came of these imaginative ideas. I went down to Eastbourne with Sean for the last rehearsals and the dress rehearsal. Sean and the director could not agree, and the play never came alive. It was too late to do much about the London production, and the whole experience was miserable; we stayed in a large hotel where Sean never went to the dining-room but had his meals upstairs. It was cold weather; he was depressed; both of us felt hopeless. The play did not do well at Eastbourne; afterwards it had a month (with Mary Hinton, Fred Johnson, and Sheila Sim in the cast) at the Lyric Theatre, Hammersmith,* where, though it did draw an audience, it was – so poorly directed – only a ghost of Sean's work. Breon got a night's leave to come with me to the première; we felt strange and embarrassed; during the intervals, not wishing to talk to anyone, we disappeared to our several cloakrooms until the curtain rose again. Sean, who did not go to Hammersmith after the trouble at Eastbourne, was never fully satisfied with *Oak Leaves*, but he never saw it properly staged. One day I would like to see it done well; I still believe that it is good and that Sean's scenic descriptions need to be translated to the stage just as imaginatively.

V

Shivaun, at Totnes, brought back from school one afternoon a cap called a 'beano', which she had made for Sean; a brightly coloured little cap in felt. Trying it on, he found it most comfortable, and this was how his collection of caps began. Frequently he was photographed in one; people would send him others from many countries, and he would make his choice for the day as the mood took him. Hence the title of his last book, *Under a Colored Cap* (he used the American spelling).

* John Whiting, who would become a distinguished dramatist, had the small part of Pobjoy.

Life magazine wrote from America at this time, asking if it could do an article with photographs of Sean's family and home. Though at first he hated the idea, it was a good offer and he accepted it. Soon Gjon Mili and Robert Emmett Ginna, who would be our endeared friends, came from London. Mili, a fine-looking Armenian, was *Life*'s top photographer. Bob Ginna, now an American film producer, was to do the story; he had a frank, boyish personality, and the occasion was both enjoyable and exhilarating. Making their base an old Dartington inn, the Cott, they arrived at Tingrith to photograph Sean in the house, in the garden, going upstairs, coming down, out for a walk, typing in his room, sitting in his chair, and smoking his pipe: pictures by dozens and dozens. The children were caught coming from school, and in the house and garden; I was photographed as well. Mili was so lively that nobody minded what he did. At night either they would eat with us or we would go out. Bob, who knew about cooking, would sometimes do lunch. We might dine at the Cott where the food was good, and Sean who, because of his eyesight, normally preferred to stay in, would come also, an achievement for Bob and Mili. Talk never flagged; after dinner it would be Tingrith again, and again talk until all hours in Sean's room, with a midnight pot of tea before they returned to the Cott.

When the article was finished, Mili thought, as there was time to spare, he might make for his own personal collection a small talking film about us as a family. Sean entered into it delightedly. Having always fancied himself as a singer, in any scene he would discover some excuse for a song while the children and I winked at each other despairingly. If I appeared to spend most of the film in taking Sean off to help with something, it was simply Mili's device to get me to stop him from beginning a third or fourth verse. When Mili asked for a scene of Sean washing up, as he usually did, we were photographed in the large, dilapidated scullery, Sean washing the dishes and singing away all the time, while I dried. The children were filmed bicycling from school, and Shivaun at piano practice. Breon being absent on the farm, Mili, who was anxious to include him, drove up to Sussex, and there is a shot of Breon, with his beard growing, leading a bull. Mostly, though, the film is just an ordinary day in our Tingrith life. I have heard from friends in America that it has been among the attractions at the New York studio party to which Mili invites hundreds of professional people every Christmas.

VI

Sean, completing his third volume of autobiography, *Drums under the Windows*, went straight into the next, *Inishfallen, Fare Thee Well*. He lived these books intensely, writing often as a dramatist would write in scenes and dialogue theatrically vivid. In the evenings he would talk a great deal, not only about his own years in Dublin, but also about Irish politics and its troubles. This was the time of the release of the thirty I.R.A. men the British Government had gaoled in 1939 for bomb offences. Most of them were young men who had obviously been possessed by patriotic enthusiasm, and who had received stiff sentences, up to twenty years. Sean was in the habit of sending books, magazines, tobacco, and letters – which meant a lot – containing any encouragement he could give. At Christmas 1947 several of the men wrote in warm gratitude. Frequently Sean pleaded for their release, and he continued to work steadily with Eoin Mahony who, from Dublin, had taken up the prisoners' cause as his main task. They were finally released in 1948, a considerable reduction in sentence.

Besides his other work, Sean was excited about the creation of a new play, *Cock-a-doodle Dandy* – as excited as when he had got the idea for *The Silver Tassie*. Once more, as so often when beginning a play, he sang a good deal; it was as if the rhythm, mostly of Irish folk-songs, helped his thoughts. I am sure he was excited because of his resolve to break from realism – not just in a single act, as in the war scene of the *Tassie*, but through the entire piece. *Cock-a-doodle Dandy* was his favourite play, and it is mine. He spoke of it in an article entitled 'Cockadoodle Doo', that he wrote in 1958 for the *New York Times*:

The first thing I try to do is to make a play live: live as a part of life, and live in its own right as a work of drama. Every charac-

ter, every life, however minor, has to have something to say
comic or serious, and to say it well. . . . But there are other parts,
phases of life, and these, to my mind, should be prominent in
the play. Above all, there is the imagination of man and that of
the playwright; the comic, the serious and the poetical imagination; and, to my mind, these too should flash from any play
worthy of an appearance on a stage; the comic imagination, as in
The Frogs; the sad imagination as in *The Dream Play*. Blake
thought imagination to be the soul; Shaw thought it to be the
Holy Ghost, and, perhaps, they weren't far out; for it is the
most beautiful part of life, whether it be on its knees in prayer
or gallivanting about with a girl.

To me what is called naturalism, or even realism, isn't
enough. They usually show life at its meanest and commonest,
as if life never had time for a dance, a laugh, or a song. I always
thought that life had a lot of time for these things, for each was
a part of life itself; and so I broke away from realism into the
chant of the second act of *The Silver Tassie*. But one scene in a
play as a chant or a work of musical action and dialogue was not
enough, so I set about trying to do this in an entire play and
brought forth *Cock-a-doodle Dandy*. It is my favourite play; I
think it is my best.

Often people ask if he discussed the plays with me while he
was writing them. Certainly I knew when a fresh play was coming,
and usually something of its theme. While he was writing he
would not talk about it, though he might give me a completed act
to read. A man of Sean's power needed no help from outside, for
the ideas that caused him to write were enough, and nobody could
interrupt. Where, perhaps, I did help was when a new play was
not produced for a while; my admiration for Sean's work helped
to keep him alert and to encourage him. From *The Silver Tassie*
onwards he was ahead of his time, and one had to look for an
adventurous impresario; they were few. Still Bobbie Lewis, the
American director and expert theatre-man, had read *Cock-a-doodle
Dandy* and wished to stage it. After a letter to Sean, he turned up
early one morning at Totnes, having taken a sleeper so that he
could spend the whole of Sunday. He told Sean then that, though
he had tried everywhere to raise money, he had not got much but

hoped still to find backers. He described how he had rung up
various rich Americans, men and women, who were accustomed to
backing plays. Once, arriving for an interview with one of these,
he had begun, 'I have this wonderful play by the dramatist Sean
O'Casey that I want to read to you.' Whereupon the rich woman
said knowingly, 'Ah, that's the man who wrote *The Playboy of the
Western World.*' No, said Bobbie, it wasn't; it was the man who
wrote *Juno and the Paycock* and *The Plough and the Stars*, and he
would like very much to describe the new work. He did so – and
the interview was over. Going on to another of the so-called
'angels', a man this time, he explained that it was about the production of a work by the dramatist O'Casey. 'Yes,' replied the
man; 'he wrote *The Playboy of the Western World.*' Hearing this
again, Bobbie wondered if he was going mad, but kept patient,
talked about Sean, and was invited to come later. Even so, he had
not yet received enough to put on *Cock-a-doodle Dandy* in the style
of production that both Sean and he desired. It was an exciting
day. Alas, Bobbie never directed the piece; but I am sure that if
he had had any chance during the years through which he was
striving the production would have been superb. That night at
Totnes he left Sean with a genuine feeling of sympathy and
affection; also real hopes for an American showing. Afterwards
Bobbie asked me up to see his London production of Miller's
Death of a Salesman; some years later, too, I was his guest, with
Shivaun, at the first night of *Teahouse of the August Moon*.

Breon, who loved *Cock-a-doodle Dandy*, had done some sketches
for the settings. That day in Totnes Sean showed them to Bobbie.
He liked them so much that, had the play been staged in New
York, he would have asked Breon to allow him to have them
revised by somebody with technical knowledge of the theatre; for
Sean they were right in the spirit of the piece. Not long after this
Breon met Augustus John, who wrote from Fordingbridge in
Hampshire (7 July 1949):

My dear Sean,
I was glad to make Breon's acquaintance and only regret he
didn't bring some drawings for me to see. When I went to
meet him in the town I recognised him at once as he approached,

for he has something of you but still more of his beautiful
mother in his face. He was rather reserved and it was difficult
to guess what he was thinking of. I shall expect and hope
to see more of him in London. I'm sure young students
are apt to be bewildered by all the nonsense talked about Art
nowadays.

I have been pretty well anchored down here over some
imaginary compositions: they seem to be crystallising at last.
You have had influenza; I have had laryngitis: but we are both
unbeaten. There's still time for experiment and we're not
locked up yet.

Love to you both:
AUGUSTUS

Breon had recommended to Sean Barrows Dunham's book, *Man
Against Myth*. Sean had just heard from the author in Pennsylvania,
and wrote now to him in enthusiasm (14 July 1949):

Dear Barrows Dunham,
Thank you very much for your kind letter and generous words.
Indeed, I've no mantle of purple or planets in my care. I am –
as I was – in hodden grey and homespun, and even homespun, or
'utility', isn't anything like what it used to be. I've three
children to care for (most of the work is done by Mrs O'C),
and they are as important as the planets, bar the one on which
we live and move and have our being. I was in your great
country fifteen years ago, and spent some days among the hills
of Pennsylvania.

I was very pleased to receive such a letter from the author of
Man Against Myth. I have read it. Our elder boy read it in
London and wrote to me about it, and the other lad bought it
for me – the issue published by Frederick Muller, Ltd. of
London. It has been a godsend to me, for, as you can guess, I am
often found arguing, and the *Man Against Myth* is at once a
buckler and a thrusting spear. It has but one drawback – it is
so splendidly written and so full of sense that one wants to
memorise it from cover to cover, a feat that my age makes
impossible. But I keep it near me. The spear is always within
reach. It is lively, too, a fine characteristic; and colorful, which
such books rarely are. It is a grand work, and I am proud of it.

It is another sign of Man's worthiness, and a call to him to
stand firm on the earth our home. And so we will.
I thank you for it from the heart out.

Yours very sincerely,
SEAN O'CASEY

VII

I was feeling run down just then and inclined to have the odd
weep about nothing at all. On waking one morning I found that
my face was blown up, that I had no neck, and that my hands were
swollen. Looking at myself, even though it was a shock, I could
not help laughing: I seemed to be like a friend's baby who was
enormously fat, and who had the same kind of balloon-face without a neck. When I went as usual to call the children, I had never
known them get up, have their breakfasts and rush from the house
so quickly. Niall, anxious for me to see a doctor, suggested that I
ought to take a picture of myself as I really was, so that the doctor
could understand something of what had happened. Sean, fully
sympathetic, said, 'It's a terrible thing to have happened. But it's
a strangely interesting face, rather like some of those in Aesop's
fables.' First, I hurried to the local doctor who assured me it was
not an allergy, and who gave me some stuff – which did not help
in the least – to put on my face. Next I went to a Torquay doctor
named Lees, who was an excellent nerve-specialist: Breon, a good
driver though, so far as I know, he had not taken any test, took
me in daily for treatment. When, after four weeks more or less,
my face was better, Dr Lees told me that it had happened because
of a nervous breakdown. I needed more gaiety, he said. It was no
fault of Sean's. Afternoons when I could have gone, perhaps, to a
cinema with a friend, I had had to fill by racing into Paignton
where my mother had rooms, and listening to her complaints;
generally it ended in a search for another lodging. When she was
not drinking I would take her out to tea. The whole business irritated me: I had always to be told what a fool I had made of myself,
and to listen to the same sing-song nagging about the way I had

brought up the children. Further, she never ceased to criticise my appearance. These were my only regular outings from Totnes. Mother came to us hardly at all and the children would have to be persuaded strongly to go to see her in Paignton.

In the circumstances, I began to wonder what I might do for a little relaxation. Several policemen's wives lived opposite; one in particular, a pretty young woman, Mary Gibbs, said she was going to try Old Time Dancing, and would I join her? So once a week I attended these classes at the local hotel. We never took the thing dead seriously; but for others it was a grave and competitive evening: it astonished me to see how proficient these people became and how jealous they were of each other. Five or six of us went wholly for fun; as dancing I do not admire it a bit – it is far too regimented and precise. I did not carry on with it through the rest of our life at Tingrith; but afterwards, in Torquay, I did go one morning a week to a private class in modern dancing where there would be about three couples taught by a professional: I liked this far better.

Sean hardly ever went visiting from Tingrith: maybe half a dozen times in fifteen years. The Elmhirsts invited us to lunch at Dartington Hall once or twice; when Lady Astor was there she had asked if we could come up. Sean dined there one evening and read *Finnegans Wake* to some of Dorothy's guests, concentrating on the first chapter and explaining the special narrative method with which Joyce summoned Dublin city, its history and its people. I recall, too, that Sean dined with William Curry at the Dartington headmaster's house. Another time we were asked to lunch; but Marsie Curry, one of the nicest women one could hope to meet, had mistaken the day, so we had to return home. We went twice to Dr Varian's for tea; also to a lunch with the Liddell Harts who had rooms in a house near us; he was the famous military correspondent. They came to Tingrith once, and the Elmhirsts at another time. I must say truthfully that I was not at ease, worried indeed whether it would go right. I regretted that Dorothy had no affinity with Sean; he missed his visits to G.B.S. and it would have been such a help if he could have talked to somebody who really loved the theatre and who was in harmony with him. But

Sean, thoroughly honest and down to earth, had nothing arty-crafty in his make-up; he had no admiration for the Chekhov Theatre at Dartington. While appreciating that Michael Chekhov was a clever man, he could not endure a set-up in which the actors wore long blue robes and went round capering and bowing to each other. I might have accepted it; Sean would not have done so in a hundred years. To talk of great drama, to discuss plays by past writers or his contemporaries – this Sean would have revelled in, and as Dorothy ran a theatre I felt she was ignoring something splendidly worthwhile upon her own doorstep.

VIII

I had not met G.B.S. for a long time; Sean missed him exceedingly. Throughout the years he wrote to us, on and off; I heard from him when Shivaun was born, and (he could be pleasantly con-ceited) he sent a packet of signed postcards of himself so that Breon might make money by selling them at Dartington. When I did get to London I wrote before arrival to ask if I could call, and gave the address of the friend's flat where I was staying. A very long letter awaited me, one I am sorry to have lost; it said that Charlotte was ill, and that the illness was disfiguring, a disease of the bones that would affect the contours of the face. He was look-ing after her, and would love to see me; so would she but it would be too painful and difficult for her. It was time, he went on in his facetious manner – knowing such a thing could never happen – that Sean produced a 'money-spinner'.

For many years Charlotte had not been strong; even when we visited Whitehall Court before moving to Totnes, she was feeling the cold extremely and needed to have heat near her. Realising how grieved G.B.S. would be, Sean was greatly upset when we heard of her death. He wrote immediately in consolation, and in October 1943 received one of the familiar G.B.S. postcards:

> We came up to London, after an absence that ran into years, on the 26th July, my birthday (87); and Charlotte's death on the 12th of this month involves a heap of business that will

keep me here for weeks to come. The spate of letters, 80 a day for a fortnight, was overwhelming; I had to acknowledge them in the lump by a notice in The Times; but still there were several that had to be answered.

The end was to be expected at our ages (86 and 87). It was quite happy; and I was tempted to put into the notice 'No letters: no congratulations.'

A letter has just come from Cosgrave – along with yours! Very friendly.

G.B.S.

Two or three times after Charlotte's death I managed to get to Ayot St Lawrence to see G.B.S. Still very much himself as a talker and a wit, he was lonely and said that he was. One visit I made with John Dulanty, the High Commissioner, who had business to discuss; G.B.S. had thought it would be a chance for me to be taken by car from door to door. It was of this visit that Dulanty wrote to Sean on 13 January 1950:

> As you will have heard, Herself and myself had a pleasant hour with Bernard Shaw, who greeted her with 'Well, Eileen, you've still got your good looks.' He was obviously glad to see her. (I wandered out of the room to give them the opportunity of a mild flirtation!)
>
> Amongst other things he talked to us, God help us, about his super super super tax income poverty, and how but for an annuity which he bought years ago – 'the first time I came into money' – he would now be in Queer Street. It was all said good humouredly. Not being quick at mental arithmetic, I couldn't follow his accounting, but equally I couldn't ask for an exposition.

At another time I told G.B.S. about *Cock-a-doodle Dandy*. He doubted whether a play with a Lourdes theme could come over as a commercial success; he never believed in miracles, and curiously he was always a bit of a sprucer about Sean writing plays for money. Time would pass quickly at Ayot: he would chat and laugh and joke and give me much advice about the children in the strong and lovely voice that never weakened. We heard from him in the early summer of 1950 (6 May):

My dear Sean,

Eileen, still lovely as ever, gave me a photograph of the lot of you which pleased me so much that I have had it framed and look at it quite often. Your marriage has been a eugenic success: the Heir Apparent is a stalwart who must count me as a Struldbrug which is what I actually look like. I keep my wits about me much better than my legs; that is the best I can say for myself.

Ireland, no longer under Dublin Castle and Grand Jury government, cannot now brood on her wrongs, for cash from America and heroic and romantic sympathy from the rest of the world. In the old days we were the first fine flower of the earth and the first gem of the sea, our only rival being Poland where hope for a season bade the world farewell, and freedom shrieked when Kosciusko fell. Now we are an insignificant cabbage garden in a little islet quite out of the headlines; and our Fianna Fail party is now the Unionist Party and doesnt know it. I have nothing to tell them except that the Ulster capitalists will themselves abolish the Partition when the Labor party is strong enough to threaten them with an Irish 1945 at the polls, and they must have the support of the Catholic agricultural south to avert it. But all they do is to send me medals of the Blessed Virgin, guaranteeing, if I say a novena, that she will give me anything I ask from her, to which I reply that the B V needs helpers and not beggars.

I have no news for you except the quite uninteresting item that I am having a bout of lumbago. They are trying to bake it out of me by Radiant Heat.

G. BERNARD SHAW

In July 1950 I read that G.B.S. was ill, having fallen while pruning an apple tree in his garden and broken his leg. In hospital he developed pneumonia which set him back. When I journeyed to Ayot in October they had turned the downstairs room at Shaw's Corner into a bedroom for him, its window giving upon the garden. Under the window was a high couch-bed where during the day he could lie for some hours. He seemed very frail and ill and clearly hated to be looked after by nurses; he was both the most fastidious and aesthetic of men. I tried to persuade him that he would certainly get better and might yet see the hundredth birthday to which he had looked forward; but he said he was not sure that the time had not come to leave everything, for he could not bear the idea of being helped from his bed to the couch; the whole idea, in fact, of being obliged to depend on others.

Dulanty had told me that G.B.S. had asked him how the O'Caseys were financially, and he had replied that he did not think we were all that good. G.B.S. commented that somebody had told him we were 'in clover'. Though I said this was hardly the time to worry him about our situation, Dulanty answered, 'I really think you should tell him, Eileen.' When I was with G.B.S. this time, and he was asking about the children and what they were doing, asking me in fact to describe our daily lives, he put in of a sudden: 'And how is Sean financially?' I could not possibly have replied other than I did: 'Of course, we are perfectly all right.' He said he had heard we were in clover and was now relieved about it. He passed on to talk of his loneliness and the deaths of his contemporaries and friends, and appeared to be extraordinarily tired. I could not help thinking that, because this great man had given in mentally and had almost willed himself not to live on, he must die very soon. I felt this so strongly that, on getting back to London, I telephoned Sean, saying I was certain G.B.S. could not last much longer: it was impossible to rid myself of the belief. Sean, who could not imagine the world without G.B.S., replied that of course he would overcome anything.

A few days later, when calling at Dulanty's, I had a compelling urge to go down to Ayot again, though I did not want to be in any way a nuisance. Dulanty was just coming downstairs. He exclaimed that he had telephoned Sean asking where I might be found; G.B.S. had said that he wanted to see me. At once I rang up Ayot, and they told me to come, if possible, that afternoon. On arrival I found Shaw dozing and very pale indeed. Before he woke I had time to study the room in detail; except for its pictures of Stalin and Gandhi, it did look like a small room in a hospital, with its collection of medicine bottles by the bed. Finally G.B.S. opened his eyes. Turning to me, he said, 'I really think I am going to die.' His voice was weak and he spoke softly; one had to move close to him to hear what he was saying. But he rallied for a moment and began to talk in his old humorous way, asking what was going to happen after death and whom he would meet, treating it as a new experience instead of being in any sense frightened: 'If there's an Almighty, Eileen, I'll have a hell of a lot of questions to ask Him.' I said that perhaps he would be able to tell Sean what there was to meet. Sean, he answered, would have to carry on. 'No,' I said, 'Sean is too old'; and he replied, 'It's up to one or both of the boys if their lives aren't wasted in another war.' His long white hands on the coverlet, he stole back to sleep again, first asking me not to go yet. Though he was so sick, his brain was as clear and bright as ever.

I crept from the room, believing I ought to go. I was talking to the nurse when the bell that was fastened to G.B.S.'s shoulder suddenly rang. He asked if I had gone, for he would like to say goodbye. Though a little reluctant, the nurse whispered to me: 'Yes, if you are not too long with him this time; he was so anxious to see you.' On my return he gave one of his lovely smiles, and said that his head was aching always. Would I stroke his forehead? Feeling that he was back again as a small child wanting a mother's comfort, I spoke to him very gently. It was wonderful, he murmured, to have the soft touch of a woman's hand and the sound of a gentle voice. Then I stroked his forehead until he dozed off, practically to sleep. 'Kiss me goodbye,' he asked. I kissed him; he smiled quietly; and when I said 'Goodbye and God bless you,' he answered, in his old quick manner, 'He has blessed you already.' He sank back into sleep. When I left I knew I should never see him again.

That evening, after leaving Ayot, I was to meet Breon in London; we were going to see Tyrone Guthrie's play, *Top of the Ladder*. I told him that G.B.S. was dying and that I had been much enriched to be with so great a man in his last moments. Two days later the expected news came; it was the loss of someone I had dearly loved, and Sean had lost probably his best friend, the man who had stood by him and defended him through all his literary life.

IX

At the end of the nineteen forties, and early in the nineteen fifties, Sean had been engaged upon *Rose and Crown*, the sixth volume of his autobiography. He wrote about it to Daniel Macmillan on 7 March 1951:

> Thank you very much for your letter dated the 6th March and for your kind interest in the present work.
>
> I don't think there is anything libellous in it. I certainly had no feeling of writing anything so derogatory while I was working at it. If I be inclined to libel anyone, I am inclined to libel myself. But, as you wisely say, it is better to make as sure as assurance can be by getting a lawyer to look over it.
>
> I am sure that no one can write anything worth a damn without annoying someone: Joyce did; Yeats did; Hardy did; and so did Tennyson. And Jesus annoyed a crowd of people. However, I haven't written anything just to annoy, but simply wrote down what I felt I must write down. And that was done, not to annoy any person, but to free myself from annoying God. Of course, some of my conceptions may be wrong – nay, all of them may be so – but they are all honest, though that isn't saying that they are true or proper. Let a man examine himself, says St Paul, and I have done this often, and must often when I am writing, so as to try to prevent anything malicious creeping into what I am setting down.

Soon after this he was writing to Harold Macmillan:

> I cannot expect, nor do I expect, that everyone should like and agree with my 'judgment'. I don't think 'judgment' to be the right word about what I state or seem to imply in play or biography. They are opinions only: honest ones taken after thought and long and wide experience of men and things; but they are, for all that, far from being infallible. Only God or Time can vindicate the judgment of man. To me one thing alone is certain – we are all one in the tremendous and glorious bond of humanity. Jew, Gentile, bond and free, Tory and Communist, can never break away from this. We are born, we

die, and we must do the best we can between the day of birth
and the night of death.

Also in his head at this time, the autobiography apart, were
three short plays, *Hall of Healing*, *Bedtime Story*, and *Time to Go*.
He continued, moreover, to write his articles for Russia; and this
was the period when Caedmon Records asked him to make a personal recording from his work, extracts from plays, perhaps, and
from the autobiographical material already published. Mostly he
went to this: such passages as the trip to America and the storm
('Sean seemed to be standing in a glasshouse tossed about in a
surging greenery of waves'); also he read his first conception of the
famous 'jeep' scene which went afterwards into *The Bishop's Bonfire*. The recording was less good than we had hoped; the weather
was frigid and Sean had slight bronchitis. Years later the entire
thing was revised and made into an extremely good record.

Denis Johnston, the Irish dramatist, arrived at Totnes to write
an article on Sean: the first time we had met Denis since soon
after our marriage and the move to Woronzow Road. Then, I
remember, we had tea together in the kitchen, and Denis was shy
and respectful, speaking as if he loved every word Sean had
written. Now he appeared to be a different man. He sat there at
Tingrith, getting nowhere near Sean either as a person or a playwright. It was a clever article, but though people liked it I
regarded it as a sugared pill with many unpleasant criticisms.
Writing from his upper middle-class background, Denis could not
credit Sean, a working man, with a natural genius and the personal love of art that accompanied it. Thus he reported that a
Gauguin hung on one wall of Sean's study and Giorgione's 'The
Sleeping Venus' on another, the implication being that Sean's
taste was muddled. But it is not a muddle when one great artist
is in company with another. Denis took no notice of the portrait
of Sean that John had given to us; he did not see our other John –
the head of a Gitana – and he did not speak of the other prints by
other artists that were round the house. Not, I dare say, that this
would have mattered if he had not made a point of the pictures he
observed in the study. I felt sad that, a dramatist himself, he could
not appreciate reasonably the tastes of another.

I may not have described Sean fully as the man he was. Deeply home-loving, he showed both his affection for us and his great simplicity in one regular observance: his resolve to bring us all breakfast in bed on Sunday mornings. For him a Saturday evening was a ritual. He would lay two trays on the kitchen table, one for Shivaun and myself, as she would come into my bed for breakfast, and one for Niall who by then was quite grown up. Sean took the sharpest delight in doing this for us; and boiled eggs, tea and toast have never seemed so good as when he prepared them. (But in the kitchen there would be piles and piles of crumbs and scrapings from the toast.) His home and his children were his world, his room, his books and his work aside. The children had a lot of freedom, for in a house the size of Tingrith all could have rooms of their own. Through the years they never played with Sean's typewriter or muddled his papers, and I think this was because they were lucky to be so free. If they had indeed touched any of Sean's work it would have been chaos; he laid his papers out on the floor in odd piles, knowing himself where everything was and hating to have the room cleaned or dusted. After it had been cleaned he could never settle back into it quickly enough.

X

Sam Wanamaker, the actor and director, visited Tingrith early in 1953 to consult Sean on a production of the fantasy, *Purple Dust* (the wearing to dust of old traditions), which had been written in 1938–9. Its principal characters, a pair of Englishmen named Stoke and Poges, want what they think is the simple country life and come to Ireland to live in the shell of a crumbling Tudor mansion. Often Sean made notes of people and events that struck him; though he might not use them at the time, he stored them in his mind and he preserved the notes. When we were in London, and I was on the stage, he met some attractive and intelligent girls who were being 'looked after' by older men, and this suggested to him a situation in *Purple Dust*; amused by the entire set-up, he created a play full of fun and imagination. I believe that one of the men, Poges, had a hint of his friend Billy McElroy, who had backed his early plays, who had a country cottage, and who even owned some racehorses in a rather casual fashion. Undoubtedly he was an odd character. None of *Purple Dust* was factual, but it did derive from Sean's experience during the thirties.

The Old Vic company at Liverpool had done it in 1945. It went well; even so, it was not staged again until Sam Wanamaker asked for it. Sean liked him, agreed to let him direct, and even went to London for some rehearsals. Before these began he wrote to Sam from Tingrith (5 April 1953):

> Charade, is it? Oh, Sam, Sam, Sam! I don't write charades. *Purple Dust* is a comedy if ever there was one. . . . Here's a quote from Brooks Atkinson: '*Purple Dust* has never been produced on Broadway, though it is a more practicable play than *Cock-a-doodle Dandy*. It is closer to both people and theater. Under the robustiousness of the satiric *comedy* and behind the occasional scenes of phantasy, there is a tangible problem to deal with and recognisable people to fool with.' . . . If I hate one thing more than another, it's talking of or writing about my work, and only do so, Sam, when I think I must; so forgive this egotism made to do away with the thought that *Purple Dust* is anything in the way of a charade. If we change it any more, it will cease to be the play that has been praised by so many; and, in my opinion, would then stand a far less chance of succeeding.

When we went up, Sean stayed with the Wanamakers at Abbey Lodge which made it easier for him to get to and from rehearsals. I had taken Shivaun, and she had a room with me in a small hotel near Baker Street. Rehearsals seemed to go with a bang; the Stoke and Poges, Miles Malleson and Walter Hudd, were perfectly suited. I remember Sean asking John Trewin, the critic, whom he admired, to come along to the church hall near Kingsway to talk over the production; he respected Trewin's judgement, and both of them were enthralled with Malleson's performance. Opening in Glasgow, *Purple Dust* ran there for a fortnight, though how it fared I do not know for somehow we never saw the notices. We had returned from London; but Sean resolved to travel to Edinburgh for the opening there, a tremendous decision and a visit we never forgot. The change in the play at the Lyceum Theatre was startling: we were utterly mystified by the half-hearted manner in which Miles was acting, a style that meant trouble for Walter Hudd who relied upon every line of Miles to hold up his own part. As they had to be the life and soul, it was simply not the same play we had enjoyed at the London rehearsals. Siobhan McKenna and Eithne Dunne had as much vigour as before, yet because of Miles much of the life had ebbed. It was, of course, a big theatre for such an intimate comedy; audiences were disappointing; and in the end, though nobody could have tried harder than Sam to do it worthily, a fine play got little further. Terribly worried – not least about finance – Sam could not understand what had happened, and we could get no explanation from Miles; when he came to lunch the warmth between us had disappeared and it was merely an ordinary polite meal. Possibly Coronation year was bad for a piece that might have been mistaken for a skit on English life and a laugh at the system as it was. I think myself that it could be called a prophetic play in the mood of *The Cherry Orchard.*

Away from the theatre, we were glad to meet in Scotland such people as Hugh MacDiarmid (Christopher Grieve) whose work Sean greatly relished, and Sydney Goodsir Smith. MacDiarmid and Sean were guests of honour at a party in an Edinburgh house for thirty or forty people and members of the *Purple Dust* company. It was a large top-floor flat. Many wore kilts; there were singers and bagpipe players; poems were read and stories told; and the younger guests danced Scots reels in the kitchen. With bagpipes in full volume in the hall the noise was fierce. Though Sean never drank much, whisky that night was so plentiful that he did not realise how much he was drinking; we began to feel the effect of the party when we went out into the air and someone gave us a lift home to our temperance hotel. As the porter opened the door both Sean and I stumbled over a small brass step neither of us had noticed and went down, flat on the mat, like ninepins. We could have been on the halls. Getting up, we clutched our bedroom keys, and the porter asked carefully, 'Are you all right, sir?' 'Oh yes,' we told him, 'we're all right.' Carefully we mounted the stairs, the porter behind us at a safe distance: it was just as well because we could not get the key into the lock. He did this for us. We both bowed politely and thanked him over and over again. He closed the door, and at last we were safe at home.

More soberly, while we were in Edinburgh, we were shown over the printing works of R. & R. Clark; Sean met the man who looked after his books and the proof-reader who had so impressed him by spotting the smallest error even in Irish history or a religious rite. That was a glorious day for Sean. He loved Edinburgh so much that he felt, if it had been less cold and far off, that it was a place in which he could have lived. Actually it was because he had found in Hugh MacDiarmid a man with whom, as with Nathan in New York, he could be entirely at ease: a poet and a writer and with the same political opinions.

Sean wrote to Sam Wanamaker (26 May) as soon as the brief tour had ended:

> Dear Sam,
> A bad situation for both of us. Here I am broken-hearted – nearly, and you, I'm sure, feeling the same damned way. It can't be helped now; and we just must face it, fight it, and overcome it – God knows how; but overcome it, in some way, we must. Forget it all as soon as we can and go on to other things. It was a grievous disappointment. Pity I didn't first take the American offer, for its acceptance would have saved you and me a hell-long time of trouble, anxiety, and hard work; and a fearful waste of time. But – as we thought – I chose the better way which so often turns out to be the worst one. Still there was good hope and bright prospects in the beginning in play and cast, and the decision, at least, was a reasonable one. It is a puzzle how the play failed to succeed, even on tour, though of course it did reasonably well in Blackpool. . . .
> I am still being congratulated on the idea that C. Chaplin is to film the play – even *Variety* in the U.S.A. has carried the news to its readers. It is curious how this canard spread about everywhere. Makes one's feelings worse. It's just as well the play didn't go to the Arts Theatre; that wouldn't have been

much good to you or to me. I certainly shouldn't have been enthusiastic about it. All our little plans have gone west now, and we are far worse than we were; for I was confident that *Purple Dust* would hunt uncertainty away for a year or so. It was a sore tumble, but all we can do is to work ourselves up to our feet again. . . .

Yours very sincerely,
SEAN

XI

I was shopping in Totnes on a Friday not long after this when a woman who helped in the house came rushing to the town to find me. 'Mrs O'Casey,' she cried, 'you must go back immediately. Mr O'Casey is in a terrible state; I'm sure he'll be ill. He's shouting at a tax-man at the top of his voice – I was afraid he might throw him downstairs. The man has gone now, but Mr O'Casey is sitting in his room, looking very upset.' I hurried home where Sean told me that the Inland Revenue had sent a man to collect the tax, about fifty pounds, that was owing. It was the final demand, said the intruder: if it could not be paid it would be taken in goods and he would have to put in a bailiff until it was settled. Then he asked about the furniture and the small Ford car; Sean told him that the car was mine, also the furniture which I had brought with me when we were married. Sean's own belongings were his hundreds of books, his typewriter, and the furniture in his study. The man, who roamed round the room, summing everything up, had apparently seemed quite charming: they had shaken hands and agreed that Sean would do his best. It was only at this moment that Sean, glancing down, saw by his typewriter a piece of paper saying that everything in the room would be confiscated, and the bailiffs put in, until the account was settled. Nothing could have fired his temper so much; he practically threw the man down the stairs, shouting at him: the noise that had sent Winnie to find me. In the end Sean wrote to the Chancellor of the Exchequer, R. A. Butler, a detailed letter in which he said:

I have been resident in England for the last 28 years, and during that time, each year, like everyone else, or almost everyone else, I have paid taxes levied yearly. They haven't been paid 'on the nail', but they have been paid off when circumstances allowed, and at the moment he who writes this letter has cleared off all that had been owing. Recently, for the past four years, however, things have been made difficult by the curious attitude of a Head Inspector of Taxes who, to my mind, acts in a way contrary to the spirit of the law calling on citizens to meet their dues. . . .

I hope, sir, you do not stand for this sort of bullying persecution. I don't believe you do. A record on my part of 28 years as a taxpayer (one year a tax of £1200) is surely enough to show that there is no intention on my part to evade payment, though I like paying tax no more than most persons. . . . It may be that the Collector considers an Irishman something of an alien, and he may be right. He may, as some do, resent it, thinking that I, as some do, live on the English people. I don't, and owe nothing to this in this respect. More than eighty per cent of my income comes from the U.S.A. and half of the remaining percentage from my own country; so that I pay in tax more than I get from the country in which I live.

I respectfully suggest that I shouldn't be subject to this bullying pressure on the part of one who, to me, is an ignorant and unimaginative beaurocrat (spelling deliberate).

Certainly, if this bailiff comes again, I shall not permit his paws to roam over the books so precious to me; and, if he carries away anything, he'll have to carry me away with them, a job that won't be quite so easy as he may think it to be.

Yours sincerely,
SEAN O'CASEY

Immediately the letter reached Whitehall, a telephone message to Tingrith told us that the Chancellor was sending a high official from the income-tax world to sort things out. As Sean had said, if they took his typewriter and books, how in the name of God could he ever hope to earn a living and to pay these people? Presently a charming man arrived, talked to Sean in the study, and asked if he might look through the account. 'It's all in the top drawer here,' said Sean. Going carefully through the papers, the official discovered several post-war credits, and at last, after totting everything up, he leaned back and said, 'Well, you may owe the Revenue fifty pounds, but they owe you a hundred.' That was that: would we dine with him at the Totnes hotel? Sean, who did not like going out, thought that I should, so we had a pleasant meal and the problem was solved. All later tax demands, we noticed, were signed by somebody with a different name.

CHAPTER ELEVEN

Ways and Means

ALWAYS I was thinking of ways and means of enjoying life and seeing that the children had a chance to enjoy it while they were still young. Probably this was because I was longing myself for the theatres. For local fairs and the occasional cinema I kept a box into which, at the end of every day, I put any odd pennies and sixpences. Then, when Shivaun was five, I opened a Post Office savings account in her name, so that I could withdraw nothing myself, and put in from time to time a pound or ten shillings; when she was eight the account had run up to forty pounds or so. If the cheque from Samuel French was not above five pounds in a month, Sean would give it to me to use as I liked. To keep the hire-purchase of the car going, and to pay bills that became too oppressive, I would sell wedding presents and any bits of jewellery I had. Sean, at Billy McElroy's persuasion, had given me a ring when we were engaged; though I never wished to part with it, I knew that before going to London I could always pawn it and easily raise thirty pounds – not more as I would try to pay this back before the next visit.

In later years at Tingrith we had a Devon man, Harry, who came over on two days a week to do the garden for us, to look after the vegetables, and to help generally in the house. A grand character, he would take on anything to help me, wash the scullery floors, clean the kitchen grate, carry the wood in, and dispose of anything else that was wanted. All of us liked him. Once, when I was explaining to him what to do while I was away in London, he said to me, 'You won't mind my asking you, Madam, but I did hear you saying you were a bit short of money. If you would

like some to spend on your London trip, I could always let you
have five or ten pounds. You could pay me as you liked when you
got back.' If he had not meant this, he was talking to the wrong
person; at once I jumped at it. 'But how can you spare the money?'
I asked. He explained that he kept his savings either in his house,
under a floor-board, or about him. At this he retired to the outhouse, and when he came back he gave me ten very old pound
notes, all rolled into each other like a concertina; I gathered that
he kept most of his money fastened beneath his shirt in two
yellow oilskin bags. To lend to me was a real compliment because
undoubtedly he was a miser, and here he was taking a certain risk.
Still, by adding to his wages every week, I was always able to
repay him.

That was another method of raising money for holidays. Often
I think to myself that, without friends or kindly souls I could
borrow from, I might well have stolen. I was determined to get
some enjoyment from life, even in my clothes; though at that
time I could not possibly have been extravagant, I did make up
my mind to get the best I could.

Harry was unfailing. When the lavatory seat in our back
garden was broken, he told me not to go to the expense of
renewal; he had several in his shed, and I could bring one back in
the car. His house was a joy: a small bungalow with a single big
room for eating and sleeping, and at the end divans where I suppose Harry and his wife slept. His main pride was his fireplace.
I could not help exclaiming: 'But, Harry, it's immense!'; and he
replied, 'Yes, that's the beauty of it. I put it in myself. It does
burn a great deal of coal, but you've just got to get it going, and
when it's dying down it's very comfortable. Of course, when it's
going full blast, the wife and I have to sit outside. Nobody could
stand the heat.' Obviously he had taken the grate from some large
house; the amount of smoke from the chimney was astonishing
for so small a place. His shed he had built himself of odd gates
and doors, all fitted into a square, with a bit of tarpaulin over the
top. Inside were stacked old fenders, old pokers, old lavatory
seats and bowls, old refrigerators, old spring mattresses: anything,
I imagine, that people where he worked had discarded. When we

parted with our own refrigerator, one brought from London that would have cost us more to repair than the hire of another, it went immediately to Harry's room for use as a cupboard. It was an old-fashioned type with a sort of beehive on the top; this he sawed off for his junk-shed. As he kept on repeating, 'You never know when a thing may be handy.'

Harry was fond of his wife; there had been no lass like her when she was young, he said; and every Sunday, wet or fine, he walked six miles to meet her. Now, though thin and worn, she kept an uncanny sense of humour as well as her own slightly miserly touch. Thus they still had all the sheets, much too good to use, that were given to them on marriage; bleached ones were far better for the likes of Harry and herself.

On an afternoon when Leonard Elmhirst, of Dartington, called at Tingrith, Harry, who happened to be in the conservatory, greeted him as an old friend. 'You must remember me, I was up at Dartington with the farm horses when you first came there. Are you wanting to see the O'Caseys? I'm sure they won't mind if you want to come in.' Taking Leonard inside, he told him to sit down and be comfortable, and called up the stairs, 'Mr Elmhirst from Dartington Hall is down here to see you; I told him to come in; we knew each other in the old days.' When Sean and I arrived Leonard was both amused and a bit overwhelmed.

I looked forward to the days when Harry worked for us. He wore very large riding-breeches; if he bent to put coal on the fire, Niall especially would find it hard not to go into peals of laughter. He had a tot of rum in his tea every morning to keep himself going. Gassed during the First World War he would be in bad pain sometimes; it did not stop him from arriving at Tingrith, but once with us he would retire to an old armchair, or, if things were really bad, to a camp-bed with a mattress, both of which he kept in an outhouse where normally he would eat his lunch alone. (Nothing would induce him to have it with us.) On his bad days I understood that he needed to be left there alone. Sean had so warm an affection for him that I wondered frequently why Harry never figured in any of the plays. Maybe there is a trace of him in the old man, Codger Sleehaun, of *The Bishop's Bonfire*, who has a curious philosophy and a strange way of talking that Harry could well have suggested.

II

It was exciting to go to London as the children grew older. We stayed generally at a Lyons hotel, the Regent Palace or the Strand, each of them most reasonable; having our breakfast round ten o'clock, and eating everything we could get on the menu, we did not have to bother too much about lunch. Lee had now remarried and made his own new life, but I was assured that when in London I could ask him for tickets for the children and myself. At this period several of his musical hits were running; I would take the children to matinées where he arranged tea for us and came now and again to see that we were fixed comfortably: the only times I met him. I have never forgotten the afternoon in September 1953 when I was leaving Totnes Post Office, and Niall, who was in town, ran across to me. 'Eileen,' he said, 'it was on the news that your friend who used to take us to the theatre has died – Lee Ephraim.' For a moment I could only stand there quietly, remembering a man I had loved, thinking of my strangely different life and hoping that his own had been happy.

On our post-war visits to London Sidney Bernstein would get me tickets as well whenever I asked for them. Sean realised, of course, that I needed these changes; though he hated to be on his own, he was all right then with the help of the daily maid; moreover, Father Russell or Dr Varian made sure of joining him in the evenings. Every evening I telephoned, and he wrote to us daily with some amusing sketches; in youth he had wished to be an artist and he spent many hours sketching until his eyesight prevented him from doing more. We can see him as an artist in those lovingly described stage-sets which would be beautiful if his directions were followed: he had always a fine sense of colour.

During one of the war years I hired a caravan and took Shivaun and Niall on the moors; Breon stayed with Sean in Totnes and, like some other people there, would come up for the day to meet us at Buckfastleigh, the next little town. We went twice also to Treyarnon in Cornwall; Marcus Tyrrell was a school-friend of Niall, and his mother – with whom I worked on the Aid to Russia Fund – had a permanent site with two caravans and a large tent. Close to a farm, which saved us from worrying about food, it was an enchanting place by the immense North Cornish sands, though in war-time there was rather too much barbed wire round the coast. I think, too, of trips to Exeter, or Torquay, or Bristol, with Shivaun, to see the pantomimes at Christmas. Those were great days. Sean, without going himself, was as excited as we were and eager to get us off in time in the old Ford; at night we would come home singing the hit song of the panto. I loved to go out with children, and to this minute I would sooner be with children I am fond of than with many older people.

III

Because Glen Byam Shaw, whom I had met while playing for Cochran in *The Miracle*, was a co-director of the Shakespeare Memorial Theatre, we would sometimes visit Stratford-upon-Avon for the festival. Glen, who admired Sean's work, would see to tickets for us and invite us to meet him in the intervals with his wife Angela Baddeley, his fellow-director Anthony Quayle, and others from the company. We went first – the children and myself – in 1950 when John Gielgud headed the cast and we were lucky enough to catch him as Lear and his celebrated Benedick. As a rule I could scrape enough money for us to stay at a hotel; but Shivaun's Post Office account was our other source. We would drop in at the Post Office every morning to draw the three pounds that in those days was the limit; I think we must have looked like gangsters as we stood about Shivaun while she struggled to fill in the form, and then hastily piloted her to the counter to get the money that she handed over to us to spend.

Two seasons later Siobhan McKenna was playing Celia to Margaret Leighton's Rosalind in *As You Like It*. She was spontaneous and fresh, and when Sam Wanamaker was casting *Purple Dust* in

Sean and Eileen at Tingrith after the war

Sean and Shivaun, 1955

Breon and Sean at Totnes

The family at Torquay, 1955: left to right, Sean, Eileen, Niall, Shivaun, Breon

Niall in the last year of his life

Sean in a Devon lane

Barry Fitzgerald and Sean O'Casey meeting at Torquay after
thirty years, 1959

Sean's room at St. Marychurch, his colored cap on the table

Eileen and Sean at Torquay

Sean at St. Marychurch, Torquay, with the Augustus John
portrait behind him. This was one of the last pictures, taken
within a week of Sean O'Casey's death, 1964

the following spring, I proposed her for one of the girls, Souhaun. In 1953 Sean came to Stratford himself. We drove up in the old Ford; Niall stayed with a Dartington friend who was walking on at Stratford where his aunt lived, a charming woman who for some years had been a Festival costume-designer. Sean knew and liked Peggy Ashcroft; but, though we had planned for him to see her as Cleopatra, he had one of his mild attacks of bronchitis. It worried him to feel that he might cough during the performance, so he did not go: he had a dramatist's horror of coughing during a play. Still we lunched with Peggy and later met Michael Redgrave and his family who lived in another part of the same house. If Sean did not get to the theatre, he certainly enjoyed the Shakespeare country as a tourist, the cottages at Shottery and Wilmcote, the sturdy Birthplace, the Grammar School, Holy Trinity Church by the Avon, and Hall's Croft where the prescriptions of Shakespeare's son-in-law, Dr John Hall, fascinated him. He and Niall liked to probe into everything and they would spend a long time looking at the books in the show-houses: they loved Dr Hall's eccentricity. In fact there was nothing in and about Stratford that we did not examine thoroughly; and as it was such a success we repeated it in the following year. Sean, who hated hotels, was quite at home in the Shakespeare and would sit happily at night in its lounge.

He and Niall got on very well because they had each a keen and sarcastic sense of humour. Breon was a sympathetic type; he and Sean would talk a lot about the stage, arguing their own points of view, though Breon, more reticent than his brother, also appreciated a silent companionship. As for Shivaun, her father yielded to her in every possible way. From childhood she had loved the theatre, and Sean's knowledge of plays helped her immensely. When she was at her London drama school she rang him up about any problem; he was better than an encyclopedia and took infinite pains to check a detail.

I had been in London with Shivaun during 1951 for the Festival of Britain. Staying in a hotel near Baker Street, renowned for its breakfasts, we had a room with a large bed, a small divan, and a little shower-bath into which one stepped. Niall decided to come up. I could not find him a room but the hotel people let him use ours and we seemed to spend a lot of time arguing and squabbling, especially over the shower which squirted more into the room than upon us.

IV

In another year Sean said he would like to explore Salisbury, with Stonehenge and the country around. It was quite a business when he prepared to go away. First he would make a list for fear anything might be forgotten, especially his medicines; he had eye drops and ear drops; tweezers, and the glasses I used for taking out his lashes; socks, shirts, pyjamas, jerseys, slippers. He dressed so simply that a small case could invariably hold his clothes; in spite of this he was resolved to have a neat list of everything with him, and he would do one even when ill and bound for a nursing-home or the hospital. He would beg me to be sure to make my own list as well. It was an odd quirk, for he would probably wear the same jersey during the entire trip; I imagine it was just part of the excitement of going on holiday. I agree he could not have been excited about a hospital or a nursing-home; but habit is strong. He was a nervous traveller, bothered about catching a train, and I am certain the staff at Torquay Station must often have laughed at us when we were there on the platform at least half an hour before time. I am as bad myself; we made a fine couple.

We stayed at the Red Lion in Salisbury; possibly we got the money from a play. Daily we were out in the car: at Stonehenge perhaps, taking many photographs of the monoliths, or at Winchester which Sean liked particularly. We walked, too, for long distances in Salisbury itself; Sean, fond of the Cathedral in the evening light, would often wander in the Close with Breon and Niall. On this holiday, so happily in unison, we even wondered whether we might find a house in Salisbury or one of the places near it. We had tea as a rule in a tea-room attached to the hotel and managed by a woman who was so attracted to Sean that we teased him about her. He liked a woman with good legs and a good figure; he would peer closely, and what he noticed with his one sound eye was usually right.

For most of our summer holidays, having no money to go far, we were content with the Devon seaside; every year we had a hut at Goodrington Sands where we could spend the day either swimming or sitting round in the sun, with a Primus for cooking. Children would join us – one summer Peggy O'Flaherty, Liam O'Flaherty's daughter, who was visiting Dartington with her mother. Sean came sometimes; his eyes were painful in the sun, so he sat and relaxed in the shade among the Goodrington trees. After the war, when Dartington was able to arrange holidays abroad for its senior boys, Breon went with his group to Holland. Later Niall had the chance of a French trip, but Sean had made up his mind that we could not afford it; ready to risk anything myself, I tried to get him to take a chance, but he did have this stubborn streak and there was no shifting him. Sorry for Niall who had to spend what must have been for him a dull holiday in the hut, I got him a radio set of his own, paying a pound down and the rest on hire purchase, and this did help to compensate him. Fortunately, a school-friend whose mother had a house in France, asked him to go there during the next year.

His call-up came not long before we had to leave Tingrith. It was a distressing period for us: Breon, his own two years' service finished, was most helpful in trying to comfort Niall, who was highly strung; even in a cricket match, or acting in a play, he would work himself into a state of nerves and he suffered from migraine which the tension seemed to encourage. On the day he joined up we did not travel to London; two other Totnes boys were off at the same time and Niall himself wanted to be at home until the last minute. In the event, he left Totnes station for the camp at Oswestry: I stood on the railway bridge watching the three lads enter the train and thinking again what a waste it was; I felt chilled from head to toe.

V

Our landlord had decided that he required the house for some
relatives. I owed a few bills in Totnes (everybody knew I would
pay them), and the largest and longest was to Mrs Lampson at
the dairy where she also sold some groceries and a small supply of
excellent fresh fruit and vegetables. She was another godsend, for
my bill with her was enormous: I was in the habit of paying some
of it on account and running up twice as much, a put-and-take
method. When I left Totnes I owed her about sixty-eight pounds;
she did not worry, realising it would be safe, and it was. Whenever
I visited Totnes after our move to Torquay and life grew a trifle
easier, I would pay in small amounts.

Sean once really scared poor Mrs Lampson. On a rare occasion
when he was out shopping with me in Totnes, he told her quite
seriously, while standing in her shop, 'Money, as money, is not
worth a damn.'

Mrs Lampson turned pale. 'Oh, Mr O'Casey, you can't possibly
mean that.'

'My dear lady,' said Sean, putting his hand on her shoulder,
'when the Russian revolution was on, and trainloads of soldiers
were passing through a station, starving for food, civilians would
hand them bundles of roubles. They threw away the money at
once. They couldn't eat roubles. No, my dear lady, food was what
they wanted. In a time of revolution money is no good at all.'

Dear Mrs Lampson could not follow this. Why should all the
money she had put away cease to have any value? It must have
worried her for ages.

Sean detested the idea of moving, but it pleased me, for I hoped
it might mean settling somewhere near London. Practically every
day towards the end of our life in Totnes, Sean and I would go
for a walk, either into the park or into the neighbouring lanes.
We seldom went up Dartington drive for fear that we might meet
somebody who would talk to Sean for the sake of talking, and
would be longing to get away from him; similarly, he would be
longing to get away from them. During these later years at Totnes

he was by no means well; his nerves were bad. An extremely sensitive man, he was instantly aware of people's reactions – whether they liked and understood him. Thus he knew that, as people, the Elmhirsts were never at home with him in spite of his respect for what they had done. This is not quite true of Leonard who came sometimes to see us and for whom Sean had admiration. For Dorothy he had affection.

We knew we had to leave Totnes. At heart Sean appreciated that the landlord had every right to claim the house, and we consulted about places to go. Shivaun, still at Dartington, suddenly became a problem: she did not want to board entirely at school, so if she were to be a weekly boarder we had to find somewhere to live within a workable radius. Daily I got round to Paignton, Brixham, and thereabouts, searching for a flat or a small house: after having had such a splendidly low rent at Tingrith, everything seemed most expensive. I was handicapped because I had broken my wrist and could not drive the car; the search took much longer when one was travelling on local buses. At length I hit upon a flat outside Torquay, in St Marychurch, near Petitor Downs. Breon and Sean approved; and Niall, who was on leave, said to me as we stood on the Downs, 'I do hope you're going to like it here, Eileen. You like the sea so much.'

Rooms in this flat led off a large central hall. Sean's and the living-room were in front, both looking finely across the Downs. We had a large bathroom, a fairly big back room, a small, long and quite well-equipped kitchen with convenient cupboards on one side, and one other bedroom, all light and with good views. Still, in aspect the flat was sombre, so Breon and I planned to drive over daily and paint it. We were short of money as usual. I collected loads of the children's old books and sold them on the way at a second-hand bookshop; at that time a few pounds could buy a lot of paint. We sold, too, the children's old projector that had given so much pleasure at parties. Every room except Sean's, which remained a darkish brown, was painted in white or in light colours; previously the walls had been covered in a sort of bumpy brown paper, thoroughly depressing. We did go gay in the hall by painting one of the walls in a really bright orange, so bright that I think it shone through the glass panels of the front door. Mr Norman, our landlord, practically screamed in horror. 'Oh, my God,' he cried. 'What *have* you done! I thought you were only going to do the front room. Oh, it's frightful, frightful – all that lovely embossed paper gone!'

'But surely, Mr Norman, it does look a little brighter.'

'Perhaps it does,' he conceded, 'but *violent!* Don't do any more. You've only a three years' lease, and you must not spoil the flat.'

I remember distinctly the day of our move. The vans reached Tingrith early, about nine in the morning, and the men in their white overalls streamed in to survey the old Victorian house and our belongings. They went up to the bedrooms, and until they entered Sean's study appeared happy enough with what they had to do. Sean, almost despairing, sat in his armchair, his head in his hands. Early though it was for him to be up, dressed and break-fasted, he waited as if ready for the doom. 'Good morning,' he said in a pleading voice with an ingratiating smile. 'Are you come to pack my books?' Plainly he thought of nothing else: the whole room was lined with shelves. His typewriters we were taking our-selves by hand.

'That's right, sir,' the two removal men who had entered said together. 'We'll bring in the packing-cases.'

'Then,' said Sean, 'maybe you would be kind enough to pack them from each bookcase as they come? It will be easier to put them in order at the other end.'

'Never you worry, sir. We'll put them as they are from the shelves and mark the boxes.'

'Oh, thank you,' said Sean. 'Those from my mantelshelf are very old. You will be careful of them, won't you?'

'Never you worry sir,' the men answered again. 'Now why don't you go for a stroll or sit in another room while we pack them.'

They went out to fetch the empty cases from the van. I glanced at the men from the window and it seemed to me that they were standing motionless. My neighbour next door came running in to tell me that they were absolutely taken aback by the number of books and did not know how in heaven's name they were going to pack them.

Innumerable people have recognised the awful look of the furniture when their armchairs are carried into the open and exposed to general view. It was like that with us. All our upholstery looked utterly appalling. Anyway, Tingrith at last was empty, and nothing was left for us to do but take a taxi – Sean, his two battered typewriters, and myself – to our new home in Torquay. The typewriters which he had brought from Dublin were the only ones he had ever used; he had guarded them so carefully that, as we sat in the cab, Sean lost and disconsolate, we might have been travelling with the Crown Jewels. 'So it's goodbye to Tingrith,' sighed Sean. It was.

CHAPTER TWELVE

Flat in St Marychurch

BREON was at the flat, awaiting the furniture vans. When Sean and I drove up in our taxi, we walked round to make certain which of the rooms Sean would really prefer: something vitally important to him. His choice was the same: a large front room with a window upon the Downs. Presently, when the vans appeared, we knew that somehow this room must be straightened before anything else; Breon worked hard with me, and at top speed, as the several pieces were brought in. There was parquet flooring so it was easy to lay the rugs. The removal men put the table in the centre, Sean's divan at the side, his bookshelves along a wall, his armchair by the fire – there was a good gas-fire – and it soon began to look reasonable. But the books followed. They had not been packed in order in the cases, merely pushed in anyhow, batch upon batch of them; and now the men, seeing that time was short, dumped them down in piles. The rest of the flat was in the same state o'chassis, books toppling in nearly every room. At about six in the evening the men shut the door, leaving us to arrange the place as best we could. Sean's room was in not too bad a shape, and he brightened slightly; if it had not been ready for him to take possession, to write and think, he would have had a terrible sense of unrest. During the next few days he, Breon, and myself worked together to try to get the books into some logical order, drama separated from art, history from poetry, and so on. Shakespeare, Shaw, Ibsen, O'Neill, George Jean Nathan, and the rest were established where they should be; over the mantelpiece, as usual, were the shelves that held some of Sean's favourites: the Mermaid series – Marlowe, Greene, Chapman, Ford, Jonson,

Massinger, Wycherley and others – rather the worse for handling and general wear; the Bible; a few favourite Shakespeares; and the Poetical Works of George Crabbe.

Within a few days, and with a huge sigh of relief, Sean settled into his armchair. His room was never just sleeping-quarters, somewhere to dress and undress; it was his home. The remainder of the flat was there to wander in, but when Sean spoke of 'home' it was his room he meant, filled with his strong personality; over-coat and mackintosh and caps behind the door – never in the hall – his boots, from which he changed into slippers immediately he came in, set in the same place by the fire. He hated his boots to be disturbed. We had to steal in and carry them off secretly for cleaning. I dreaded the times when they were worn out and he had to buy new ones. Shopping he hated; throughout life, since he had broken his instep while working on the railway, he had to wear much the same kind of boots which he got from a shop called Trueform; it terrified me that the number might one day be discontinued. Other shopping he had not to worry about, for I could get his clothes, his jerseys and his shirts.

In the St Marychurch flat, where he was lucky to have a screened-off basin with hot and cold running water, he could bathe his eyes more often in water as hot as it could be borne. I have not yet mentioned one of the most complicated domestic matters, Sean's bath. It was a ritualistic exercise, especially notice-able after we had reached Torquay. In the winter his shirt, pants and socks were draped over a radiator to be fully aired. The towel, too, was hung over a radiator in the bathroom. Sean would spend a long time in the bath, and unless under great stress I would never be out of the flat; latterly because I was worried about his health, but in the early days because when he had finished and dried himself on the warm towel he would call me to carry in the shirt, all aired, for him to slip his arms into, and then to hand him the pants and the socks. Normally he planned to have his bath in the afternoon before his rest; I would have liked a pound for every repetition of 'Thank God that's over until the next time.' This performance happened about twice a week.

II

Slowly we accustomed ourselves to the flat. Like any move, and especially one from a fairly large house, it did take time. Shivaun, starting as a weekly boarder at Dartington, caught the bus to Totnes on Monday mornings; customarily I went on Fridays in the old Ford to collect her. Breon and Niall had a large room at the back of the flat, though Niall at first was seldom there as he was in the Army and later at the London School of Economics. Breon, completing three years at the London art school for which he had received a grant, was sharing a flat in Abbey Gardens with another boy from Dartington.

Sean had got down to work without delay. He had completed a play called *The Bishop's Bonfire* and was ending the sixth and last volume of his autobiography, *Sunset and Evening Star*. He chose such good titles for his books; it was great fun when the time came to decide. He would put down three or four titles that he thought likely, and go over and over them until he settled on the one he preferred. *Sunset and Evening Star*, published in 1954, had splendid notices. Almost everyone praised the last paragraph:

> Even here, even now, when the sun had set and the evening star was chastely touching the bosom of the night, there were things to say, things to do. A drink first! What would he drink to – the past, the present, the future? To all of them! He would drink to the life that embraced the three of them! Here, with whitened hair, desires failing, strength ebbing out of him, with the sun gone down, and with only the serenity and the calm warning of the evening star left to him, he drank to Life, to all it had been, to what it was, to what it would be. Hurrah!

Sean was happy with letters from George Jean Nathan, and from Hugh MacDiarmid to whom the book was dedicated in these words: 'To my dear Friend Hugh MacDiarmid, Alba's Poet and one of Alba's first men.' Nathan wrote from the Royalton Hotel, New York:

My very dear Sean,
Sunset and Evening Star, which arrived a few days ago, adds to
your lustre. I have read it with unceasing admiration and
delight. The autobiography in toto is surely a master-work of
our times and is scarcely approached in its kind by any other
work of this century in the English language.
God bless you –

GEORGE

MacDiarmid's letter was from Brownsbank, by Biggar, Lanark-
shire:

Dear Sean,
How can I thank you for the dedication of *Sunset and Evening
Star* – and for all you said in it about me, and for the copy of
the book itself with your holograph on the flyleaf? I am
immensely proud of it – and a little ashamed, because I do not
really deserve it.
Save in one respect. My regard for you. I know no other man
I feel so close to. There is scarcely anything you say in the book
that is not just my own opinion and in my own spirit too – if
only I'd had anything like your genius of expression. I've seen
The Times Literary Supplement review and *The New Statesman* –
and your brief letter in reply to the latter. These homunculi
are multiplying and practically monopolise the literary field
now in all the so-called 'free nations of the West'. I think we
are bound to go right down. You are the only survivor now in
English Literature of a breed that produced many great figures
in the past – but yields hardly the veriest midget of a throw-
back now. . . .
I have read and re-read with immense appreciation, much
laughter and pride, and I will often turn to it again when I feel
in need of reassurance that our portion of the human race once
produced a real man or two, and the English language can still
even in these diminished and dubious days furnish a medium
for passionate and worthwhile expression.

Ever yours, CHRIS

Those were letters my mother would not have understood.
During our last period in Totnes she had grown steadily more
difficult: in any new lodging she raised some fault or other with

the landlady. Fortunately for everyone, she did have rooms in Paignton where she stayed through the weeks of our move. Her health – though there was no serious trouble – was not good, and she was in and out of hospitals and nursing-homes. I should have felt sympathetic; but I just could not, for I never knew whether she was genuinely ill or simply imagining she was. When out with her she exasperated me because she would walk much slower than she needed; I developed a horrible sense that I wanted to push her; she could get along far quicker, I knew, because if you saw her out on her own, unaware that she was noticed, she would be walking at a normal pace. Occasionally I would try taking her to a cinema; but there she would move her seat several times, to the annoyance of everyone near us. Worried about being horrible to her, I would resolve to be patient next time. Now we were in Torquay she soon discovered lodgings quite close. The relationship was the more awkward because she had no affinity whatever with Sean or, after our marriage, any interest in his work. *Juno* and *The Plough* were the only plays she would tolerate. As much of the Irish Press also criticised Sean, she would put in, 'It's not only me – look what other people are saying.' There was no possible point of contact and she could not think in modern terms. I suppose her drinking began because she was lonely; the habit, which nowadays would be treated as an illness, increased as she got older. It was in secret; such solitary drinkers as these – who worry about making friends – do not go to a pub in the ordinary fashion. It was embarrassing to deal with her in her various rooms; yet somehow, when she was not drinking and for weeks on end chose an entirely religious slant, this was equally hard to accept.

III

On the publication of *The Bishop's Bonfire* early in 1955, Cyril Cusack wanted to stage the play in Dublin. He visited us, excitedly, in Torquay where he and Sean, who saw things in the same way, agreed to ask Tyrone Guthrie to direct. It is a powerful piece. I know what prompted Sean to create in it the part of the girl, Foorawn: he remembered a young Irish girl who wrote long letters to him over the years in Totnes, telling him that she had taken a vow of chastity and therefore could never marry. Her photograph proved her to be good-looking; her letters made it obvious that, though she longed to be married, she dared not because of the vow. Sean says of Foorawn, 'She tries to keep her eyes turned modestly towards the ground, but doesn't always succeed, for her years are few and her heart is young and yearning.' The priest in the *Bonfire*, Father Boheroe ('a man to the world as well as a man of God') showed how forward-looking many of his type had become. In a sense, Sean was foretelling quietly much that has now happened: Catholicism in most matters is more broad-minded.

The play was to be acted at the Gaiety Theatre, Dublin, at the end of February 1955. Sean would not go; indeed, none of us would have gone if Sidney Bernstein had not telephoned one evening asking about the *Bonfire* and inviting me to be his guest, with Shivaun. He booked rooms for us at the Shelbourne where he and his second wife Sandra were also staying. I enjoyed watching Guthrie at rehearsals; it was an imaginative production, cast extremely well with such artists as Seamus Kavanagh ('the Prodical'), Cyril Cusack himself as the Codger, and his wife Maureen who was exceptional in the difficult part of Keelin. Tyrone Guthrie wrote to Sean on 26 February:

> Cyril and I are differing – but very amiably, no squeals or pouts – about the style of the production. He wants it quieter, more sentimental and Tchehovy than I do. He thinks I'm making it both too farcical and too melodramatic. Well, God knows he may be right, but I'm sticking to my guns. I think the theatre in general, and your work in particular, must be highly-coloured, larger, louder, funnier, more rumbunctious and disastrous than 'Life'. . . . I don't think there'll be much fuss – a hiss or two and maybe a flutter of scurrility in *The Standard*, perhaps even a vote of protest from the Sewage Disposal Committee of the Letterkenny Urban Council.

At the dress rehearsal, I recall, Sidney was particularly nervous over the shooting scene in the third Act when Foorawn is killed.

The play has, of course, its melodramatic side; I am certain it was influenced by Sean's sustained admiration for the nineteenth-century dramatist, Dion Boucicault.

Before the première Sidney and Sandra took Shivaun, who was only fifteen, to the shop of Sybil Connolly, noted for her exquisite dresses and her use of peasant materials, pure Irish linen, lace and flannel; they bought for Shivaun a lovely full red flannel skirt, a white blouse of Irish embroidery, and a large plain black woollen shawl. So to the first night which was almost electrically exciting. Shivaun and I got to our seats in the dress-circle, accompanied by a young Irishwoman, Dr Madeline Solomon, who lived in Torquay and who chanced to be in Dublin. The theatre, practically deserted when we arrived, soon began to fill, and before the circle was crowded I saw Gabriel Fallon come in; clearly knowing that we would be there, he walked over to us and shook hands. I introduced Shivaun to him. At this distance I really cannot remember what I said, but he reported in his book, *Sean O'Casey the Man I Knew*, that I asked him to 'be kind to the old man', and this is something that for the life of me I cannot imagine: I never thought of Sean, or referred to him, as an old man. Possibly I said, 'Be fair to the play': naturally I would have been excited and tense, and thinking far more of Sean's work than of how Gabriel Fallon might receive it. During the first interval we were left on our own. Madeline had gone off to look for friends in the house: Gaby we did not see at all, and anyway as a critic he could hardly have discussed the piece with us. Sidney and Sandra were down in the stalls. It was then that Lennox Robinson came over, taking us courteously to a table and getting drinks: he saved our lives, for first nights are agonising to anybody concerned with the author. Again, during the next interval, Lennox looked after us. At the end there was a mixed reception; sustained applause and some boos. A few people close to us were shouting in Gaelic, and I wondered whether they were condemning Sean to the depths of hell. Seeing how upset I was, my neighbour whispered, 'They are just saying what a marvellous man Sean O'Casey is!' Cyril Cusack, small in stature but brave in bearing, came downstage to defend the play in Gaelic. We heard that students who could not get in had lit a bonfire outside, not a comment on Sean and his work, merely youth protesting because it could not get into the theatre. A Catholic organisation, the Legion of Mary, made its own protest.

We were asked to go round to see the cast and stayed fairly late. Back in the Shelbourne, we found a note from Tyrone Guthrie, asking us if we would join them at supper in their room; it was the first time I had met Judith Guthrie except for a how-d'ye-do at rehearsal. They both sympathised wonderfully with my own way of thinking: it was the right sort of relaxed time after the ordeal at the Gaiety. As soon as we were in our own room, Shivaun fell asleep; Tyrone suggested I came back to talk, so we went on into the early hours of the morning.

Criticisms, on the whole, were not good. When we entered the hotel lounge next morning, with Sidney and Sandra, who were bound for London, the English critics were sitting about, waiting to leave for their flight home: it was a curiously frigid, detached atmosphere. After all, there must be an odd feeling on both sides when a critic has not liked a play and the dramatist's wife is introduced to him. On the previous night, during the performance, I could not help looking carefully at Gabriel Fallon: it was at the time when he and Sean had quarrelled. During the 'jeep' scene, which went over splendidly with the entire audience ('An' what would the ordinary cars and pedestrians do, an' the roads buzzin' with jeeps?'), he was doubled up with laughter. Next day, in his review, he said nothing of the humour in the second Act; indeed, he criticised the play rather badly. I did telephone him to say that there was no reason why he should have liked the *Bonfire* – his criticism was his own affair – but I believed he should have made it clear at least that part of the night's humour had appealed to him.

Notices had little effect on the bookings, though Maureen Cusack said in an amusing letter to Sean:

> I hope you will be able to come over; the weather for the last few days has been lovely and the sun is quite warm. . . . We are doing a steady business with the play but it would give it a real gee-up if you came over. The audience love it but the Irish

notices and the *Standard* advance campaign have had an effect.
One lady, a Civil Service spinster, was there and she was
regaling her friends at coffee the following morning: 'Oh, I
couldn't stop laughing. I knew I shouldn't but I couldn't help
it, but of course I didn't applaud at the end.'

With the house booked solidly, the run had to be extended for a
fortnight; audiences seemed to enjoy it. I went to several performances and found that every time the playing had improved;
the more responsive the house, the better the cast. At this period
Mrs Pandit Nehru, with whom Sean had corresponded, was at
our hotel for a few nights. She applied for tickets, but in a house
so crowded she could have them only in the back row of the
circle. The manager asked us to meet her in his room during an
interval. A gracious person who appreciated Sean's work, and
seemed to have read it all, she was unhappy to be sitting so far
back, for she could not catch everything clearly and the Irish
accent made things worse; she said she would buy the text. At
length the play, 'the sad play within the tune of a polka', as Sean
called it, had its run extended by a fortnight. Though there was
one offer to transfer it to London, the cast – which was not all
that well paid in Dublin, certainly not enough – asked for larger
salaries, and the plan lapsed. Further, Seamus Kavanagh, who had
a regular Dublin radio programme, did not want to go over; and
so excellent an actor might have been hard to replace. This need
to recast, with one thing and another, killed the project; a pity,
for Guthrie was anxious for a transfer, and so of course was Sean.
Happy to hear of the houses and the merit of the production, he
saw few of the notices at the time; he had reached a stage when
he hardly read criticisms at all.

IV

Niall, having finished military service, had entered the London
School of Economics in the University of London. Off duty he
was extremely fond of music. When, as a senior at Dartington, he
got home late from activities at school, he would spend hours with

his record-player, It is hard for me now to hear Isobel Baillie in the *Messiah*, or singing one of her records, or Dennis Brain playing Mozart's Horn Concerto, without visualising Niall as he listened intently. Classical music aside, he liked traditional jazz: King Oliver, Louis Armstrong, Bessie Smith, Ma Rainey, Jelly Roll Morton, and the rest. When he was in the Army and knew I might be going to London, he would list several rare titles and I would go to an obscure place in Charing Cross Road where three doped-looking men, up flights and flights of stairs, would sell me the records and, I felt, study me curiously, wondering all the while what in the name of God I was doing to be collecting the things. Niall, at school, had joined a band called the Strumpers in which he played the trombone. He used to drive us all mad while prac-tising this instrument; it really does make a hell of a noise. When we had moved to St Marychurch, our landlord came tearing up the steps and rang the bell so loudly that I was convinced it must be either a burst tank or a fire. I rushed to the door. Mr Norman, generally a very quiet man, screamed at me, 'I beg of your son to stop that noise. It has got right inside my brain.' After this Niall would stuff a great wad of rags into the mouth of the instrument.

Just now the American company, N.C.B. Television, wanted to film Sean and his family in his home: earlier they had done Picasso and some others. Yes, said Sean. Bob Ginna and Bob Graff were to produce it, but this time Wolfgang Suschitzky, and not Gjon Mili, would do the camera work. For Sean to be with Bob Ginna and Bob Graff was an old friends' reunion. When they came to talk over the film they proposed to do the whole thing in a large hotel-room to save the disruption of our flat. Sean knew, and so did I, that we would not feel at all easy or natural in these cir-cumstances; so we kept to the flat though neither of us pictured the upheaval it must mean. For a week the place became a film unit's delight. We did leave Sean's divan in his room so that he could get some rest; the other rooms appeared to be full of equip-ment, electric flex trailing about the floors. It was heavy stuff, and I wondered whether it might fall into the flat below. Fortunately, it did not.

I had myself to get a room at a hotel, the Links, quite close to us in St Marychurch, where so many of our American friends would put up for a night. Sean entered marvellously into the whole thing. As soon as he had agreed, he was unsparing in his concentration upon every detail, studying questions to be put to him and running through them with Bob Ginna, his interlocutor. Anything that involved going outside the flat he would study earnestly on the night before, knowing that when the film was being shot he would have to contend with his eyesight as well as his nerves. He was in full accord with Bob, who had a quick sense of humour, a lovely boyish personality, and an affection for Ireland. In fact, we were fortunate with all who worked on the film: Bob Graff, naturally, and Suschitzky, whom we had not met but who proved to be a magnificent camera-man, gentle and considerate with Sean. Every day at lunch there would be an extra break so that Sean might lie down for his rest. Before filming began, as it was at the end of the season, and the flowers we had in boxes on the steps up to the flat were looking pretty sad, a nurseryman we knew and had bought plants from, Geoffrey Dobbie, arrived to fill the boxes with petunias, to bring some splendid fuchsias in tubs, and, in a word, to transform the entire steps. Geoffrey Dobbie owned a fine nursery in Babbacombe. When I called on him for plants on our move from Tingrith, we were chatting, as I would do with everyone, and he said to me, 'So you've taken a flat in Marychurch. That's where that Sean O'Casey man has gone. I should think he was difficult. Sounds to me terrifically argumentative. A bit like Shaw.' I said: 'Well . . . he's not bad. I happen to be his wife.' Immediately Geoffrey started to apologise; but both of us thought it very funny. When he delivered his plants, he and Sean got talking and a friendship grew. A Norfolk man and a plant-lover, he looked after our small garden entirely.

Those petunias would give Sean his opening speech in the film dialogue. He was in fine spirits; the rest of the family, though serving only as a background, were less professional; any notion of acting I ever had flew out of the window. Besides being nervous, I was busy looking after Sean. We had one family scene with him, round the tea-table in the dining-room; Breon and Niall appeared

from London for this and Shivaun from school. Though given a
bare dialogue outline, we lacked Sean's wisdom and had rehearsed
nothing beforehand. Somehow we managed to carry on, getting the
tea, putting it on the table, and sitting down as if we were
thoroughly enjoying it. Incorrigibly, Sean began to sing; the
director was gesticulating to us to try to break the song up so that
we could get on with our conversation, and the trickiest part was
not to laugh. Listening to ourselves later was curious; Breon
and Niall's voices sounded so loud and deep. It is strange to hear
one's voice on tape for the first time; though I cannot say we were
good in the film, I did think it was all most comic.

For Sean it was a happy business because he could spend the
evenings with Bob and the others, and when in form he was an
unmatched story-teller. Our feelings were mixed when the film
was done, everything packed up, and the flat in order again.
Though glad to have our home to ourselves, we could not help
feeling wistful that our friends had left us. Bob Ginna had wondered during the shooting whether Mr and Mrs Greenwood, who
lived below us, might not be inconvenienced by all the equipment
in the drive-way; he went to apologise and to ask also if half an
hour of the film could be taken in their part of the garden. They
said charmingly that they were enjoying the occasion. 'But', Mr
Greenwood added, 'who *is* this Sean O'Casey, and what do they
want to film him for?' I am glad to say that curiosity made him
get Sean's autobiographies from the library and read them.

Again Sean turned to work. He was receiving a vast amount of
correspondence from students; several of the letters he answered,
and though I thought he wrote too many, I could understand that
it was his longing for an audience that kept him at it. We heard
that *Red Roses for Me* would go on in New York during December
1955, with Eddie Marshall as Brennan o' the Moor. He crossed
from New York to spend a day with Sean and to discover how
the part ought to be played. Sean took him right through it. I
believe that Eddie in performance was admirable.

v

I had started to take evening classes in French. One evening I had
been out to a class; on returning, and coming up the steps, I heard
groans and almost a scream: it occurred to me that Sean must be
listening to a thriller. But when I got inside I found him in agony:
the doctor opposite us was out so I telephoned Dr Maurice Lees,
who responded at once, gave Sean a drug to stop the pain, and
immediately ordered him to hospital: it was a stone in the kidney,
and after a week he was operated on for this. It developed into a
long illness, some twelve weeks; when the operation was over he
had severe bronchitis as well as further complications: it astonished me that so frail a man could stand up to it as he did. Breon,
who had come to the flat, would drive me to the hospital twice a
day, at eleven and six, along dangerous, icy roads.

Sean received many flowers and telegrams after the news of his
illness had been broadcast; and one evening, after asking me into
her room and telling me how Sean was progressing, the good-
looking Sister said, as Mr Greenwood had done, 'Who *is* your
husband, Mrs O'Casey? So many telegrams and flowers. Is he
famous?' I explained that he was a dramatist much loved in
America from which most of the flowers had come, though there
were numerous messages as well from England and Ireland. Sister
made friends with Sean and would talk to him when she had an
opportunity. The Press could be a nuisance. After the operation,
while Sean was dangerously ill, nobody was permitted to talk to
him; I would just look into his room. But one journalist contrived somehow to enter the hospital, and a nurse discovered him
attempting to get Sean to speak; furious, she turned the man
away, but when he called on me afterwards at the flat he insisted
that somehow he had to have a story on returning to town. I
talked to him; not that there was anything to say beyond the customary phrase that Sean was as well as one could expect. None of
the more responsible newspapers would have bothered me at such
a time as this.

During that period of three months nobody went to Sean

except the children and myself. Niall would travel from London at the week-end, and Shivaun from school. As he got better I would bring his letters to him day by day and read them to keep up his interest. Visiting anybody in hospital restricts one's talk; the nearer you are to a person, the less you have to say: you feel entirely unnatural. The children did too, though Shivaun fared best. Dr Doran, who was Sean's doctor now, a tall, handsome Irishman, later one of our dearest friends, helped Sean by seeing that he was forgiven if his bed was untidy, with letters and papers scattered round it. He had a private room which helped; even so, hospitals are the devil for straightening up your bed. As soon as Sean improved, he longed to be home in his room, and on the day we were genuinely excited: always thin, he now resembled a child, he looked so small and frail in his greatcoat. A setback after returning obliged him to remain in bed some time; he never seemed to be without discomfort or pain. Every morning he had to pour spirits of wine into his ear to prevent a polypus from forming; though I never understood entirely, I presumed that, while too near the brain for an operation, the polypus could be controlled by a slight daily burning. Then Dr Doran, whom he would see twice a week, either at the surgery or at home, decided to treat the ear now and again himself, and Sean had never before known such ease; Doran had been trained as an ear specialist, and it was lucky that Sean met him as a general practitioner specialising in the ear and throat.

While Sean was away in hospital, we felt so unsettled between visits that Breon resolved to decorate the kitchen. We would have liked to do Sean's room which was still in that peculiar pale brown, but it needed too much work and would have taken so long that we delayed beginning it in case Sean returned in the middle. With his eagerness to get back, it was not past reason that he would have used his persuasive gift to leave hospital before he was really fit. Until his death his room retained that pale buff wallpaper. We did brighten it immensely with curtains and colour, and its feeling was always remarkable.

VI

As at Totnes, Sean in Torquay went visiting hardly at all in spite of his friendship with Dr and Mrs Doran, Dr Lees, and Dr Madeline and Louis Solomon. This was the stage when everybody called on Sean. Late in life, after his illness, he dreaded meeting even the local people he liked; some were hurt, but others sensibly understood. When out for a walk in those days, we would first drive for a few miles, either to the front at Torquay or to some neighbouring gardens, and begin our walk there: we might stay out for two hours on a clear summer evening. Sean and I then were closer to each other than in the flat: it was as if, full of love for each other, we were reviving walks before our marriage. Sometimes, when Breon and Shivaun were at home, they would go out with Sean as well.

If Tom Curtiss and Dickie Watts (often together), or Brooks Atkinson (always on his own) happened to be in London, as they were, on an average, twice a year, they would run down to see Sean; often, as they were theatre critics and this was their freest time, it would be on a Sunday: arriving for lunch they would stay until late in the evening. Tom was drama critic for the *Herald-Tribune* in Paris, Brooks for the *New York Times* in New York, and Dickie for the *Herald-Tribune* there. Brooks, who loved the country, its trees and birds, invariably hoped to see trees and shrubs unfamiliar to him in America, or to hear fresh bird-song: much of his later correspondence with Sean was about birds and trees. Tom Curtiss has written in a letter to me:

> O'Casey and I corresponded regularly after our first meeting, but I did not see him again until 1950. I settled in Paris and frequently came to London to cover the theatre; on each visit I would entrain for Devon to spend an evening with the O'Caseys. Each of these sessions, which continued until the year of his death, 1964, was a rich experience, for though O'Casey lived far from the bustle of great cities, he was ever in tune with what was happening in the world. He lived long, but he never grew old in spirit. He wrote great tragedies, but

he believed that there was hope for man. He was opposed to the dead-end pessimism of Beckett and his imitators. 'After all', he said once, 'Hitler seemed to have the knife at the throat of civilisation, but he didn't win – though it cost the lives of millions. There are terrible things in life, but I do not think life itself is terrible.' One wants to believe that he was right, and his great courage in the face of terrible personal tragedies is an example and an inspiration.

Barrows Dunham, author of *Man Against Myth* and many works of philosophy, to whom Sean wrote the letter I quoted earlier, had first visited us in Totnes with his son; now, with his wife Alice, he saw us in St Marychurch. He was one of the courageous few who, during the McCarthy period, acted as a so-called 'unfriendly' witness before the Un-American Activities Committee. 'Friendly' witnesses would co-operate or inform; 'unfriendly' ones, such as Dunham – a man who had, like Sean, a grand integrity – would give only their names and answer nothing else, however fierce the questioning: it was an amazing test of will, faith and endurance.

David Krause, as a young man, called on us often; after war service he studied Irish dramatists and literature at his American university under Dave Green, and later he would begin to collect Sean's letters for publication. I remember how he, Sean and myself walked on Babbacombe Downs, Dave in his warm, generous way, talking excitedly about Sean's work and what it had meant to him. He slept near us where Clare, our help, had a small house, but he would spend the days at the flat and we looked upon him as one of the family. Ron Ayling, too, then a student at the University of Leeds, asked to come. Ron, who had lost his parents in the Blitz when he and his sister were in an air-raid shelter, had been cared for by his uncle and aunt, working-class people, and this meant that he had had to study hard for his place in college. The story, and his love of literature, appealed to Sean. Ron came to St Marychurch frequently while in England: when he taught at Rhodes University in South Africa, he carried on his friendship by letter, with visits when he was on annual leave.

Paul Shyre had written to ask if he could direct *Purple Dust* off-Broadway. In 1956, after an applauded production had opened its long run, Sean began to make more money; the regular income from *Purple Dust* helped us to buy new carpets and curtains, and in general to do up the flat, Sean's room in particular. I planned to get a new carpet for it, but when the patterns appeared for him to choose he rebelled: 'I can't possibly have the men coming to lay the carpet. My entire work would be disrupted and the place in terrible order. I would far sooner not have the carpet.' I wanted it very much, for I knew that with it the room would look and feel warmer. Thereupon, asking the men to do the measurements, I got them to make the carpet up so that Breon and I might lay it ourselves. It was an exhausting experience. Sean left us after lunch to have his rest in my room. First we removed the old mats, then put one lot of furniture aside, took the great, heavy new piece of carpet, and stretched it out on the other side of the room where it proved to be far too large. We had to fold it in at the edges, and it was a miracle that we did not fold ourselves in as well. Next we had to take out the books, lift the cases, and put back the books again – all at such a speed that we were practically tired out. Breon said reasonably, 'We can't do it. We must go far more slowly.' By the time Sean had got up, refreshed, we were hot and fit to drop, and I had practically nothing on but an overall: we had worked, without ceasing, for two hours. Sean just looked and said, 'When on earth can I get back to my room again?' At this I blew my top. 'You've only been out of the room for a few hours,' I told him, 'and you'll have to wait until the evening. It's going to look very good when it's done, Sean, and it will be much warmer for you.' I felt inclined to weep; Breon walked off silently; Sean vanished to put on the kettle for tea. Relenting, he said later that he was sorry; he saw how we had worked and told us that we should not have done it, for the room was perfectly all right as it was: 'I hate to be out of it.' After tea we set to once more, Sean helping this time by replacing the books. By the evening, thanks to Breon, it had been done. The carpet was to have been cut to fit round the skirtings of the room, and to be resewn; but the men never had a chance to come to do this, and for the whole of the time Sean was there, that carpet was left folded in at its edges.

Shivaun had resolved suddenly that she did not want to stay any longer at Dartington, but to go to the Central School of Arts and Crafts in Holborn to study design. I was dumbfounded. After all, we had chosen Torquay so that we might be close to Dartington where at first Shivaun had refused to board weekly, and I had to take her in every day; she had become a weekly boarder, and now she planned to leave altogether. Her headmaster, Mr Curry, who should have had a term's notice, was understanding; after I had taken some of her drawings to London and interviewed the Head of the Central School, she was accepted – a year before the usual age of eighteen. She got a room in Abbey Gardens with a Dartington parent who took in students, opposite the flat that Niall shared with a friend. Breon was in Torquay now, having a room he could use by day as a studio.

Sean's love for his children was intense. He never forgot them; though money was short he managed to send them what he could afford. His telephone talks with Shivaun were amusing. He would go on and on until I had to whisper at last, 'You really must ring off, Sean; it's costing a lot of money.' Then I usually added, 'Let me talk to her a bit,' and I would hardly have time to say a word before he cut in, 'You're talking enough, goodness knows. Think of the telephone bill.' Though we would agree regularly to make the next chat brief, this never seemed to happen.

Niall, up at London University, was always concerned with politics. When he and many of his friends were going to march in a students' protest against the Government's Suez policy in 1956, Shivaun was anxious to go herself. Niall, sure that there would be violence, was troubled about this but she went all the same. Towards the end, when things had grown complicated, Niall did force her to leave the march. One of his closest University friends was an Indian who, when the police came to remove him, was sitting in a meditative position, cross-legged, on a wall. 'You can't

touch me,' he exclaimed, 'I'm a Buddhist.' Somehow the word had
a magical effect, for they turned and left him.

Now the Russians suppressed the 1956 rising in Hungary. Once
or twice, Niall, deeply worried, drove from London in the old
Ford van, which the children shared, to spend the evening arguing
with Sean, and to return in the early hours to join his University
class in time. Sean insisted that the Russians were in the right.
Among his papers I found a letter that explains a little of the
argument. Headed in Sean's hand, 'Last letter written by Niall',
it runs:

> Dear Daddy,
> I hope you find the enclosed press cuttings of interest from
> today's *Daily Worker*. The Old Guard is having quite a tough
> time at present. Resignations on the staff include Malcolm
> MacEwan, 'Gabriel', Philip Bolsover; on the verge are many
> others, including Sheila Lynd. The attitude of the executive
> over Hungary on many matters has been quite untenable. One
> can imagine the mistakes that have been made in Eastern Europe
> as being the same here, as if the Soviet Union had liberated us
> from Hitler, and had set up J. R. Campbell and his gang as
> Government. This isn't Communism at all. The double-think
> reminds me of Captain Waterhouse.
>
> Love,
> NIALL

Sean wrote underneath this:

> A very forthright letter. He hasn't hesitated to say what he
> thought. He was really very distressed about the Soviet inter-
> ference in Hungary. He hides the distress he felt under the
> careless scorn of his letter-wording. Two weeks later he hurried
> down from London to talk with me about it, for he knew that
> whatever I might say would be what I believed. We talked long
> and seriously and earnestly, but could not come to an agree-
> ment. We had to agree to differ.

Niall had had little experience of the cruelties of strife, for
he was but six when the Second World War was alive, whilst
I over a long life had known the Boer War, the First World
War, the Easter Rising in Ireland, the Black and Tan terror,
the Irish Civil War, and then the terrible strife let loose by

Hitler, not forgetting the Western refusal to open its eyes to what Hitler did in Spain, leading to the first growth of his gigantic egomania that finally slew five million Jews, and sent to the grave many millions of old and young in almost every country in Europe, in a vast and deep attempt to make himself the Lord of Creation and stamp out the power of Socialism, fully grown in the USSR and bud-ripening in many other countries.

He did not, and could not, see the implications of having such proud and ignorant and narrow-minded 'gets' as Mind-szenty, head of Hungary, Prince Primate; and Niall had never read what the Prince Primate had been in Hungary or what he could be as dictator of the country. But his hot and honest opinions, put out without hesitation, were at any rate a tribute to his home where, at all times, in every circumstance, free thought was the genre of our family life.

Though disagreeing, we ended by putting my arms around him and looking at his face which was full of eagerness and honesty and sorrow. Little did I think that when he returned to London to come down again in the second week of December, within a month this gallant and darling boy would be dead.

I could realise why I did not understand Sean's view of the Hungarian situation; any type of cruelty would distress me, even if it were supposedly in the right cause. I remember that when Niall, so anxious to settle his own mind one way or the other, drove from London to talk over the matter with Sean we would sit absolutely silent round the table at meals. In considering such problems as these, Sean, in spite of his normally gentle nature, grew strangely stubborn and hard. He would hold that anybody against the leaders, anybody who had blacklegged or informed, should be shot; he believed with sincerity that it was the only course to take. Though he had always been like this in political questions, I was still surprised that, hating cruelty and oppression as he did, he seemed completely to accept the need for those harsh measures in Hungary.

He was not merely a theorist; though frail, he was genuinely brave. I know that, if the hour had come, he would have faced everything for his beliefs. In the Irish Troubles he had been put up against a wall and just escaped with his life. In a minor domestic way, when I was frightened of tramps (to whom I gave money), it would be Sean, frail as he was, who would go to the door, ready to fight for me.

VIII

The Christmas of 1956 was the most awful I had ever spent. Niall, arriving for his holiday, seemed to be ill: I imagined he had been overdoing it, coming down as he had to see Sean over these political worries. Also he had been to a number of parties: the band in which he played the trombone had been round quite a bit during the term. After seeing him, Dr Doran said he would like to bring a specialist that evening and told Niall to remain at home and to keep quiet. Niall played his records; then, as he felt dog-tired, he got to bed. The specialist and Dr Doran were with him for a long while. When they came out to me I was alone in the front room. Sean was in his room, working. The flat was des-perately still. It was the specialist who said, as if he must get the awful sentence over, 'Niall has not got long to live. He has leukaemia.' I managed to say: 'Have you told Sean?'

'No.'

'Then, please, I think I had better tell him. . . . Have you told Niall himself?'

Dr Doran said he had, and I felt utterly shocked, a dreadful feeling that returns to me sometimes when I think about Niall: I felt cold, ice all over. I just left the doctors and went to Niall. There was little to say. I had not felt the full impact yet, and I could not even begin to imagine life without Niall. He was part of the family. He sat there at the side of the bed, looking so young and handsome – life, I thought, must be before him. In a way he tried to help me. He actually said, 'Poor you!' I told Sean, but what do details matter? Niall had to bear the full dreadful sentence.

It was decided to take him to Exeter Hospital that night. I was with him in the ambulance. Though the doctors did not believe that this was necessary, and said I could follow next day, I could not think of Niall in those long, dark lanes between Torquay and Exeter with the terrible verdict on his mind. I was determined to go with him and see him into hospital, and a room was booked for me in a hotel. The journey was dark and gloomy, but at least Niall had me to talk to; mostly, of course, our conversation was hopeful and we told each other that treatment might save everything. I still could not begin to understand the word death in association with Niall.

When we arrived at the hospital, where Dr Haddon was in charge, it was late, one o'clock, and Niall was put to bed in a small ward of about eight people: the doctor told me I could return about noon. After I saw Niall then he was given some treatment and appeared to be ill; his throat hurt him a good deal. Realising I could visit him several times a day, I knew it was better for me to remain in Exeter, so I telephoned Sean, and we agreed that he and Breon should come up to join me. Everything, the usual turkey, the usual Christmas fare, had been ready for us in the flat; as it was we settled into the hotel in Exeter. Daily, Niall grew worse. On Christmas Eve he was in great pain with his throat and could not swallow. On Christmas Day Sean and Breon went to see him, but Niall could not say much. We gave our presents to each other, Niall's a watch which he put on. He was a little livelier with Shivaun, joking as they had always done together, and she told him she had been accepted at the Royal Academy of Dramatic Art: he had helped her by hearing the piece she was to do at the audition. It was tragic that this was the last time she saw her brother. It was also the last time that Sean would see his son.

The rest of the family returned to the hotel. I stayed at the hospital while Niall had his lunch. Doctors and nurses were having Christmas drinks in a room close by, and a nurse came to ask me if I would join them. I did not feel like it, but Niall wanted me to go; his ward had three or more very sick people in it. The lunch, turkey and the customary Christmas food, was brought in. Niall was sitting up; he had always loved food, and it was horrid now to see that he could not swallow.

Nurses had worked hard to decorate the hospital with Christmas trees and paper-chains; it looked very bright. There was, too, a parade in which the doctors wore fancy dress; patients who were well enough loved it as it went through the wards while carols were sung. Sean, Breon, Shivaun and I had our own meal quietly at the hotel, and Christmas Day was over. The nurse had told me that I could return later and stay with Niall. He had been put on his own now in a small private room where he had a dreadful night with a high temperature and chill. A kitchen was right opposite his room, and I was allowed to fetch ice cubes and to rub them on his head. He did not sleep; when he shivered I put more blankets over him; then he would get so hot that only a sheet was bearable, and he wanted ice in his mouth to suck, or ice rubbed on his head. It was good of the hospital people to let me stay; the nurses would not have had time to relieve the discomfort he was enduring.

My mother had been anxious for Niall to see a priest, and Sister asked me if I thought we should send for one. I explained to her that Niall had not been brought up as a Catholic; he was twenty years old and must decide himself whether he wanted a priest or not. Niall did not wish to see one, not from any antagonism towards the Catholic faith or any other; it was just something he did not want. But after my mother had got into a state and telephoned several times Niall asked if it would help me and appease her if he agreed to see the priest. He did not mind, he said. However, I felt that he was fighting his illness in his own way and that the answer must be No.

Dr Doran had been trying over Christmas to get in touch with Dr Bodley-Scott, who was considered to be the country's expert on leukaemia, and whom he knew. At last he managed it. Niall was accepted for St Bartholomew's Hospital, and we went to London by train on 27 December, travelling in a special carriage with a nurse in attendance. Niall, a trifle better, talked now and again; he was never gloomy, and if in despair at times it was in a slightly cynical way. The young and pretty nurse was looking forward to an evening in London; when she had seen Niall into hospital she would return next day to Exeter.

During our drive to Bart's from Paddington we passed the Polytechnic Cinema in Oxford Circus where an Italian film was advertised. 'You must go and see that, Eileen,' Niall said. 'It's very good.' I said, I think, that there were many other good films he would like to see, and he made no real answer. We both had hopes.

At Bart's that evening Dr Bodley-Scott had come especially to see Niall; Dr Doran had told him all about us. I said that, if it would help, Niall could have a private room, but Dr Bodley-Scott said he would prefer Niall to be in a ward with constant attention. So Niall was put in a bed beside Sister's desk, again in a ward where the patients were very ill: it was light and the beds were curtained. I got a room at the Strand Palace Hotel; Breon had come to join me in London, and Shivaun stayed down at the flat with Sean.

Next morning, when I saw Niall, he was a little better; hope might have returned to him. Nursing and treatment at Bart's were so fine, and he realised that every conceivable thing that could help him was at hand. The days passed. Breon stayed at Abbey Gardens in the flat he had lived in when at the Art School and where Niall had lived while at University. Every day I was allowed to be with Niall for a long time, and he could also see a few of his London friends. He was brighter and able to get out of bed to go to the bathroom; he liked one doctor who was young and who talked to him quite a lot about the possibility of getting better. I believe he felt once that he might live for a year or so, and that during that time research into the disease would have found a cure.

Really, Shivaun at Torquay had the hardest task of us all. Left to look after Sean, her fortitude was amazing. At least Breon and I were able to see Niall. But Shivaun had nothing to distract her from the tragedy; Sean was in great distress and she had a double problem.

The day before Niall died he felt much better. We were on our own. He had been through the heat-and-cold treatment, and his bed was curtained off. Blankets were put over him when he was cold; when he was hot he was in a bath of sweat and had to be sponged down. All the time he had tubes attached to him that transfused pints of blood. The nurses were splendid; they got tea early for him that day because he loved it and it was wonderful to be able to swallow again. He asked me to bring him fruit in the evening. I went to the hotel where Breon was to have dinner with me, but felt too uneasy to wait for the meal; as soon as I could I dashed off. Though it seemed foolish to us as it was the first evening when we could have relaxed a little, some premonition drove me on. The fruit Niall wanted we bought at a stall in the Strand; I think Breon got it for me. Then I jumped into a taxi and told the man to drive to Bart's as quickly as he could. I rushed up to the ward where Sister was surprised to see me back so soon. Niall was delighted; his throat was beginning to hurt and he seemed desperately anxious to taste the fruit. His nurse said that though it was possible for him to eat it he must not swallow the pips from the grapes and must just suck the orange and swallow none of the pith. It was a breathlessly quick task for me to skin the grapes and give them to Niall, also the orange and the peach. He had a savage desire to taste before his throat gave out; a savage desire to taste and live, to live – live – live. Suddenly he grew very quiet. Sensing danger, I asked Sister if I could telephone his brother as I really thought Niall was worse. 'No,' she said, 'the morning will be all right.' Then she looked at Niall and said, 'Yes. Telephone.' I did. Niall became delirious and excited. All the tubes were still attached to him. He looked strong and well; it was hard to hold him now when he wanted to get up and go places. He talked only in a gay mood. 'Let's go to America' (he knew *Purple Dust* was on there); or 'Let's get the Hillman' – we had just bought this new car – 'and go anywhere.' He imagined Shivaun was with us and getting a meal; he talked about jazz, and talked and talked and talked. He tried to get out of bed, the nurse and I holding him in. Breon arrived and Niall seemed more relaxed, lurching no longer. Suddenly he regained consciousness. He knew he was going to die, and quietly and sadly he said so. A nurse came and removed the tubes that were giving him blood. He received oxygen, and at intervals I was handed a mask to put over his mouth to help him breathe. I knew Breon was there, but in my mind now I see only Niall, Niall going from life. He said 'Goodbye.' I did kiss him, and from a corner of his eye a tear was trickling, the one sign of sorrow that his fight to live was over, at the age of twenty years.

Breon and I walked long into the night on the Embankment, saying little. I felt numb; I could not have left Niall for ever. We thought it better not to tell Sean and Shivaun until the morning but to let them have one more night in hope. Poor Shivaun had been magnificent; no matter how great the sorrow, it is easier to be taking an active part in it than to be many miles away, longing to see the person who is ill. Shivaun and Niall were very close. Now, while suffering so deeply, she would have to console Sean who must have been inconsolable.

At the hotel we went to our rooms to rest. After a bath I resolved to go back to the hospital to see Niall, to look at him. The Strand was fairly quiet; it was about seven in the morning, and the flower-shop at the corner was open. I went in, bought a large bunch of freesias, and took a taxi to the hospital where the Irish porter who knew me by now told me that my son was in the Chapel of Rest. I went in; Niall, laid in a coffin, looked very handsome and so young; his hair was thick and his hands looked so fine; he had just a slight mark on his forehead, like a big bruise. I laid my flowers beside his face; I was glad I had come, and I drank in every moment of that last glance.

We had to stay in London for the cremation a few days later; Breon helped with the formalities, the certificates, and the arrangement of the service. However, the hospital authorities asked me if they might have Niall's body for a day for research into the disease. As we felt that it would have been his wish, we agreed. The actual service was very simple. I had told nobody of Niall's death except my own friends, but somehow friends of his own age must have known of it; they must have been thinking about him when he was ill. That small chapel was crowded with young people; I suppose that another Dartington mother and myself were the only older people there. It was final now. I should never see or hear Niall again; he had died.

CHAPTER THIRTEEN

Mainly New York

WHEN I reached home with Breon, after Niall's cremation, I knew that in an effort to help her grief Shivaun had tidied every drawer, every shelf, every corner of the flat. It had been a drive to keep herself going; all was perfect, even my work-basket, with the smallest strand of cotton in place. It touched me deeply, more than anything she said, for I understood how completely she had sought to control her sorrow, so that she would not break down and find herself unable to help Sean. On my arrival she could give way to her feelings. Sean, almost numbed, went through entire weeks of misery; it was terrible to see him overwhelmed, engrossed in sorrow, and to hear him keening. It made it twice as hard for me, as well as for young people like Breon and Shivaun; we tried to hide our grief and to carry on almost relentlessly with the daily round. Once, when Sean was keening and upsetting me badly, I said to him, 'Sean, dearest, Breon and Shivaun have lost a brother as we have lost a son'; and he answered, 'I have tried, but I cannot stop grieving.' The tears would well into his eyes, and one could only caress him; nothing could take away such sorrow. After his death I discovered among his papers a diary he had written every day about Niall; it spoke, too, of all the other young people who had died of this same horror, leukaemia.

Presently I was alone with Sean. He continued to grieve, and I realised then that I was not too good myself. In the evenings I began to drink more; it was useless, and because Sean hated drinking anyway I was adding to his burden. Those three to four weeks were intensely difficult. Niall had been so brave over the loss of his life that, having seen his courage, I tried to be equally brave about losing him.

The days were bearable; one had plenty to do, and the mind could be distracted. But in the evenings, those long evenings of late January and early February, there would be a feeling of deep depression. On one fatal night Sean was keening softly in his room. After supper I tried to talk to him, but we seemed to have no way at all of helping each other. I kept taking an extra drink; it did not help. Then, suddenly, a wild impulse came over me to take all the sleeping-pills I had and to end it there and then. I had no thought of Sean; I was just utterly selfish and self-pitying. What happened after I had taken the pills I do not know. Sean, it seems, came to my room to talk, found me unconscious, and was terrified. Immediately he telephoned the doctor who drove over at once.

I suppose an ambulance arrived to hurry me to the nursing-home where the doctor did what he must to save me. When at length I revived, he said nothing but: 'Eileen, how could you do such a thing to Sean?' Not a word to me. How could I indeed? I thought. Thank God I am here alive! Sean, who had come to the nursing-home, had been nearly demented while he waited to hear if I had recovered.

Next morning the doctor said to me simply, 'You can go home, dear. Let us say no more about this. It is far best forgotten.' At noon I reached home. Between midnight, when they had taken me off, and my return at midday, the whole drama had happened. Nobody had seen me leave the flat or come back to it. Again Sean embraced me in deep emotion; not one word was said then, or ever after; we both knew it was essential to carry on living instead of indulging in selfish grief. Sean threw himself into his work; I went on with my everyday life, and we got over the time somehow, as one must.

II

Over in New York the off-Broadway production of *Purple Dust* was still running. At home Sean tried gallantly to immerse himself in his writing: his articles for Russia, answers to students' letters, and the group of essays that would be published one day in *Under a Colored Cap*: this contains the requiem, 'Under the Greenwood Tree', that he wrote after Niall's death. Paul Shyre, who had adapted *I Knock at the Door*, Sean's first volume of auto-biography, for a stage reading, flew over from America, an alert theatre man who was then on happy terms with Sean and who made an excellent thing of his adaptation and production.

Shivaun, in spite of a most promising report, had not settled at RADA and decided after a single term that this was enough. She happened to be at a St Patrick's Day party with some Irish players led by Jose MacAvin who used every year to take pro-ductions round the New York colleges; and Jose asked her if she would join them as an assistant stage manager. Being extremely restless and unhappy after Niall's death – for they had been much together in London and she missed him intensely – Shivaun decided to go with the players: a worry to me until I met them myself. After rehearsing for a few weeks in London, she went to Dublin, and on to America, where, in New York, she found many friends of Sean: Brooks Atkinson, who was charming to her; George Jean Nathan, not long before his death; and Eugene O'Neill's wife, Carlotta. Difficult though she was, Carlotta liked Shivaun greatly and gave her several photographs of Eugene and herself to bring back to us.

Though Sean, in spite of disliking casual visitors, would see many American students who came at this period, he could not be so gay and full of gusto as he was. Daily he grieved over Niall; often I would find him, broken, his head in his hands; one cannot measure sorrow. Extrovert though I am, I could not release my one grief; it was like a stone within me. My mother, too, was hard to bear: she could not forget that I had allowed Niall to die without a priest. His cremation had shocked her and also my Irish relatives who wrote accusing letters, saying that I had been wrong and wicked. Because they were sincere in their Catholic views, I did not resent this.

I would go to see Mother when Sean lay down in the afternoons. It was essential because now she was constantly drinking and apparently could not help it; after all, she was lonely, but Sean would never accept any excuse for drinking, a practice he hated. Mostly I tried to satisfy the landlady: Mother was fortunate to have a good woman, a Mrs Davies, to look after her. An old man named Charlie, a character who lived beside us in St Marychurch, had an ancient car for hire work, and I engaged him to take Mother out. He was a general help and messenger, a godsend to me and a lovable person whose wild yarning amused Sean. Thus he knew, he said, where treasure was hidden on the moor; he believed in pixies and the Little People; if he liked, any day he could have made enough money to be a millionaire, but he really didn't want to: some fabulous lord would leave him money in a will. In spite of his fairy-tales, he was invaluable. He would call for Mother whom he liked, and take her out in his car, and I could rely upon him to buy the drink and ration it: it was mostly brandy then. If needed, he would even sit and drink with her in a pub. He never lost his respect for her, treating her as she wished to be treated, as a lady. Several other old ladies he would drive round to do their shopping, or for pleasure; he spent hours in mending his battered car and patching its dilapidated upholstery. On the after-noons when I left Sean and raced off to see my mother, her talk would usually be about my wickedness with Niall. After this I would be fearful unless I got back to Sean to make his tea; his eyesight was so poor that it frightened me to think that he might scald himself with the kettle. On the way home in the car I would find myself crying and indulging in self-pity.

III

The Tóstal was an annual festival of plays and music held in Dublin during the spring. When its Council asked Sean to send a play for production in 1958, he let it have the work he had just completed, *The Drums of Father Ned; or, A Mickrocosm of Ireland*, a light-hearted and extremely funny comedy about another Tóstal, in the town of 'Doonavale':

This comedy's but an idle, laughing play
About the thing encumbering Ireland's way;
A flag shoved from a window, and a cry
To wake up drowsy girl and drowsier boy,
To snatch from Erin's back the sable shawl,
And clothe her as she was before her fall. . . .

Breon and I thought, when we read it, that it was the one play
Sean had written that was not in the least controversial, or out
against anything. After the Tóstal Council had accepted it, he
wrote (October 1957) to Brendan Smith, the Festival Director:

> Some time ago, Eileen (Mrs O'Casey) read *The Drums of Father
> Ned*, and, talking about it a little later on, said she didn't like
> the taking-of-the-money episode between Skerighan and Berna-
> dette. She thought that an Irish girl could hardly be so sophis-
> ticated (big word), so ready to seize a chance. Thinking it over,
> I think she is right. Irish girls (or Irishmen) aren't clever at
> taking advantage of a condition of things which would mean
> money if they were a bit more brassy. They find it hard to
> make a bargain – bar at cattle fairs where everyone is doing it.
> Alone, they are pretty hopeless, or dealing with one whom they
> know. They refuse what they are longing to take. Even the
> occasional lass on Leicester Square isn't in it with her other-
> race conspirators. We aren't good for standing up for our rights,
> unless they are political ones, and when dealing with these, too,
> we lose sense, and become frenzied.
>
> So I send you herewith the amended part of the play and shall
> be glad if you would give it to the Director chosen to act the
> play out on the stage.
>
> > With all good wishes,
> > SEAN O'CASEY

All well so far; but the Archbishop of Dublin would not have
the play as it was; he refused indeed to open the Festival with the
customary Votive Mass if Sean's work and a dramatised version of
Joyce's *Ulysses*, called *Bloomsday*, were performed. In consequence,
Jim Fitzgerald, who was to direct, came to ask Sean if he would
make certain 'structural alterations': a request to which Sean
could never agree, though obviously in any work a tightening-up
or some minor amendment is possible. Jim returned to Dublin. It

was apparent that the Tóstal authorities were not prepared to defy the Archbishop by putting on *Father Ned* as it was; and Sean was told that the play had been rejected. When Samuel Beckett, who was to have been represented by three mime plays, heard that the Council had banned both *Father Ned* and *Bloomsday*, he withdrew his own work: it still seems utterly absurd to me that the word of an Archbishop should have caused the abandonment of so grand a programme by three great Irish writers.

Sean wrote to the *Irish Times* (17 February 1958) a letter in which he said that he had not asked the Tóstal to take an interest in his play; when he was engaged on it he had no idea that the Council wanted it for production in Dublin; in fact he thought that the event should be used for the benefit of some younger or newer dramatist. Ultimately he sent *Father Ned*: its script reached Dublin at the beginning of September 1957, 'so that those concerned had plenty of time to consider the play, yet it was only after the Archbishop had issued his fiat that the discovery of structural changes was made.' Sean added:

> When the script returned, I found – though it was quite obvious that it had been read by far more than one person – there wasn't a single mark on it (other than the alterations I had already made myself) to indicate any tentative idea of questionable construction. To this day I haven't the slightest notion of what part of the play, in their opinion, needed an alteration. It is rather comic to think of a frightened Archbishop frightening the Tóstal Council into closing the gates of Dublin on Dubliners. Shut the gates! Quick! We have not a moment to spare. The Archbishop doesn't know (or doesn't care) that a work by Joyce or Beckett, or even by O'Casey, performed in Dublin, is of more importance to Dublin than it is to any of those authors: that outside Dublin is a wide, wide world, and that this wide place is Joyce's oyster, Beckett's oyster, and even O'Casey's oyster; or that these voices, hushed in Dublin, will be heard in many another place.

And again:

> Where are the indomitable Irish about whom the poet sang? Gone to cover? Looks like there isn't an arm or a leg of them

left. They have left for other lands to get outside of the ecclesiastical iron curtain; a cause of emigration that is never mentioned. It may be just as well that Ireland's population is getting less and less, for it will leave plenty of room for the elect people of God, the faithful few, with all the rascals gone; those that stay safe from any touch of pitch that might defile them; for at present, reading the Lenten Pastorals, it would seem that the Irish people are becoming a nation of delinquents. All the same, citizens of the Republic, bad or good, have a claim on the state. His Grace the Archbishop, in a democratic state, is no more than a citizen of the Republic, even though such a claim comes from an accident of birth; well, so am I a citizen of the Republic, not only by accident of birth, but also by definite intent.

So, by demand of Dublin's Catholic Archbishop, this citizen, with a tear in his eye, a pain in his heart (while the other Archbishop doesn't say a word), has to say a second time – Inishfallen Fare Thee Well.

'He could hurl a thunderbolt as fiercely as anyone,' commented Brooks Atkinson. It would be six years before Sean allowed a play of his to be presented in Ireland.

IV

Cheryl Crawford, who was going to stage *The Shadow of a Gunman* on Broadway, asked Sean to go over with me for the opening, at a time when Paul Shyre was to direct *Cock-a-doodle Dandy* in an off-Broadway theatre. Sean was not enthusiastic; his doctor said it would be bad for him to fly, and in any event he was not constitutionally strong enough for the trip. Brooks Atkinson wrote that it would be a good idea if one of the O'Caseys went; and it was decided at length that I should go and that Breon would stay with Sean in the flat. The Cheryl Crawford management, hearing I was to come by myself, did not offer to pay my fare or to put me up in a hotel; obviously they had just wanted Sean. The decision – for I had to think of the fare – was difficult until Lucille Lortel, who financed *Cock-a-doodle Dandy*, said that she would like to look after

my expenses and to give me an apartment in Hampshire House
Hotel to use during my visit. That made the whole thing possible.
Much excited, I prepared for the journey, thirty-two years after I
had been in New York and the reading of *Juno and the Paycock* had
unconsciously decided my life.

When I landed at midday in New York, Sean's agent Jane
Rubin and a friend, Cathy Fannon (who had visited Sean at
Torquay in the previous year), met me at the airport. I was among
V.I.P.s to be let off first, and a chair was in waiting for me to be
wheeled to the Customs; presumably Jane had thought I was a
very old lady. Still, the chair came in handy for my luggage. I was
surprised that even the Customs officials greeted me warmly as
Sean's wife: they appeared to know all about him. Next it was
an excitement to reach my hotel and to find the room filled with
flowers and plants from so many people, all over New York, that
had been sent to greet me as Sean's wife: flowers from friends I
had known in London, flowers from Peggy Wood, with whom I
had acted in *Bitter-Sweet*; from Norah Howard, who had been in
the same company; from colleges; from Brooks and Oriana Atkinson; from S. Y. (Yip) Harburg, who wrote the book and lyrics of
Finian's Rainbow, and his wife; and from the various publishing
houses. Julie Haydon, George Jean Nathan's wife, had sent a
beautiful orange tree in a pot.

The room, bright and welcoming, had huge french windows
that opened upon a balcony looking across Central Park; the curtains were of white frilled muslin, and the effect was fresh and
feminine. I had a small kitchen, a bathroom and shower; it was
luxury, and I loved it. At once I was whirled off to lunch with
Lucille Lortel at the Plaza; but I managed to get back to rest
before meeting the cast of *Cock-a-doodle Dandy* which would open
in two days at a little off-Broadway theatre beneath Carnegie Hall.
Many young people were at the first night. I did not think myself
that it was a good production, though Lucille had done everything
she could for it; it is an uncommonly demanding play and perhaps I was expecting too much. After a fortnight of satisfying
houses, the public dwindled and the run had to be brief. On these
occasions I lack the courage of my beliefs; though I never rave

over anything I do not like, it is hard to be courageous enough to tell friends who are working anxiously that I do not like their efforts. Sean had written for the *New York Times* a preliminary article in which he said:

> The Cock in the play, of course, is the joyful, active spirit of life as it weaves a way through the Irish scene (for, like Joyce, it is only through an Irish scene that my imagination can weave a way), within the Irish shadows or out in the Irish sunshine, if it is to have a full, or, at least, a fair chance.

Presently *The Shadow of a Gunman* opened its Broadway run, staged at the Bijou Theatre by Lee Strasberg of the Actors' Studio, with Susan Strasberg, a pretty, petite girl, as Minnie: this was the production to which Sean had been asked, and the company had been rehearsing in the 'Method' style for something like three months. I appreciated what I saw at a crowded première with Brooks Atkinson as my companion. The scenery mingled the tenements of Dublin and New York; I liked the fact that a Jewish actor had been cast as Seumas Shields. The entire revival differed from an Irish one; but I have always believed that any good play, concerned with the human struggle, can be acted in several different styles. Many Irish people who objected to Strasberg's treatment could have been accustomed to the familiar Irish manner: obviously admirable, but one must have an open mind. I sensed during the performance that Brooks approved. Afterwards, at a large party with Lucille and all my friends as well as the Strasberg cast, I met the film star, Greer Garson, elegant in white mink to her toes.

The *Gunman* ran profitably for six weeks. I telephoned Sean quite often to keep him in touch with everything; Lucille insisted that I should do so when I wished, and I found that on going to friends they would say immediately, 'Wouldn't you like to speak to Sean?' Again he was unlucky when having an apparent success: a newspaper strike intervened, and when houses begin to drop off in New York it normally means that a play is over; expenses are fantastically high. I met Cheryl Crawford for the first time: a woman, stimulating and intelligent, who had plans for putting on other works by Sean. But though we lunched once or twice to discuss this, Sean heard no more.

Lucille, at the week-end, would ask me out to her country house; there she showed me the Barn Theatre in which she staged so much during the summer months with leading players from New York. Her husband, Louis Schweitzer, was one of the most lovable wealthy men I have met; I knew nothing of his business activities, but at home he was full of humour and exceedingly fond of music, with a special room to hold hundreds of records and his tape recorder. He also owned a radio network over which I spoke about the play, my fondness for New York, and things in general. Lucille's mother and family came to dinner that night, and during the meal I said cheerfully, 'After visiting New York, there's one thing I don't want – a brown mink coat. Every woman who goes down in the lift in my hotel seems to have one. It's become a sort of uniform for rich women. So many of them, toddling along on their high heels. They look just like rich penguins.' I heard Louis chuckle: 'Eileen, you really have said something now. It's likely that all the women at this table, except yourself, have a mink coat.' There was a roar of laughter and Lucille asked me what I would like if I had my choice. I said I would prefer a blond beaver or a Russian sable and left it at that.

With Lucille I went over to see Peggy Wood at her country house. David, her son, married now and living in the neighbourhood, was the same age as Breon; they were not much more than eighteen months when *Bitter-Sweet* opened. David called to meet me, but I can hardly say that we recognised each other.

V

Joseph Stein, who contemplated a musical version of *Juno and the Paycock* on Broadway, invited me to his house. I had known him and his wife in Torquay when they first tried to get Sean interested in the musical plan that did not altogether please him: he considered that *Purple Dust*, which had so many songs and a comedy theme, would be more suitable. However, Joe was persuasive, and so was the money; and Sean said Yes. Shelley Booth was to be Juno, and Jackie MacGowran would go over to play Joxer. The work was only in the making when I was in New York and listened one evening to the music, Marc Blitzstein's, that on its own sounded right. As it fell out, *Juno* in production (Winter Garden, New York, 1959) had a very rocky experience. Sean felt that it should never have been called, simply, *Juno*. Thinking back, I believe it might have been quite a success if it had been re-written in parts, treated less as a musical comedy than a musical play, and retitled.

Yip Harburg and his wife were extremely hospitable. I had seen him at a London party where he played the *Finian's Rainbow* music to us. Later, when I was up from Devon, the Harburgs, who were in London, took me to dinner and a theatre with Niall, then on army leave. Niall that evening had a bad migraine. After the theatre, while we were having coffee outside a place off Brompton Road, Yip returned all the way to his hotel apartment for some pills he believed might help. Now in New York, late one night, I walked for miles with him round a city he loved: we went down to a part of it in which through the night the shops remained open, and it startled me to observe how many people were about.

Dave Green, who introduced his wife to me at lunch, we had known first as an American naval lieutenant at Totnes; after this, as a university teacher and specialist in Irish literature, he saw us at St Marychurch. Dave had been doing a book on Synge in which I could help a little, for I had acted with Pegeen Mair, Maire O'Neill's daughter, in *Riders to the Sea*: she left the stage for her own pottery works (and mending china for the British Museum). Getting in touch with her, Dave was allowed to read her mother's letters. I am sorry this friendship with Sean had to be marred when Sean, late in life, was progressively tired and weak. Dave had asked once whether he might bring his family to see us at Torquay, and though Sean had replied that he would love it, when the time arrived he was not equal to a visit. Still, Dave had brought his wife down to show her where he was stationed during the war, so he telephoned from Torquay to say that, as they were so close, could not Sean see them? Sean was stubborn; no, he would not see them. He was unwell and sleeping badly, with a certain amount of pain into the bargain. I urged him not, at any rate, to sit on the balcony in case the Greens might walk by; Sean, again cussed, said why shouldn't he sit on his balcony? I had gone out; evidently Dave did pass the house, and seeing Sean up there felt they could well have met and was hurt by the refusal. I was sorry, and I think Sean was; nothing could alter him in that mood. Here the fault was on both sides; they did continue to correspond, and Sean always kept a fondness for Dave. (There was a similar problem when the two young people who ran Caedmon Records, found after years of warm correspondence with Sean that he refused to see them – simply because he was feeling ill.)

VI

Carlotta O'Neill, Eugene's wife, had me to lunch with her in the exclusive hotel where she lived. She had already met and admired Shivaun. We argued a lot about Irishmen; because at that time she was full of resentment against Eugene, she imagined I would not have a good word for Sean. It was a lively argument, no malice in it; I had no intention of yielding and agreeing that Sean was the dreadful Irishman she wanted me to picture. When I left about four o'clock, we had been at it for three and a half hours. Carlotta was most particular about her health and almost daily had a doctor to visit her. I saw her husband's *A Touch of the Poet* which was on then at the Helen Hayes Theatre, with Kim Stanley and Eric Portman, and I was introduced to Helen Hayes.

Julie Haydon, the actress, George Jean Nathan's widow, was a lovely young woman, overwhelmed by the memory of George who had died six months previously. She took me to a house, a little way from the city, that she had bought as a museum for everything he had done; she had put up a stained-glass window in his honour, and was arranging to give talks about him and readings from his work. Sean, she knew, had regarded him as the best of all critics, and she must have read the letters Sean had written during a long friendship. Julie, in her generous manner, got toys and dolls for me to take back to my friends' children. I saw her often, a romantic person who told me the entire story of her romance with George and their wedding at sea; she could not speak of him without being overcome. Though I liked her greatly, I did feel that she was still almost too obsessed by her memories.

That November I was in New York for Thanksgiving Day, a great American occasion, like an old English Christmas, when families unite and people travel for miles to be with their folk. I was lucky to be in the heart of its hospitality on an enchanting, crisp day, with a gay air over the whole city. In the morning the Bob Graffs asked me, with Cathy Fannon, to a party at their flat. In the evening I went with Cathy to *West Side Story*, vital and exhilarating; and after it we joined Lucille's party at the Plaza where we were the only persons among the twenty-five at a large long table who were not members of the family: some of them, meeting only at Thanksgiving, took the chance to catch up on each other's news, and it became really animated. Finally, on my last night, Lucille told me to invite anybody I wished to a party she gave for me on a top floor of Hampshire House, a beautiful place below which the lights of New York stretched off into the dim distance; on one side you could look down upon skaters on the floodlit rink in Central Park. It reminded me of a strange setting for a ballet; the rest of the view could have been for drama or tragedy. I did understand why Sean had so loved a city that could throb, as this did, with excitement and sadness and drama.

Next day I was to leave for England. Cathy stayed with me overnight, and in the morning Lucille came. A marvellous hostess, she wanted now – remembering what I had said at dinner – to make me a present of a blond beaver coat, but I just could not make myself accept such a gift. It was sad in one sense to leave New York and the finest holiday since our marriage. Still, beyond everything was an overmastering wish to be back with Sean, Breon and Shivaun in my home. It was in a moment like this that I realised our loss so sharply. Back to Torquay to see Sean and Breon and Shivaun, but not Niall.

CHAPTER FOURTEEN

St Marychurch Still

I WAS happy to be back with Sean, and we talked endlessly of his American friends and of New York itself, the city that had so strong a fascination for him, and of which he had written once, in *Rose and Crown:*

> The streets were deep and Dantesque, dizzying the mind when one looked up to the tops of the buildings towering up as if they sought a way to the blue sky and the sun ashine therein; and the whole city in its aspect and its agitated life grew into a rosy, comfortable, and majestic inferno; life so busy and stimulating that all but the sick in soul and very sick in body forgot the time they would come to dust in the cool of the tombs: a grander-patterned background than many of the grand ones Sean had threaded in his hasty way through life.

While I had been there he had been working at home on his play about Irish religious bigotry, *Behind the Green Curtains.* Every day he received the Dublin newspapers and followed everything that went on; one of the new scenes, I think, would have derived from the report of a celebrated Irishman's funeral and the question whether Catholics – not supposed to attend the services of another religion – would have been allowed into a Protestant cemetery. (Robert Hogan directed the first performance of this piece, at Rochester, U.S.A., two years before Sean died.) Another two plays were on hand, *Figuro in the Night* and *The Moon Shines on Kylenamoe;* all three were published together in 1961. *The Moon* is just an exceedingly funny and good-tempered sketch about an English peer who arrives by train in the middle of the night at a tiny Irish station in the back of beyond ('Stoppin'', says the Guard, 'at Killcolm,

Ballyfunbarr, Kylenamoe, Kylenatorf, Killcormac, an' all the rest
o' them, depositin' eager passengers without harm or threpida-
tion!'). The theme of *Figuro in the Night*, which is set in a district
on the environs of Dublin, is best suggested by its dedication:

> This Work is prayerfully and solemnly dedicated to what is
> known as 'The Ferocious Chastity of Ireland', and has been
> written and printed for the one and only reason of warning to
> Gael, Gall-Gael, and Gael-Gall, including those decent and
> law-abiding members of that section of the Irish Community
> who live, work, and worship within a religion and political
> belief contrary to, and at enmity with, the life, worship, and
> political activities of those domiciled within what is regarded
> as the twenty-six counties of Southern Ireland; in the abiding
> hope that all, North and South, will combine against, fight, and
> destroy this communist and insidious effort to overthrow the
> age-long virtue of the Irish People; to prevent this rock-built
> chastity from corrosion, so that it may outlive all red-like
> attempts to frighten or weaken its determination by a godless
> and ruthless ridicule. Amen.

Besides the plays, Sean was collecting articles for a book that
he called provisionally 'Reveries in the Dusk', but which appeared
in 1963 as *Under a Colored Cap*. He had cheerful news, too, of *The
Drums of Father Ned*; Robert Hogan had staged it, judging from
the slides he sent to us, in a gaily pictorial production at his college
in Lafayette, Indiana, during 1959; one of the photographs Sean
used as a frontispiece to the published text. There was also an
English production, the only one so far, at the Hornchurch
Repertory Theatre in Essex. Its young director, David Phethean,
interviewed Sean and sent in November 1960 photographs that
pleased him; but neither of us could go up.

A year earlier the English Stage Company had chosen *Cock-a-
doodle Dandy* for the Edinburgh Festival. Sean Kenny, its designer,
had been to Torquay to discuss the sets; though they hardly followed the precise textual descriptions, Kenny had, of course, to
work on a low budget. George Devine, who asked me to go to
Newcastle for the play's preliminary week, was worried about
his leading man, Wilfrid Lawson; dominating though Lawson

could be at his best, he was by no means consistent and it was now something of a problem to hear what he was saying; through the run his Sailor Mahan could be unreliable. Even so, the production had a triumphant Festival première – one that impressed Lord Harewood, the administrator, who telegraphed his congratulations to Sean. In the circumstances, when *Cock-a-doodle Dandy* reached the Royal Court in London, Sean welcomed an invitation to see his favourite work. It was a good many years since he had been in any London theatre; with his bad eyesight he had to sit fairly close to the stage, but in spite of it, and though he could not hear half of Lawson's dialogue, he acknowledged the general quality of the acting, and, curiously, was not in the least critical: happy, I think, that ten years after it had been published, the play had achieved this major production. I had a job to get him to attend George Devine's party on the stage after the performance, but he gave way and met there John Osborne with whom he was photographed, Sean as the Angry Old Man and Osborne as the Angry Young One, tags invented by the theatre's press representative, George Fearon.

II

With *Purple Dust* continuing in New York, money was easier; so instead of staying at a London hotel when I came up to discuss Sean's work, I rented a little mews flat at the back of Cromwell Road. While I had this, Sean, who hated any disturbance more and more, travelled to London only three times. He had loved the city when we met first, and the flat was in the district where we used to walk together, not so far from Clareville Street. Now we never visited art galleries or any places from the old days; the bookshops that had once delighted Sean; the shops near the British Museum; Zwemmers in Charing Cross Road; even any theatre. Always tired he had to rest as much as possible. During that 1959 visit George Devine inquired if he might bring round Peter Hall, the young director who was soon to take over the Royal Shakespeare Company; Jackie MacGowran, Harry Craig, Lovat Dickson (of Macmillans) and others were there, and Sean talked of the plays he was finishing, those in *Behind the Green Curtains*. Peter Hall said he would much like to read them. On publication Sean sent a copy, but, whatever happened, we heard no more. Lucille Lortel, who crossed during two summers especially to see us, and who stayed at a Torquay hotel, hoped at one time to do *Figuro in the Night* in her celebrated Broadway matinée series.

In London Sean consulted an eye specialist who had known Dr Cummins in Dublin. After examining him, Dr Lyell said, 'Well, I have done all I can. One eye is useless, as you know; but I do not believe you will lose the sight of the other completely. It should last you.' When Sean joined me in the waiting-room, he said, 'How strange, Eileen! When I was a small boy and went with my mother to the hospital in Dublin, the specialist told her, "He'll have life-long trouble with his eyes, but I don't think he'll ever go blind – not in his right eye, anyhow."' The good eye did see enough for him to be able to walk alone; but in his last years reading was a hopeless task, even if by holding a book at a slant and peering at it out of the corner of his eye he could make out an odd word or two. He felt it was a startling coincidence that two doctors, separated by so long a gap, should have said the same thing.

Early one afternoon in Torquay, Donald Ogden Stewart, who was living over here – he was a Hollywood script-writer for Katharine Hepburn and Spencer Tracy – called on us with his wife Ella and a Russian named Boris Izakov: they brought caviare and vodka. Boris, there to discuss the translations of Sean's auto-biographies into Russian, was excitable and friendly; he had lost a foot in the war but he moved rapidly with his artificial limb. We had dinner out and went on to the Aquarium, and I gathered that the Russian temperament was uncommonly akin to the Irish. Sean would have been pleased if Boris had lived nearer because, in a fashion, there was the same hilarious fellowship between them – no word of politics – as between Sean and Barry Fitzgerald.

Articles written for Russia were sent to a representative of the Russian magazines in London. These men and their families would stay two or three years in a flat the Soviet Embassy pro-

vided; I knew especially Vladimir and Elena Silantiev who came
to a Torquay hotel for a week-end, bringing their small son, a fine
boy, sturdy and intelligent. The Soviet Embassy asked at another
time if Sopronov, the dramatist and editor of a magazine called
Ogonek, could call on Sean; he drove down with a Mr Nazarov and
saw a lot of the Devon country. Also a Mr Alexei Surkov, address-
ing Sean as 'Dear Master', wrote to say that of all his English
journeys he remembered best the visit to Torquay: 'The talks
with you and your most charming wife helped me to enrich my
impressions of the intellectual aspects of contemporary Britain.'
Surkov wrote of the late spring at his summer home in Vnukovo
where

> the apple trees and cherries blossom in crazy fashion. The
> crocuses and daffodils have already bloomed, and now the
> cups of the many-coloured tulips are blinding the eye. And in
> the sky on the air line (we live in a mile's distance from the
> central airdrome of our country) day and night howl the engines
> of the TU, IL, Comet, Boeing-707, Caravelle, and others. But
> man is an adaptable animal – gets used to everything.

And he ended: 'I wish you to enjoy in the future the very best of
Irish health!'

Peter Balashov, an influential Russian bookman, wrote in 1960:

> In any place I visited, in Ukrainian villages, on Ukrainian
> plains, on the sea-shore near Feodossia, everywhere I saw people
> who had read your books. I enjoyed myself having talks with
> them so far as they felt the overwhelming poetic power of your
> works. There were mere milkmaids, doctors, and school-
> teachers among them. . . . One episode I would like to tell you
> about. It happened to be the very winter evening I got to know
> your book had been published in Russian. I felt myself not
> quite well and could not go to the bookshop immediately to
> buy some copies. But when I managed to get to the nearby
> shop all your books had been sold out immediately.
>   To the next bookshop I went and they grow up in the new
> districts of Moscow like mushrooms. It was a cold day, but
> my heart was warmed by the spring smile of a young shopgirl
> who offered me your book to buy. She had read it and liked it

very much. 'Such a good book,' she said to me. I commended her for her good taste and asked: 'Now then, if you like the book, do pack ten copies of it.' 'Such a lot!' she exclaimed. 'What's that!' I say. 'I am going to make a present to my friends if you are quite sure it will be a good one.' She looked at me with her big, clear eyes and answered humbly, but with confidence: 'Don't bother, it will be.'

III

Shivaun, away with the Irish company, spent the Christmas of 1957 in Mexico. In the following spring, when I met her off the liner at Plymouth, the amount of her luggage startled me. She had brought all kinds of things from Mexico in baskets and bundles and a trunk, and all we could do was to hire a car back to Torquay; I have never known anybody to carry round so much. When we had greeted each other and discovered a car – it was not easy – I was talking away eagerly, wondering what she might be doing next. The driver turned to us and said, 'You don't want 'er to work, do you? Work was meant for 'orses.' I think he believed I was going to slave-drive my daughter.

Sean was relieved to have Shivaun at home: Breon was also with us in the flat, though elsewhere he had a room that he used as a studio. Presently he decided to go to St Ives in West Cornwall, and with a friend I discovered for him a large and cheap studio; it was here, where artists gather, that he met Doreen, a Northern Irish girl, whom later he would marry. Before he left Torquay he and a local fellow-artist organised an annual exhibition of young contemporary painters; the Mayor would open it formally at Torre Abbey and one had to get a personality to speak; I tried to think of any actor or actress I might know. Mai Zetterling came first; in the second year, Adrienne Corri.

Sybil Thorndike, in Torquay for sadly ill-attended readings with her husband, Lewis Casson, spoke at one of the exhibitions and delighted Sean with a visit that reminded him of long-ago pleasure in *Saint Joan*. And we were happy to see Sir Bronson and

Una Albery, Una an old friend, Bronson a new one whom Sean had written to previously on business terms. Sean had, also, an endeared guest from Ireland. In Dublin, before the final demolition of the burnt-out Abbey (its productions went to the Queen's), it had been decided to make a film in the shell of the theatre where the stage and some of the auditorium remained. Former Abbey players would appear in a documentary, and Sean was invited with his lasting friend, Barry Fitzgerald, whom from the first he had recognised as a grand comedian. Because Sean was not strong enough to travel, Barry arrived with his invariable Dublin host, J. J. O'Leary, who was like him a keen golfer. We had met Barry only once since Woronzow Road; I happened to be in London when he was filming and he and J. J. had a West End service flat.

It was just after Christmas and very cold; snow in even the deep south-west. Sean had been intensely moved at the prospect of a reunion, and I remember the emotional moment when Barry, in aspect much the wearier of the two, entered the room. Walking towards each other, arms outstretched, they embraced, and brokenly, in their Irish voices, each said the other's name: 'Barry!' 'Sean!' Sean was over eighty and Barry must have been about seventy; theirs was the kind of affection that endures through life. Once more a film unit took charge of our flat. Paul Rotha was to produce, and our friend Wolfgang Suschitzky, who had photographed Sean often across the years, was doing the camera-work. Observing at once that Barry's memory was at fault, Sean carried him along astonishingly; their scenes together in *Cradle of Genius* are the joys of the production. Every evening Barry would turn up to sit by the fire in Sean's armchair while Sean sat propped on the divan; they talked so easily that I wished they could have seen a lot more of each other, but Barry had to go back to Dublin and thence to Hollywood. He died in 1961, and soon after his death a journalist telephoned to ask if we were aware that Barry had left Sean some money. When I asked him, Sean said it must be a mistake; it was true, though, and a letter that arrived in confirmation contained Barry's praise of Sean as the man who had realised his talents and inspired his work. It was a deeply touching remembrance.

Shivaun, just before Christmas 1958, had got a job in the design workshops of the Bristol Old Vic. She stayed there for two years; and at Christmas 1959 Sean had gone up with me to Bristol to see a Julian Slade–Dorothy Reynolds musical that Shivaun had helped to design: it was called *Hooray for Daisy*, and Daisy was a cow with marvellous long eyelashes that blinked at the audience. Unfortunately our seats at the Theatre Royal were a bit muddled, and we were so far back in the circle that I doubt whether Sean could distinguish much of Shivaun's cow. Her friend then was Robin Phillips, now a successful director in the West End and at Stratford, but at the time a Bristol Old Vic actor; we had a cheerful Christmas dinner at our hotel near Clifton Suspension Bridge, and Sean stuck it out manfully. I think Shivaun might have carried on in her small room in Bristol, making her props and hats and getting little further. But, agreeing that one had, whatever one's talent, to get some definite training, she decided to return to an acting school; after acceptance for both the Central and for LAMDA (London Academy of Music and Drama) she chose the Central, and later, when a number of students broke away to form another group, she went with them.

IV

Right through these years Sean had many foreign students' questions to answer. Even if we could often laugh about them, they could involve a good deal of work. Consider these notes on the fifth volume of his autobiography, *Rose and Crown*:

> *Cochran's Backer:* The Man who supplies the money to the Producer to enable him to do the play; a damned nuisance, for he will back only what he is sure will make money. Thank God, he is often wrong!
>
> *Joyce's 'Thunderclap':* Joyce combined the names of many languages for 'Thunder' into one long, reverberating word, as a show of how primitive man heard it in terror and anxiety; the 'sacred frogs' of Ireland yelled their croaking against the production of *The Silver Tassie*, and the clamour linked them up with the frenzied, ignorant fear of early man.

Hearseman, pass by: Hearseman is one who drives a hearse, the car carrying a corpse to the cemetery. The words are a play on the last few words of the epitaph written by Yeats himself for his headstone. They are Horseman, Pass by. My term tries to show the wide difference between horsemen and hearsemen.

Bulldog Drummond: A celebrated but ridiculous character in the stories by one calling himself 'Sapper'. A lusty, beefy fellow of great strength, belonging to the upper class; daring against all kinds of spies and criminals; never daunted – a ridiculous and fictitious hero. Churchill had the build and look of Bulldog D.; but he was, of course, a very different type, full of decision, daring, imagination; vital, and a great leader; but he did bluster occasionally, and, at times, even bullied. But in the war he was a godsend to England.

Ballaghadereen policeman: One from this tiny town in a wild part of Mayo, the far West. Such a one, as distinct from a Dublin man, would be mystified by what he saw passing, looming up before him in the cool mist of the morning.

Joxer: Joxerian: Yes, Joxer, of *Juno*.

Sean O'Faolain: A novelist and short story writer; very clever. . . . What he wrote appeared in AE's (Russell) paper, *The Irish Statesman*. All their opposition, including Yeats's, is proved silly now.

Sinclair: Arthur Sinclair had a company touring England with Irish plays. It was he who first acted 'Capt. Boyle' in *Juno*, with Sara Allgood as Juno. It was a fine company of actors, and Sinclair, though a comparatively ignorant man, was really a great actor, though given to taking too much drink at times. He toured England with my plays and died a few years ago. All but one of the company are now dead.

Cuneiform Order of Impassionate Canons Irregular: Jocular play on words. Cuneiform is, of course, name of the word symbols used by Babylon and Assyria, wedge-shaped, ancient, and dead. . . . like the methods of the Orders. Impassionate as against the Passionists; Irregular – there is no such thing as Irregular. There are Canons Regular, signifying that though they be connected with a cathedral, they are bound by canons or rules, therefore becoming a regular Order as distinct from the ordinary priest. The real name of the visiting priest was Father Leo, whose birth-name was McLoughlin. The order was that of

the Discalced Carmelites, Friars who wore sandals over bare
feet.

The Crosby touch: Yes, the sort of song Crosby sings, the same
kind of sentimentality.

The end, thank God!

We met another kind of student, Saros Cowasjee. Ron Ayling
wrote to ask Sean if he would see a young Indian, a colleague from
Nottingham University. Saros appeared to us to be an extremely
pleasant and enthusiastic young man, and he came again, with a
friend. After a few months he wrote to me to say that he was
engaged on a critical study of Sean's work entitled *Sean O'Casey:
The Man Behind the Plays,* and would I contribute a preface? Though
I had no intention of doing so, Sean persuaded me, saying he was
certain I could manage it and that it would be good for me, anyway. When the book was published I did not much like it; probably I would not have accepted if I had read the text, though there
was no malice in Cowasjee's writing and he was obviously stating
facts that had been told to him. My preface was written as a letter,
and I said in it, among other things:

> After lunch he rests, mostly to give his eyes a rest. This is a
> regular habit now, over many years. Then tea, and around five
> p.m. he starts to get into action on his typewriter, and he writes
> on and off all the evening. He has his evening meal and goes on
> again, of course on some days with more gusto, and naturally on
> some days he thinks or relaxes – looks at odd TV pictures,
> mostly sport or Zoo series, listens to music. He likes Mozart,
> Mendelssohn, and Haydn and others, and traditional airs of
> most countries. All must depend on how far he is in the
> creating of his work. . . .
>
> Sean's great love for Ireland is very true and real. It is as
> clear to read in all his works as in Shaw's and James Joyce's.
> Not a sentimental love, but a hope that the great intelligence,
> humour, and energy of the Irish people will be used to the best;
> education to thrive, ignorance and superstition to pass away. . . .
> He does not believe in a pessimistic outlook, he always sees the
> way of a better living, and better life for all human beings. All
> Sean's plays have a note of hope and going on further with
> life. . . .

I must mention his admiration for Gael Linn in Ireland, the Gaelic movement; they run a 'pool', and with the money do various things, such as getting new motor-boats for the Irish fishermen and more up-to-date equipment. Also the cultural side has a collection of songs and poems; they have recently made a very fine film of Irish life. Sean, who speaks Gaelic, is in close touch with them.

Well, the O'Casey day ends in much the same way whether we be one, two, or more. Around midnight Sean gets up from his armchair and goes to the kitchen to see how much milk we need. He asks me each night, 'How much shall I ask for?' and I say one or two more pints. Sean makes a piece of paper in a dart and puts this in an empty milk bottle, with the words 'one or two pints' written on it. That is the last O'Casey writing on most days. He may go back and listen to more music, or write, but often he just sits and thinks – having written his request for the morning milk.

v

On Sean's eightieth birthday, 30 March 1960, he was astonished to get so many telegrams from people in America and Russia who were hardly names to him, as well as from his friends, Dickie Watts and Brooks Atkinson, and from Samuel Beckett, who also wrote in the *Irish Times*: 'I send my enduring gratitude and homage to my great compatriot, Sean O'Casey, from France where he is honoured.' A telegram from Providence, Rhode Island, said, 'We celebrate your life and work on your birthday. – 155 Students studying your plays at Brown University.' From Moscow: 'Warmest greetings to you, great son of Irish people blazing new trails in literature, outstanding playwright, tireless partisan of peace and progress, on your eightieth birthday. Red roses for you of our friendly feelings and our heartfelt wishes of many more years of life-giving creation. – Chakovsky, *Foreign Literature* magazine.' Joan Littlewood, of Theatre Workshop, sent eighty red roses, and there were many other bunches. Sean would never celebrate birthdays except for the children's sake when they were young, so that they could have the excitement of blowing out the candles on the cake. On this occasion, the messages apart, he passed quite an ordinary day.

David Krause's excellent book, *Sean O'Casey: The Man and His Work*, came out in time for the anniversary. Later an American publishing firm asked him to collect Sean's correspondence. Though I did not myself see any reason for this during an author's lifetime, it proved in the event to be a good thing, for Dave could ask Sean questions about the early letters and sort out hundreds of them. He used to spend several days with Sean and leave with his bundles of letters in a suitcase to have them typed. All the while there were negotiations for Sean's work. He agreed, for example, to a Granada television performance of *The Plough and the Stars*; when it was complete, Sidney Bernstein promised to send a copy to Torquay; because our flat was not quite big enough for even a small film show, Dr Doran and his wife Mary offered their own flat and had to deal with the setting-up of the film and the onrush of technicians. Different from any *Plough and the Stars* I had known, I found it only intermittently right, on the whole distorting the play without adding to it. Nora, in particular, was over-acted.

Then Bernard Miles, of the Mermaid Theatre, London, presented *The Bishop's Bonfire*, first travelling to Torquay with his wife Josephine and bringing a tape-recorder with him, so that the entire talk, with Sean's ideas about the production, could be preserved. (The recorder appeared to be so simple a machine that I wondered if, now Sean's sight was dimming, he might use one to relate any incidents he could casually recall: it would be something to do in the evenings.) Ultimately Frank Dunlop directed the *Bonfire* at the Mermaid in July 1961, and Sean contributed a programme note: 'The play shows an aspect of Irish life – the terrible fear of the sight of a lover and his lass among the rye or half-hidden in the bracken, in a dance at the cross-roads, or walking together down a country road or lane: a land where chastity has become one of the worst vices.' He said modestly, 'At the age of eighty-one, counting up all that has been done in play, book, and article, what does it amount to? Very little; very, very little indeed.' His public did not think so; and in the following year,

1962, Bernard visited us again, now about a season of three plays:
Purple Dust, directed by Peter Duguid; *Red Roses for Me*, directed
by Julius Gellner, with Donal Donnelly as Ayamonn; and *The
Plough and the Stars*, directed by Joss Ackland, with Donnelly as
the Young Covey. I went to some rehearsals before going to St
Ives where Breon's first child was to be born, and later saw the
three productions, managed with much credit on the big Mermaid stage. Bernard had afterwards a Sunday-night reading of
Paul Shyre's treatment of *I Knock at the Door*, with such people in
it as Peter O'Toole, Maggie Smith and Jackie MacGowran.

Soon, too, we received from Bob Graff an offer to buy for the
cinema Sean's six autobiographies, published together under the
collective title of *Mirror in My House*. Though I was against any
film, especially during Sean's life, Sean himself was determined
to accept. In a state of health far worse than I knew, he wanted to
leave me as comfortable as possible; at heart he did not believe
that he had all that time to live. The film contract provided that
the money was to be paid over three years. Once Sean had con-
sented, Bob Graff and Bob Ginna had a script prepared by John
Whiting, an able writer, but far in style from Sean, with nothing
of the same tragi-comic sense or the gift for Irish characterisation.
When the script of *Young Cassidy* arrived, I read it myself as I was
now going through all scripts and theses, trying to ease the strain
upon Sean's sight. Bob Graff told me it was suitable; but, without knowing the technique of a film script, I was conscious that
the warmth and beauty of Sean's work had not come through.
Sean, very tired and suffering from his bad nights, was weary of
it, and Dr Doran was anxious for him to be free from any care; he
did rewrite a few scenes but naturally they were not in key with
the remainder of the script. It was an unhappy period, though the
deal did not alter Sean's regard for the two Bobs, who were
striving hard; we hoped the film might be better than we imagined. Personally, I consider that because Sean had devised his
autobiographies much as a dramatist might the entire film could
have been worked up from the dialogue as in Joyce's *Ulysses*.
(Other films can be made from the books; perhaps they will be
one day, especially the tragic life and death of Sean's sister, a

poignant story in waiting.) *Young Cassidy* was not released until after Sean died; again one has little courage in saying what one believes when friends have toiled so sincerely. There was bad luck here in both the casting of the main characters and in the production, but I do think of Donal Donnelly's magnificent performance as an undertaker's man and of another by Maggie Smith – an actress I have never ceased to applaud – as Sean's first love. The cast included such names as Flora Robson (Sean's mother), Michael Redgrave (Yeats), Edith Evans (Lady Gregory), Jack MacGowran (Sean's brother) and Sian Phillips (his sister). Rod Taylor played Sean.

It was a relief, at any rate, that our finances had improved so sharply. Sean had been accustomed to complain that the only big things he could leave me were his manuscripts, and he hoped somebody would buy them.

VI

Steadily my mother had become less agile. Now she was so much older, I had got her to return to the one Torquay landlady, Mrs Davies, I knew would look after her; also I had Charlie who was ready to take messages and to drive her out when needed. I had invited Mrs Earle, now a dear old lady almost eighty, to stay with me for a few weeks, and in the evenings this left me free sometimes to go to Mother. Suddenly her landlady telephoned me to say that there had been an accident; Mother had fallen downstairs and split open the back of her head, and it was unlikely that she would live. Even after so appalling a shock she had not lost her memory; she had, as Sean often said, a good brain and will-power that was exceptionally strong. But the thought of death alarmed her; I was glad that, with Mrs Earle at the flat, I could remain with Mother that night; several times the priest came, and her doctor, while admitting that she had been a difficult person, respected her courage; I tried to console her by saying that she would probably see again the son she had loved, and whom she had never, I think, forgotten. I was desperately distressed that she had to die without ever having had the kind of home or anything she desired; all taken from her when my father lost his money in Dublin. I tried to help her to get through the last hours in peace, and about one in the morning she died. Mrs Davies attended to everything, and I was able to get back to Sean. The funeral was on a fiercely cold, ice-bound day: Sean had suggested that Geoffrey Dobbie, the nurseryman who was in the habit of staying with him when I went to London, might go with me, so there were just the two of us, and Mrs Davies, at the funeral Mass in the Catholic Church. I was grateful to Geoffrey Dobbie for helping me through.

Just after this, Sean, who had been exercised about the need to make full use of the material scattered in drawers and cases round the flat, resolved to draw up his will. Financially, we were easier; it was grand to have productions on the Continent and a renewed interest in Sean's work, but he recognised that I was careless with money and dwelt on the lack of it when it was too late and it had gone. He talked things over with Dr Doran, and one day, when Ron Ayling was there on leave from Rhodes University, and Geoffrey Dobbie was tidying the garden, he asked them to be witnesses to a document that said simply:

Last Will of Sean O'Casey
Written on 15 September 1962
I bequeath and leave to my beloved wife, Eileen O'Casey, all I have and hope to get: all royalties due, all contracts, all manuscripts and typescripts, all royalties to come, fees of every sort – in short, all I am possessed of, and all moneys my work may earn in future years. I give all my goods, estate valuation, and all else, to her in gratitude for many, many years of happy and fruitful companionship; and with all I bequeath to her my deep love, as deep now, deeper indeed, than the love I felt for her in our earlier years.
Witness my signature this day, 14 September 1962
SEAN O'CASEY
(Witnessed by Geoffrey Youngman Dobbie and Ronald Frederick Ayling)

Later it was drawn up in a proper legal fashion.

Sean was grieved at the news of President Kennedy's assassination in the autumn of 1963. The fact that a young man had been cut off from life so suddenly took his thoughts back to Niall; and he wrote this letter to Rose Russell, head of the Teachers' Union in New York. She sent it to the *New York World-Telegram* for publication on 27 November:

Oh, my dear Rose,
What a terrible thing has happened to us all! To you there, to us here, to all everywhere.
Peace, who was becoming bright-eyed, now sits in the shadow of death; her handsome champion has been killed as he walked by her very side. Her gallant boy is dead.
What a cruel, foul, and most unnatural murder!
We mourn here with you, poor sad American people.

Mrs Joseph Kennedy, the President's mother, wrote from Palm Beach, Florida, in January 1964, thanking Sean for autographing copies of his *Selected Plays*. 'I am sure,' she told him, 'that these gifts will be deeply appreciated and always treasured by the members of the family and will be bequeathed with pride to future generations of Kennedys.' At first Sean had been uncertain what to write in the books; but he had a fellowship of sorrow with the family in the loss of an adored son, and he wrote simply, 'In grief there is a great kinship.'

This was in the last year of his life. That spring, the English manager, Peter Daubeny, then beginning his World Theatre seasons at the Aldwych in London, hoped to bring over the Abbey company from Dublin in *Juno and the Paycock* and *The Plough and the Stars*. The Abbey management informed Sean; and, having banned any of his work in Ireland since the Archbishop's interference in 1958 and the rejection of *Father Ned*, he had to consider changing his mind. Peter Daubeny persuaded him to do so. He agreed, moreover, that because Dublin had not seen the plays for so long, it would be fair for them to have a week's preliminary season, a needed work-out for the Aldwych. I saw them in London; though they crowded the theatre, these productions, with their lack of vitality and imagination, keenly disappointed me.

Sean remained at home; he had no wish to travel, and I doubt
whether people understood how much his health was deteriorating.

VII

In the previous year Breon was up from St Ives to stay with us for
a few days with his wife Doreen, who had a five-year-old daughter,
Alison, by a former marriage. Doreen, a Northern Irish girl with
lovely auburn hair, slept with Alison at the house of our daily,
Clare; they would come across in the morning after breakfast.
Alison, observing that Sean was always in his room, alone, felt
that we were deliberately shutting him away, and she crept in one
afternoon to sing consoling nursery rhymes to him. On sitting
down to tea, she said to Sean, as one conspirator to another, 'You
do feel cheered up now, don't you?' Breon came afterwards with
the baby, Oona: the children delighted Sean, and he dedicated his
book of essays, *Under a Colored Cap*, to 'Little Alison and Littler
Oona – to be read when the sturdy airs of womanhood blow
round them – should they desire to do so.' He did see Divna,
Breon's other little girl, when the family visited us again; he was
very weary then. On the last night Breon sat and talked to him,
and when Sean said goodbye in his usual warm way, I did not
think it was the last time they would meet. Sean would never see
Breon's son, Brendan, or Shivaun's son, Rubin; Shivaun was
married after his death.

During the late summer of 1964, while the film of *Young
Cassidy* was being made in Ireland – Shivaun was acting the small
part of Lady Gregory's maid at Coole – Sean, stricken with acute
bronchitis, had to enter a nursing-home. I did not want Shivaun
to hear how bad he was until she had finished her part; he was ill
indeed, but as ever hated to leave the flat. Geoffrey Dobbie had
been a comfort; Sean now needed somebody to attend to him
every hour or so, and one night Geoffrey offered to take on the
duties so that I could have a full sleep.

When Sean was in a hospital or nursing-home, he dreaded that,
with his failing eyesight, he might possibly knock something over.

On this occasion he reached the home about six, and a nurse saw him into bed while I waited outside. On going in I found him settled and sitting up, with a weak smile on his face, and, beneath it, the desperate look of a man trapped. The nurse, bustling round cheerfully, said she knew Sean's work and wasn't it wonderful to meet him? His eyes had begun to hurt: unless they were bathed three times a day in almost boiling water, they grew very sore. Immediately we were alone I turned on the hot-water tap in the basin; though not boiling, it was the best we could do. Next, Sean asked me to lead him around the room. On the right-hand side of his bed was a small table, and on the other side a table with a lamp. He had his small portable radio on his right hand; his medicine, water-glass, and a jug on the other. He had brought the large bowl of tobacco that held his pipe. The placing of all these he had to learn by touch, so we toured the room, feeling the edges of the bed and the tables, the chair at the bed's end, the wash-basin by the wall, the oddments at the side of the basin, the position of the towels and the large sponge. Six or seven times we circled the room. 'Now, dear,' he said, 'let me do it alone as I shall have to when you are not here.' He did it himself until the items were memorised, touching everything separately with sensitive fingers; when sight is bad, touch is emphasised. To my knowledge, Sean never did knock things over, or let them drop, and he was not slow in his movements.

At length, when he seemed to feel certain of himself, I went home. Sister said I could come back when I liked, after eleven-thirty in the morning; and when I arrived next day he was unwell and low-spirited; I sensed that it was something other than his health. He said, 'Eileen, I don't appear to see so well. The water is not really hot enough to relieve my eyes. These damn trays! I don't know what is what. I spill things. This morning I knocked over my cup of tea.' Anybody could do that, I answered. 'Ah,' he said, 'but it meant that the nurse had to come in to change my top sheet; I felt just terrible.' After first persuading the nurse to let me be there at every meal except breakfast, I asked, too, if I could pour his breakfast tea, leaving no pot or milk-jug on the tray, simply a cup of tea where he could feel it. The thought that

Sean might have to forego the cup of tea he loved so much filled me with horror. While at the nursing-home he was very low: he grew delirious and would wander from his room into the passages, talking excitedly. One morning I found him roaming in his dressing-gown, about to give the dinner-gong a great wallop; I stopped him just in time.

As he got better he was feverishly anxious to return to the flat. When Dr Doran told him he could, I asked if he might stay for one more night, something I have often regretted, but I was so tired that I wanted just that night with nobody to look after. There was nothing special to do; after a meal with a friend I came back early and went to bed, realising that I need not worry about anything or anybody. Wrong, maybe, but it was natural. Once having had the extra day's rest, I was excited to get Sean home again.

David Krause had planned to go through more of his letters and to hear Sean's comments. That day Sean took me aside and said, 'Eileen, you're not represented in this collection. It looks as if I have been writing to all sorts of women, advising them about acting or their love affairs, while there's not one word of anything I have written to you. Why don't you let Dave put in your letters as well?' I told him that his letters to me were between ourselves and I had no wish to see them published with others. Though he embraced me and said he perfectly understood, he still returned to the question next day: 'Surely, Eileen, you will put in the one I wrote from the Torbay Clinic?' And I said, Yes, I would. I had had enchanting letters from Sean. This is what he hoped, particularly, I would publish:

Torbay Clinic,
Wednesday, 12 August 1964.
Dearest and sweetest girl of my life; dear, dear Eileen,
Here I am like a cooped-up Cock, ragged in feathers, drooping in comb, the crow gone off into a cough. I have tried to let myself be absorbed by the Clinic, tried to fit in, but my whole being refuses to do away with my wish to be home, to be back again where you are.
That is my only home, has been so for many, many years –

where you, my darling, are: where you get up in the morning, go to sleep o' nights: where you come and go, where we eat together and talk together, and walk the well-worn paths, still bordered with many bright flowers and many blossoming bushes.

When I first set eyes on you, I thought you the loveliest lass I had ever seen; but bred straight out of the workers' way and suddenly plunged into the world of literary and drama society, I thought I had become 'a man of the world', and so girls were but pretty and gay things to play with. Impudent and barbaric idea. Yet as I got to know you more, and the dog Bobbie; as we laughed together so readily over many things, including Bobbie, I began to like you for much more than your lovely face and handsome figure. I failed as 'a man of the world', for I couldn't stop myself from talking of serious things, and your interest in the talks and your quick and sensitive responses showed me a girl with a most active, sensitive, and kindly mind, and the 'girl for a gay time' vanished, and a lovely companion took her place. Then companionship was linked with marriage, so you set out to create the first O'Casey home in 19, Woronzow Road, St John's Wood, making it colourful with much ingenuity and imagination and damned little money. Within a year the first baby, Breon, came, and here were we – I with little idea of fatherhood, and Eileen, with natural instinct, having a far bigger idea of all that motherhood meant. A hard time, a colourful time, but a testing one for both of us.

And so it has gone on for nigh on forty years, your hands alone moulding the life of the little household, dealing well with practical affairs, and wisely with the education of our boy, a matter in which I could give no hand, for I had had no jot of knowledge or experience on the way a child should be educationally brought up; and, darling, you gave all our children a suitable and artistic entrance into life.

All this time, a good many years, you had to face the barrage of incoming bills, with never enough money coming in to ever let you shake yourself free from them; they were the necklace always twisting round your lovely neck, for I had no gift whatever to write anything that would find a ready market; and the English people had decided 'to ignore O'Casey's serious work because of his lamentable political judgments',

Eileen, of course, being the chief sufferer. How you managed to stand up to it all, and go on, is a mystery to me, now that I look back at it all. This insecurity, this constant closeness to poverty, made me irritating and morose at times, and again the sufferer was the wife – and the young boy, sensing the tension around him, when, at meal times, a silent and sullen da sat like a frozen image at the table. You were a brave lass, my darling, to have borne with these oppressions. Many a time a gentle remark to break the tension was ignored, or a tender overture of affection was banished into a deeper silence. All I can say in extenuation is that many a time I yearned to take your tender efforts to my heart, and fold you and these in my arms; but proud ignorance kept me obstinate. How often have I recalled these obstinacies, and, without exaggeration, agonised over them – foolishly, for things done are beyond recall, and there can be no forgiveness for an ill deed done.

Here,* trying to shake off the effects of recent high temperature, and the swallowing of many anti-biotics; enjoying the sensation of being at home once more; for though the Clinic was first-class, the nurses skilled to their finger-tips, and full of kindliness; the room lofty, airy, with a fine view of a terraced garden and of the sea; and I was watched over by my trusted doctor and friend, Dr Doran; the Clinic was not home, for you were not there, Eileen. Anywhere, be it never so lovely and grand, is no home to me when you are not there. Wherever you are, Eileen darling, is home to me. Even when you leave here for a week to do business in London, the home is shadowed till you come back to me. The 'great playwright', the 'wonderful man' sinks low, and, relatively, becomes but a whimpering figure in a darkened doorway. The stalwart of the O'Casey home is not Sean, but Eileen; as it is, so it was always.

Take care of yourself: you have the sure gift of an irresistible personality; you are very witty, you have a gorgeous sense of humour; and you are highly intelligent. Your faults are that you are inclined to be too generous, and you are too strongly disposed to take the problems and sorrows of others into your own sweet nature.

So take care, darling, of your really glorious personality, for your own sake, for the sake of those you love; and for the sake

* The letter was completed at home.

of the community in which you live, and in which you will live
for many years after I am gone. You are, and have been, indeed,
Cuisle Mo Chraidhe, the pulse of my heart; and this heart of
mine loves you, and will love you unto the last. Oh my darling
girl.

SEAN

VIII

Sean had been back only a short time when we had a telephone
call from our friend, Gjon Mili, the *Life* photographer. Could he
come to take pictures? Thinking Sean was too tired, I rang to
make excuses. But Mili arrived in mid-morning, Sean was quite
ready for him, and during the day Mili remained with us, taking
photographs before lunch and even a few in the afternoon before
Sean had his rest. When it was over, and Mili had gone, about six,
after having tea with us, Sean simply collapsed. Though fearfully
tired, he seemed to be pleased that he had sat for the pictures.

Geoffrey Dobbie had written to Shivaun in Dublin, telling her
that her father was ill and that she should come. Though Dr Doran
said she need not, Shivaun did so and arrived not long after Mili
had left. She found that Dave Krause had finished discussing the
letters with Sean and was himself about to go. Her father, she
thought, looked extremely tired but fairly cheerful; after all, for
many months they had known him like this. So she returned to
her work with no idea that this was the last time she would see
him.

CHAPTER FIFTEEN

Sean

AMONG the last articles Sean had written were one for Russia about the dramatist Arnold Wesker, and another, also for a Russian journal, upon Shakespeare's Quatercentenary. Finally, as late as 12 September, he posted to the *New York Times* a long satirical attack on contemporary playwriting, calling it, in a hit at an Ionesco title, 'The Bald Primaqueera'. With it he sent this letter:

> The Editor,
> The *New York Times* Magazine,
> Times Square, New York City
> Sir,
> I am venturing to send you an article that is critical in a gay, satirical way, I hope, of the present-day trend in the theatre living now among the shadows where naught but dark things happen.
> To me life couldn't have achieved so much were it always busy destroying itself.
> I hope you may think it worth publication, but, if not, then, of your kindness, I shall be grateful for its return; for typing is now a per ardua ad astra task to me.
> With all good wishes,
> Yours sincerely, SEAN O'CASEY

His article ended with these words:

> Ah, to hell with the loutish lust of Primaqueera. There are still many red threads of courage, many golden threads of nobility woven into the tingling fibres of our common humanity. No one passes through life scatheless. The world has many sour

noises, the body is an open target for many invisible enemies, all hurtful, some venomous, like the accursed virus which can bite deeply into flesh and mind. It is full of disappointments, and too many of us have to suffer the loss of a beloved child, a wound that aches bitterly till our time here ends. Yet, even so, each of us, one time or another, can ride a white horse, can have rings on our fingers and bells on our toes, and, if we keep our senses open to the scents, sounds, and sights all round us, we shall have music wherever we go.

By now he was increasingly tired. We could still go for car rides or short walks, but the evenings were hard, for he could neither read nor (with any pleasure) watch television, not that he had done so often. I would have marked for him the times of radio programmes that were at all hopeful, and now and again we would do a tape-recording, though even this he had begun to find a strain. We would have our supper in his room by the fire: sometimes he might have his on a tray in bed. I would read to him, mostly Shakespeare – favourite passages from the plays, and the Sonnets which he loved – Rowse's *England of Elizabeth*, maybe, or George Jean Nathan's criticism with the irony that always made him laugh. One book he returned to at the end of his life was a biography of George Crabbe, prefixed to an edition of the poems in a small print that was trying to read. Crabbe, he told me, had had a similar experience to his. Sean knew so much of Shakespeare by heart that we could pass many hours in a test of memory: he would quote long passages and ask me to check that he was word-perfect. It was dreadful to see him there among the books he could not read, even if by putting one slant-wise to his good eye he could sometimes make out a word or two. Often I would find him doing this, trying to look up favourite texts. Books were friends to him, and it was extraordinary to watch him as he handled one, picking it from the shelf, caressing it almost, peering at the binding, and then walking with it to his chair as if he looked forward greatly to the reading.

Daily it had become routine for me to read to him the headlines in *The Times* and in his Irish newspaper (which arrived by post from Dublin, a day late); because of his sight he took fewer papers towards the end. He was determined to keep up with all the political news, the parliamentary reports, so I would plod through them. Theatre news, too, though this was naturally more compelling. Breakfast, as in most households, was not a time for talk: Sean would be anxious to reach his room where he could settle to the newspapers, the letters, and his work.

II

His fatigue grew; but in the middle of September he appeared, for a man of eighty-four, to be fairly well. Dr Doran, who was about to go on holiday, had been to see him, examined him thoroughly, and left prescriptions to carry me over: he warned me to see that Sean got a lot of rest. Early in the following morning, 18 September, about five o'clock, Sean came into my room with his nose bleeding profusely. I telephoned Dr Doran, who said at once, 'Be sure to bring him to my surgery; it will be easier to treat him there.' I drove him over, Sean taking several thick towels with him to counteract the bleeding, and the doctor managed to plug one side of the nose where the trouble was. Doran had telephoned Dr Lees, who was also at the surgery; and I was told that young Dr Haskins, who had recently joined the practice, and who was a nose-and-throat man, would be able to manage should the bleeding start again. It was imperative for Sean to rest a great deal.

Back at home, Sean lay on his divan, propped up with pillows, and I got his lunch: it was an omelette and I was lucky enough to make it very well. He enjoyed it; we chatted; and he lay down to rest. Then at about half-past two in the afternoon the bleeding restarted, and I telephoned Dr Haskins who came immediately and stopped it. He had not been gone more than an hour before Sean was in great agony with a pain in his side; he could hardly speak. Again I rang the doctor; exceedingly worried, and not knowing Sean's entire case-history, he gave an injection to kill the pain, and we decided that Sean must enter a nursing-home or hospital. The doctor went to arrange this. Sean, the pain having ceased for a moment, began to talk to me about myself. There was no doubt, he said, that he was very ill; I should realise that he must die one day. He begged me to look after myself, and not be too rash and generous; now that his plays were doing better on the Continent, and the last two years had been good for us, it would probably be all right.

I realised that Sean would probably not survive for many more years, but why think of it? Of a sudden he was again in agony, a terrible pain now across his chest. I summoned the doctor; there was another swift injection; and the ambulance arrived. As soon as the pain had stopped, Sean was able to talk quietly to me, but in the ambulance we did not speak. I held his hand; Sean had always a tremendously firm hand-grip, especially for anyone of his years; as we approached the nursing-home I noticed that the grip had lessened and I thought he was going to sleep.

They carried him into the hall and into his room which was on the ground floor. When he was in bed, I turned to the doctor: 'I do hope you can save him from any more of that agonising pain.'

In a very soft voice the doctor replied, 'He will have no more pain. He is dead.'

It was the final icy word; I had heard it when Niall died. Sean's little cap was on the side-table; his coloured cap. Neither the doctor nor I could speak. He put the cap gently on Sean's head and left us alone. Sean had gone after his long and wonderful life, his life of fighting, integrity and love. He had died between the sunset and the evening star.

III

I was absolutely quiet and showed no sign of giving way. Dr Haskins took me back to the flat, asking me if I could manage by myself. On the journey he said, much moved, 'It is a strange thing, Mrs O'Casey. Since I have joined this practice, my father, who is an ardent admirer of your husband, has kept asking me whether I have seen him or spoken to him. Two or three times a week I have seen you coming to collect medicines. Now the first time I have seen and spoken to him is the day of his death.' The doctor did not like to leave me at the flat; it seemed so still, Sean's room so quiet; I do not think that I realised entirely that Sean was dead. Then, trying to concentrate, I found myself doing so calmly, and Sean's own words returned to me that, whenever I was really in stress or grief, I became still and practical.

My first thought was to tell Breon and Shivaun; otherwise they might have heard the news on the radio. Breon, who was working on the St Ives exchange, answered as soon as I telephoned; then I got in touch with Shivaun, and like Breon she said she would come at once. Ahead lay a long, solitary evening. At nine o'clock, when the news broke, local people telephoned to ask if they could come round to be with me, and I made an excuse, saying somebody was already in the flat. As a rule I hated being alone, but at this moment I wanted nothing more. Breon reached me next day from St Ives, and Shivaun from London. Time flickered by like a strange dream; Dr Lees helped by giving me some pills that induced a calm, far-off sensation, and I managed to get on with the business one must see to after a death. Letters and telegrams poured in; letters from people I had not heard of since youth, letters from Sean's friends, telephone calls from newspapers. I would have been lost if Breon had not guarded the telephone so that I had no need to utter a word.

Our main object was to keep to ourselves in the flat during the few days before Sean's cremation. Breon drove the car, and we would go off in it beyond Torquay, slipping back to the flat in the evening and hoping that no one would come to talk to us. Sean had said that he wished to be cremated, that it should be a very quiet service for the family alone, and that his ashes should be put with Niall's; instead of flowers, for I knew he would have wished this, I asked for donations to leukaemia research. Though the Abbey Theatre and some Dublin newspapers wanted to send representatives, I replied firmly, No. The people who arranged the service on the lines Sean had desired were wholly understanding, and though at the gates I saw a few visitors from London and Dublin, it was a family occasion, no more.

IV

Life for all of us had to run on: Breon had to return to his family in West Cornwall, and Shivaun to her acting school, while I remained temporarily in Torquay to plan the future. During the last weeks Sean had asked me whom I would prefer as his literary executor. Like me, Breon had not really the right temperament to sort through a mass of papers and list them, and it would have meant leaving his family and his work for many months. Sean had suggested various names, Peter Newmark, American friends, Tom Curtiss in Paris (he, too, would have had to come from his work as Paris critic for the New York *Herald-Tribune*). Ron Ayling was living quite close, in Bristol, where he was a part-time university lecturer; Sean had a regard for him, so I invited him to sort the papers, a dusty job, a search through boxes and old chests, that I would have hated but that he did thoroughly and with affection for Sean.

Knowing I would leave Torquay, I wanted Sean's room to be remembered, it was so much a part of him. At first I had wondered about getting a local photographer to take a picture of it and some of Sean's possessions, his typewriter, his cap, his robe. But Bob Graff had telephoned several times to see if he could help; now, when I explained to him, he sent an American photographer, Erich Hartmann, a sensitive artist who was in the flat for two days creating a beautiful sequence of pictures: Sean's daily life without Sean. Sidney Bernstein was another most thoughtful friend; when I reached London, dazed and worried, he arranged for one of his cars to take me round.

Sean's papers and his manuscripts had grown so precious that they were the principal things I had to watch; Ron Ayling filled a case for me to take to London and deliver to Macmillans. At the time Shivaun and a friend, both agitated about preparations for an American tour, were staying in my small Cromwell Road flat; on the evening I arrived I was to go out to dinner. Dressing in a hurry and rushing for my appointment, I put the case with the papers behind an armchair in the flat, leaving my bigger suitcase on the floor in the centre of the room, with clothes scrambled everywhere. While I was in the middle of dinner, Shivaun rang to say that the flat had been burgled, and my immediate thought was for the manuscripts. Caring little for my own belongings or Shivaun's, I said urgently, 'Please, Shivaun, see if there is an old suitcase behind the armchair – unopened.' She came back at once – for me it was a long wait – to say that the case was untouched; the petty thieves had simply removed some of my clothes, bits of our jewellery, a small radio and an electric fire. I was infinitely grateful, for if the men had grabbed the case and seen in it simply a pile of dusty papers they would probably have tossed away the lot. Next morning, after a word with Macmillans, I took everything by taxi to their offices, feeling like a James Bond type with the documents to be delivered safely, and quite certain that someone was in pursuit.

After twenty-five years in Devon I had resolved to live in London. I had stayed at Totnes because of the children and at Torquay because it suited Sean. Now the furniture was stored; from my base in the Cromwell Road I hunted for a temporary flat and soon chose one in Drayton Gardens, Kensington; most of Sean's books were there, and the presence of the Augustus John portrait, which had been with us through our married life, made the flat feel like the home where we had lived together.

Sean had left a single unpublished article, 'The Bald Primaqueera', which he sent to the *New York Times* less than a week before he died. Ron Ayling, on my behalf, asked for the article back; its length had been the difficulty. At last it was returned, through the St Martin's Press, and, knowing how Sean had cared for it, I strove to get it published. British magazines also found it too long, but finally Robert Emmett (Bob) Ginna wrote to the *Atlantic Monthly* which took it at once and told me how proud they were to print it.

v

During a period of years when one is living with a man who is not really strong, there comes to the back of the mind, naturally but unobtrusively, the thought: 'If I were on my own, I could do this . . . come here . . . go there.' When the children were small, and I was on the beach, I had to be on the move the whole time; I would look at men, at girls, at other women, stretched out sunbathing or reading a book, and think to myself, 'Wouldn't it be lovely if I were alone, and able to do that!' Yet, when the children grew up, and on the few occasions when I was, in fact, on a beach and sunbathing alone, I heard myself say, 'Wasn't it lovely when the children were small, and we were all on the beach together!'

Here, then, I am; I can travel; I can go where I like when I wish. But when Sean was alive it was possible to go out with the knowledge that he would be at home waiting for me; now nobody, when I return, will listen to all I have done, share my moods of happiness or depression. I have had to adjust myself to a life without Sean; without having him to look after; without him to look after me; without our talk and our jokes; without anyone to admire me as he did; without anybody to whom I belong.

I dread the stillness I walk into; the solitude. Deeply now, and always, I miss opening the door and not hearing Sean's voice, warm and welcoming: 'Is that you, Eileen?'

The Works of Sean O'Casey

1918   *Songs of the Wren*, 1st and 2nd series (verse), published.
More Wren Songs (verse) published.
The Story of Thomas Ashe (pamphlet) published.
The Sacrifice of Thomas Ashe (pamphlet) published.

1919   *The Story of the Irish Citizen Army* (history) published.

1923   *The Shadow of a Gunman* (full-length play) produced. Published 1925, with *Juno and the Paycock*, in *Two Plays*, dedicated 'To Maura and to the Abbey Theatre'.
Cathleen Listens In (one-act play) produced.

1924   *Juno and the Paycock* (full-length play) produced.
Nannie's Night Out (one-act play) produced.

1926   *The Plough and the Stars* (full-length play) produced and published; dedicated 'To the gay laugh of my mother at the gate of the grave'.

1928   *The Silver Tassie* (full-length play) produced and published; dedicated 'To Eileen with the yellow daffodils in the green vase'.

1933   *Within the Gates* (full-length play) published; no dedication.

1934   *Windfalls* (essays, verses, short stories, and two one-act plays – *The End of the Beginning* and *A Pound on Demand*) published; no dedication.

1937   *The Flying Wasp* (essays) published; no dedication. Described on the title-page as 'A laughing look-over of what has been said about the things of the theatre by the English dramatic critics, with many merry and amusing comments thereon, with some shrewd remarks by the author on the wise, delicious, and dignified tendencies in the theatre of to-day.'

1939 *I Knock at the Door* (first volume of autobiography) pub-
      lished; dedicated 'To Breon and Niall'.

1940 *The Star Turns Red* (full-length play) produced and pub-
      lished; dedicated 'To the men and women who fought
      through the Great Dublin Lockout in nineteen hundred
      and thirteen'.
      Purple Dust (full-length play) published; dedicated 'To
      Shivaun'.

1942 *Red Roses for Me* (full-length play) published; dedicated 'To
      Dr J. D. Cummins in memory of the grand chats around
      his surgery fire'.
      Pictures in the Hallway (second volume of autobiography)
      published; dedicated 'To the memory of the Rev. E. M.
      Griffin, B.D., M.A., one-time Rector of St Barnabas,
      Dublin. A fine scholar; a man of many-branched kindness,
      whose sensitive hand was the first to give the clasp of
      friendship to the author'.

1945 *Drums under the Windows* (third volume of autobiography)
      published; dedicated 'To Dr Michael O'Hickey, a Gael of
      Gaels, one-time Professor of Irish in Maynooth College.
      In a fight for Irish, he collided with arrogant Irish bishops,
      and was summarily dismissed without a chance of defend-
      ing himself; taking the case to Rome, he was defeated
      there by the subtlety of the bishops, helped by a sly
      Roman Rota, ending his last proud years in poverty and
      loneliness. Forgotten, unhonoured, unsung in Eire, here's a
      Gael left who continues to say Honour and Peace to your
      brave and honest soul, Michael O'Hickey, till a braver
      Ireland comes to lay a garland on your lonely grave'.

1946 *Oak Leaves and Lavender* (full-length play) published; dedi-
      cated 'To little Johnny Grayburn, who in his sailor suit,
      played football with me on a Chalfont lawn and afterwards
      gallantly fell in the battle of Arnhem'.

1949 *Cock-a-doodle Dandy* (full-length play) published; dedicated
      'To James Stephens, the jesting poet with a radiant star
      in 's coxcomb'.
      Inishfallen, Fare Thee Well (fourth volume of autobiography)

published; dedicated 'To Walter McDonald, D.D., Professor of Theology in St Patrick's Roman Catholic College, Maynooth, for forty years; a great man gone, and almost forgotten; but not quite forgotten'.

1951 *Hall of Healing* ('A Sincerious Farce in One Scene') published in *Collected Plays*, vol. 3.
Bedtime Story ('An Anatole Burlesque in One Act') published in *Collected Plays*, vol. 4.
Time to Go ('A Morality Comedy in One Act') published in *Collected Plays*, vol. 4.

1952 *Rose and Crown* (fifth volume of autobiography) published; dedicated 'To the Young of All Lands, All Colours, All Creeds:

> Shadows of beauty,
> Shadows of power;
> Rise to your duty –
> This is the hour!'

1954 *Sunset and Evening Star* (sixth volume of autobiography) published; dedicated 'To my dear friend Hugh MacDiarmid, Alba's Poet and one of Alba's first men'.

1955 *The Bishop's Bonfire* (full-length play) produced and published; dedicated 'To Susan Gone and Susan Here'.

1956 *The Green Crow* (essays, with stories from *Windfalls* and articles from *The Flying Wasp*) published in America, then in London (1957); described as 'a nest of Ids and Trends'.

1960 *The Drums of Father Ned* (full-length play) published; produced in America in 1959; dedicated in these words: 'The Memory be Green of Dr Walter McDonald, courageous theologian in Maynooth College for forty years; of Dr Morgan Sheedy, his lifelong friend, banished for venturing to defend a Parish Priest against a Bishop, and who sent me "an old priest's blessing" from Pennsylvania to New York in 1934; of Father Yorke of San Francisco, who warned Irish Ireland of fond delusions many years ago, and who told Dr McDonald, his friend, that in the *Rerum Novarum* the Church was offering the workers no more than a string

of platitudes; of Canon Hayes, Founder of Muintir na
Tíre, bringing a sense of community life and co-operation
to rural Ireland, and brightness with them; and of Father
O'Flanagan who, when his poor flock were shivering
through a black winter, bade them go to a private-owned
bog, and take from it all the turf they needed, led them
there to do it, and was, consequently, banned from his
Parish and from County Sligo by his Bishop. Each in his
time was a Drummer for Father Ned, and the echoes of
their drumming sound in Ireland still.'

1961   *Behind the Green Curtains* (play in three scenes) published; no
dedication.

Figuro in the Night (one-act play 'In Two Scenes eloquently
and humorously related, but vilely and maliciously inspired and created by dangerous and unseemly influences
emanating from, and begotten in, the pernicious confines
of atheistic and communist lands') published. The play 'is
prayerfully and solemnly dedicated to what is known as
"The Ferocious Chastity of Ireland", and has been written
and printed for the one and only reason of warning to Gael,
Gall-Gael, and Gael-Gall, including those decent and law-
abiding members of that section of the Irish Community
who live, work, and worship within a religion and political
beliefs contrary to, and at enmity with, the life, worship,
and political activities of those domiciled within what is
regarded as the twenty-six counties of Southern Ireland; in
the abiding hope that all, North and South, will combine
against, fight, and destroy this communist and insidious
effort to overthrow the age-long virtue of the Irish People;
to prevent this rock-built chastity from corrosion, so that
it may outlive all red-like attempts to frighten or weaken
its determination by a godless and ruthless ridicule. Amen.'
The Moon Shines on Kylenamoe (one-act play) published; no
dedication.

(The preceding three plays were published in one volume.)

1962   *Feathers from the Green Crow: Sean O'Casey, 1905–1925*, ed.
Robert Hogan. A collection of stories, essays, songs and

short plays published in America, and then in London (1963).

1963 *Under a Colored Cap* ('Articles Merry and Mournful with Comments and a Song') published; dedicated to 'Little Alison and Littler Oona. To be read when the sturdier airs of womanhood flow around them – should they then desire to do so'.

1967 *Blasts and Benedictions* (articles and stories selected and introduced by Ronald Ayling) published posthumously.

Index